Ignatius Theodore Eschmann, O.P.

# THE ETHICS OF SAINT THOMAS AQUINAS
## TWO COURSES

Edited by Edward A. Synan

Ignatius Eschmann, O.P. (1898-1968) was a most distinguished interpreter of Saint Thomas Aquinas, if we take "interpreter" in the double sense of one who knows what Thomas meant and who brings to that interpretation what our century has made available.

During the First World War Eschmann served in the German Army; later he spent a year in a Nazi prison as a result of having explained *Mit brennender sorge* in German churches. He had received his post-secondary education at the "Angelicum," the Dominican University in Rome, and on receiving his degree was transferred to its teaching staff. It is a curiosity that although his official training was in theology, he always taught philosophy. But as L.K. Shook, C.S.B. pointed out in his funeral homily, the troublesome philosophy-theology conundrum may be solved better on the personal plane, as Eschmann had done, rather than by abstract definition and legislation.

English-speaking readers will be glad to find that Eschmann could cite T.S. Eliot to make a point, that he knew there is more in the OED than linguistic lore, and that he could adduce Bertrand Russell within two lines of citing Walter Winchell. Eschmann was a linguist of formidable expertise; he was the opposite of the party-line "manual" Thomist. The ethics he found in Saint Thomas is an ethics for adults, an ethics of Christian liberty, an ethics of splendour, but an ethics ruled by the virtue of prudence. Lest we misjudge all this as ethical laxity, let us remember that Eschmann obeyed his Superiors without question when he was assigned to Germany in 1936.

All those who studied under him will hear Eschmann's voice and remember his presence in reading these transcriptions of two courses he gave on the ethical teaching of Aquinas. What they cannot be expected to have known is that he had written out *verbatim* every course he gave, although his rhetorical expertise gave an impression of the *ex tempore*. For those to whom Eschmann has been no more than a legendary name, these pages will be the next best thing to having heard him for, in substance, every word is his.

Two sides of Eschmann are clear: he was a controversialist who, after his prison year, was hesitant to publish; he was also a constructive thinker, unwilling to substitute commentators, no matter how classical, for the Master. Both sides are patent in this book. Saint Thomas *redivivus* would surely recognize in these lectures the seeds he had sown seven centuries earlier.

Ashley & Crippen

I.Th. Eschmann, O.P. (1898-1968)

ETIENNE GILSON SERIES 20

STUDIES IN MEDIEVAL MORAL TEACHING 1

# The Ethics of Saint Thomas Aquinas
# Two Courses


by

Ignatius Theodore Eschmann, O.P.

edited by

Edward A. Synan



PONTIFICAL INSTITUTE OF MEDIAEVAL STUDIES

Preparation and publication of this volume was made possible by a grant from the Medieval Moral Teaching Fund in the Mediaeval Studies Foundation

CANADIAN CATALOGUING IN PUBLICATION DATA

Eschmann, I. Th. (Ignatius Theodore), 1898-1968
The ethics of Saint Thomas Aquinas : two courses

(The Etienne Gilson series ; 20)
(Studies in medieval moral teaching ; 1)
Includes bibliographical references and index.
ISBN 0-88844-720-5

1. Thomas, Aquinas, Saint, 1225?-1274. Summa theologia.
I. Synan, Edward A., 1918-1997. II. Pontifical Institute of Mediaeval Studies. III. Title. IV. Series.
V. Series: Studies in medieval moral teaching ; 1.

B765.T54E77 1997 230.2 C97-931838-6


Pontifical Institute of Mediaeval Studies
59 Queen's Park Crescent East
Toronto, Ontario, Canada M5S 2C4

Printed in United States of America

# Table of Contents

PART TWO. *ESCHMANNUS AEDIFICATOR*

# Introduction

## A. The Project

Authorities at the Pontifical Institute of Mediaeval Studies have invited me to edit these university lecture-course materials, left unpublished by their author, Ignatius Theodore Eschmann O.P. Now long dead, for he died in 1968, Eschmann taught for twenty-two years as a Senior Fellow of the Institute and as a Professor in the Department of Philosophy at the University of Toronto.

This invitation to edit a small selection of his lectures was prompted by two considerations. First, this accomplished scholar published relatively little of his very valuable work; hence an effort to make available a significant part of his writing is appropriate. Second, that the invitation to undertake this project has been extended to me stems from the fact that Eschmann was my professor in a number of lecture courses and seminars he offered to "License in Mediaeval Studies" candidates in Toronto. This second consideration is reinforced by the circumstance that during the last years of Eschmann's life we were colleagues on the teaching staff of the Institute and the University. Under both formalities, the student-teacher relationship and later as academic colleagues, we were friends. This project, therefore, has been a work of "piety" in the strict sense of *pietas*; as a kind of "family obligation" the work has been a privilege rather than a burden.

Beyond his academic affiliations, Eschmann was a priest in the Roman Catholic Order of Preachers, generally called "Dominicans," a name derived from that Order's thirteenth century founder, Saint Dominic Guzman. It is far from irrelevant to note that the thirteenth century theologian, Saint Thomas Aquinas, whose ethical foundations these two courses examine, was a member of the same Order; the thought of Aquinas was the focus of Eschmann's work in general as well as of the materials edited here. This edition presents an instance of moral doctrine, proposed by Saint Thomas in the thirteenth century, that can be read with penetration and profit as the twentieth century gives way to the twenty-first.

On the non-academic plane, Eschmann resembled physically the traditional description of Saint Thomas himself: tall and heavily built, crowned with sparse hair, Eschmann was precise and deliberate in speech and gesture. Of infinitely more importance than his corporeal presence were our colleague's impressive cultural accomplishments and these were by no means restricted to academic areas. Not only was Eschmann a scholar of international reputation, he was also an organist, a connoisseur of music and of literature, a gourmet yet no glutton. Courtly and friendly in manner, he was a cultivated European gentleman as well as an edifying Dominican friar.

Eschmann's admirers, above all his students, have long deplored the fact that his publications were so limited. That paucity of published materials is at odds with the fact that he had produced an enormous mass of course materials of the highest quality, either typed or carefully written in his exceptionally legible hand. Incredible though it may seem, he wrote out in full each class lecture. These course notes are now to be found in the Archives of the Pontifical Institute where most of Eschmann's long teaching career occurred. In their boxes, they have been described by an expert archivist as occupying approximately "twenty linear feet" of shelving.

A first conclusion to be drawn from contact with that material and with his personnel file in the Institute Archives, those documents juxtaposed with reliable anecdotal memories, my own and those of others, is that Eschmann was a figure of the sort that inevitably generates myths. Often enough such myths are harmless elaborations of facts that are striking enough in themselves. Here the pleasures of fiction—Aristotle has reminded us that we embellish the stories we tell in the conviction that thus "we do our hearers a pleasure" (*Poetics* 24; 1460a 16-18)—are renounced for the reliability of either eye-witness reports or of documented fact. On some details, my own witness will be the ground; on many the witness of friends and colleagues who remember Eschmann well; on still others documents adduced are, some primary, some secondary.

Into the class of "secondary" documents fall, for example, the *Mediaeval Studies*[1] notice, provided by the late Laurence K. Shook C.S.B. in accord with our custom of dedicating the issue of that periodical following the death of a Senior Fellow of the Pontifical Institute of Mediaeval Studies to the memory of that Fellow. The funeral homily too, preached by that same distinguished scholar in his role as President of the Pontifical Institute at the time of Eschmann's death, counts as a secondary source. Shook's respect for the truth of history is guaranteed by, to take a single

[1] L.K. Shook, "Ignatius Eschmann, O.P. 1898-1968," *Mediaeval Studies* 30 (1968): V-IX; as is usual a photograph accompanies this notice of a deceased Senior Fellow.

instance, his outstanding biography of Etienne Gilson;[2] thus these two records of Shook's words are generally reliable, if not primary, documents.

### B. History and Myth

This erudite religious, baptized as an infant under the names "Karl Theodore," was born in Düsseldorf on 13 November 1898, son of a Railroad District Supervisor named Karl Eschmann and of his wife, Anna Buschmann. Karl Theodore's single sibling was a brother named Hans who became a Doctor of Music and a professional organist. Our Karl Theodore's classical secondary school education was provided by the Royal Prussian Hohenzollern-Gymnasium in Düsseldorf.

A first insight into the mentality of this archetypal German Professor is provided by an unexpected circumstance: both his birth certificate and a transcript of his Gymnasium grades (not all of the latter *sehr gut*, as Shook mentioned at Eschmann's funeral) are in his file at the Pontifical Institute. These are primary documents which only Eschmann could have provided and which only one of his temperament would have preserved and filed as an adult. On graduation from the Gymnasium at the age of eighteen, Eschmann was taken into the German Army. His Army Pay-Book, if memory serves, was available to Shook, thanks to that same file, when the Institute President composed the funeral homily and the *Mediaeval Studies* notice of Eschmann's passing. No other staff member would have thought to include documents of that sort in a personnel dossier; we must be grateful that Eschmann was meticulous enough to have done so. The Army Pay-Book, no longer in the file, was almost certainly forwarded to Eschmann's brother on the death of our colleague. This document gave witness that Eschmann had received an honorable discharge from the Army in November 1918. On his military service Eschmann described himself as "a faithful, but unenthusiastic, soldier." His single mention to me of his war-time experience concerned the near impossibility of entrenching in the water-logged soil of Flanders where he had served with, if my memory can be trusted, the field artillery, not implausibly as a machine gunner (the assignment Shook reported) charged with defending the crew of an artillery battery against infantry attack.

Much more worthy of notice is the fact that Eschmann's service in those damp and shallow trenches was the ambience for his careful reading

[2] L.K. Shook, *Etienne Gilson*, The Etienne Gilson Series 6 (Toronto: Pontifical Institute of Mediaeval Studies, 1984).

of Saint Augustine's *Confessions*; he had brought a copy of that incomparable work with him to the front. It is not difficult to think that he may have been the only soldier in any army to have done so, but it is impossible not to realize that this reading, leisurely if in doleful circumstances, was a contributing cause of two developments that marked the mature Eschmann whom we knew.

First, after his discharge from the German Army in November of 1918, Eschmann in the spring of 1919 joined the Friars Preachers, the "Dominican Order," with its modified version of the "Rule of Saint Augustine." The horrors of the slaughter that was the First World War, seen through the lens provided by the Bishop of Hippo, most certainly steeled the young Eschmann for the sacrifices, directly owing to his religious commitment, that were to be demanded of him especially during the militant neo-paganism of the Hitler years in Germany.

Second, the incomparable masterpiece by the Bishop of Hippo, read meditatively and as a refuge from the unending pressure of survival at the front, certainly gave Eschmann experiential knowledge of the joy and peace to be found in prayer and in the love of the Holy One. Eschmann was neither the first nor the last to find the impetus for a life of prayer and sacrifice in that prolonged presentation of contrite praise by the erudite and eloquent son of Monnica and Patricius.

So it was that after his honorable discharge from the German Army Karl Theodore presented himself to the Dominican novitiate. When he made his first profession on 19 May 1920, after a year in the novitiate, he took the name "Ignatius," but retained his baptismal "Theodore" as a middle name; henceforth he would be called formally "Ignatius Theodore Eschmann, of the Order of Preachers." When in later years he was teased occasionally by his associates for having chosen, or received, "Ignatius," the name of Saint Ignatius Loyola who founded the Jesuits ("teased" because, as will be seen, Eschmann often thought it right to dissent from the views of many a Jesuit theologian) he would make a somewhat ponderous response. He would say with unfailing gravity that he venerated Saint Ignatius Loyola as, indeed, he venerated all saints; the name "Ignatius," however, designated in his case, not the Founder of the Company of Jesus, but of the early martyr, Saint Ignatius of Antioch.

## C. Rome

Although Shook had given the year 1920 for Eschmann's arrival to study at the "Angelicum" (the usual designation of the Dominican University in Rome, officially named "The University of Saint Thomas") a cryptic fragment in Eschmann's dossier corrects that date to 1922. That note, partly typed and partly handwritten, evidently by a native German speaker, provides either directly or indirectly the authority of the celebrated medievalist and Thomistic scholar, Angelo Walz O.P., for 1922 as the date of Eschmann's arrival at the Angelicum, along with other precious testimony. Walz, it may be noted, was stationed at the Angelicum while Eschmann was there. This note is worth citing in full; first, in typing:

> Eschmann came to Rome in 1922, not in 1920
> Eschmann excelled as organist in the Angelicum and in the Canadian Sanctuary of St. Joseph in...⟨no location given; Montréal?⟩
> Deep in research and knowlegde ⟨*sic*⟩ of the sources in doctrine, he was a great esthtetician ⟨SIC⟩ in music.

There follow these handwritten words:

> Spinet i⟨n⟩ room,
> Superb musician/famous as a preacher

Another two lines of typing follow:

> Eschmann ist ⟨SIC⟩ quoted in A. Walz, L'Università S. Tommaso in Roma, Roma 1966, p. 83.

Finally, stamped in blue-inked capitals, most likely by Shook or by his secretary

> RECEIVED SEPT 23 1968

(a date posterior both to Shook's homily and to the *Mediaeval Studies* notice he composed).

If a conjecture may be made on the provenance of this note (the substance of which was copied in Shook's hand on a sheet of lined paper and kept with its original in Eschmann's personnel file) either Walz or one who knew the book by Walz which is cited, had seen the *Mediaeval Studies* notice of Eschmann's death and then sent the note to correct the date at which Eschmann had come to Rome as well as to add details of real interest: Eschmann had been organist at the Angelicum and, presumably, at the Montréal shrine of Saint Joseph, that he had a spinet in his room at the Angelicum, along with what might have been guessed: he was esteemed as an exceptional musician, scholar, and preacher, even with peers who are not always easy to impress.

Related obscurities prompted an inquiry of my own (4 March 1996) that has resulted in a prompt response (13 March 1996) from Father Bruno Esposito O.P., Secretary General of the Dominican University in Rome. This letter assures us that Eschmann was enrolled there as a student in the

Faculty of Theology during the academic years: 1923-1924, 1924-1925, 1925-1926; during the 1926-1927 session he was enrolled, still as a student, in the Superior Course in Theology. His status then changed; for the years 1929-1930, 1930-1931, 1931-1932, 1932-1933, 1933-1934, and 1935-1936, he taught in the Faculty of Philosophy, but in no other Faculty of the Angelicum.[3]

A source of possible confusion may be avoided by mentioning at this point that the Pontifical University of Saint Thomas Aquinas in Rome, named in Italian "Pontificia Università San Tommaso d'Aquino" (but popularly called "The Angelicum," in accord with the honorific medieval designation of Saint Thomas Aquinas as "the Angelic Doctor") sponsors a learned journal in which Eschmann was to publish a number of book reviews as well as the first two installments of an article, left incomplete when he departed from Rome in 1936. That journal is also named *Angelicum*. Here "Angelicum" will be Italicized whenever it designates the journal, but not when it names the University.

Eschmann was ordained a priest, 12 July 1925; by 1928 he had earned the lectorship in theology and was ready to be assigned teaching duties at the Angelicum, an assignment that was recorded in a "Chronica" entry of the *Angelicum*. This notice informs us that, "As required by the new plan of studies, Fathers Amiable, Eschmann, Friethoff, Heuston, Horvath, Kuiper are assigned by the Most Reverend Father General to teach in the 'Angelicum'."[4] Eschmann had completed the training in theology customary for academically gifted priests and thus was authorized to teach on an advanced level, although, to be sure, he taught philosophy rather than theology.

In addition to his book reviews, Eschmann's first publications are two installments of an article in *Angelicum*, "De societate in genere; Quaestio philosophica," that is, "On Society in General: A Philosophical Ques-

[3] "Il Rev.do P. Ignatius Theodore Eschmann, O.P. é stato inscritto nella nostra Facoltà di Teologia Matr. A. 1240 per gli anni accademici: 1923-1924; 1924-1925; 1925-1926; e 1926-1927 (Corso Superiore di Teologia).

Si dichiara inoltre che il suddetto Padre ha insegnato nella nostra Facoltà di Filosofia per gli anni accademici: 1929-1930; 1930-1931; 1931-1932; 1932-1933; 1933-1934; 1934-1935 e 1935-1936, non risulta che abbiia insegnato in altre nostre Facoltà....

[Signed by hand] P. Bruno Esposito, O.P.,
Segretario Generale."

[4] "Ratione nova studiorum exigente, a Rev.mo P. Generali ad docendum in 'Angelicum' assignati sunt PP. Amiable, Eschmann, Friethoff, Heuston, Horvath, Kuiper." *Angelicum* 5.4 (1928), Chronica, p. 635.

tion," in the 1934 volume. This article was never completely published; its second installment in 1935, although the last to reach the press, carries the term *continuabitur*, "will be continued."[5] The *Angelicum* carried twenty-three of his twenty-five book reviews. These were written in a number of languages: German, French, Italian, and Latin. The language chosen reflects in most cases the language of the book under review.[6] As was then the custom, and it was one that would remain in force through Vatican II in all church-related universities in Rome, lecturing at the Angelicum was done in Latin; Eschmann spoke and wrote fluently Latin, German, French, Italian, and English.

## D. Germany

In 1936 Eschmann was posted to Germany. Behind this, on the direct witness of a Toronto colleague to whom Eschmann himself had recounted the episode, lies the most disastrous of the innumerable misunderstandings (or worse) that marked Eschmann's life; it had the most grievous consequences of them all. Early in his academic career at the Angelicum he had requested a transfer from Rome to Germany; he had done so in a letter to his Superior. For a time he heard nothing concerning this request, most likely because, as a promising student or as an effective member of the Angelicum staff, Eschmann was too valuable to lose. Alas, one of the *Angelicum* reviews he had published gave offense to someone who had both the power and the authority to transfer him. The episode gives a certain poignancy to his discussion below of the "virtue of obedience." That he might have given offense is easy to understand; Eschmann held firm and often idiosyncratic opinions which he expressed with a trenchant pen, as our present texts will demonstrate abundantly. His Superior sent for him, drew the letter requesting an assignment to Germany from his file, and said that the request—made years before and in a far different political climate—was now granted. Thus, in 1936, Eschmann was sent into the cauldron that was Germany under Adolf Hitler. In view of what was to follow, the fact that the article he had been publishing in *Angelicum* was left

[5] See *Angelicum* 11 (1934): 56-77, 214-227.

[6] A convenient listing of all twenty-five reviews is to be found on the last pages of L.K. Shook's memorial notice in *Mediaeval Studies* 30 (1968): VIII, IX, along with a list of twelve publications other than book reviews which include "Many notes on the Ottawa edition of the *Summa theologiae* of St. Thomas"; the linguistic range of the twelve items other than reviews is English (8), German (2), and Latin (2).

incomplete is, even in the view of an academic, a truly minor matter.

On 4 March 1937, Pope Pius XI issued a formal diplomatic complaint in German to the authorities of the Third Reich, not often mentioned when papal relations with the National Socialist government of Germany are scrutinized. That document, written in German, was designated, as such documents are, from its opening phrase: *Mit brennender Sorge*, "With burning anxiety." In it the Pope set out forthright complaints against specific aspects of the National Socialist regime in Germany; as might have been anticipated, those complaints were bitterly resented by that government. Eschmann was assigned to read and to explain *Mit brennender Sorge* in Catholic churches; this assignment would transform his life. First, he was dogged by suspicious government agents. A well-attested episode has him noticing such agents taking notes on his sermon; bending down from the pulpit, Eschmann offered to provide them with a written copy "so that this time, at least, you can report what I actually say!" These words are pure Eschmann. Whether this incident was the crucial offense or not, his outspoken courage earned him a year in a Cologne prison.

During that year he suffered as did the classical "confessors of the faith": not quite martyrs, since they were not put to death, those confessors were heroic in their degree, as Eusebius recounted of Origen, "for many days his feet were stretched four spaces in the stocks" during the Decian persecution. Under inhuman stress they gave faithful witness to their faith and to their courage. Eschmann's imprisonment took place under the Civil Police, not under the Gestapo (as one myth that grew up around him would have it). Still, the standard Police did their best; he was forced to clean latrines and, what rowelled his sensibilities even more, he was routinely beaten and kicked by his guards. "A German, I was kicked by my own people!" he would complain to a Toronto colleague. This was the year during which, so a story goes, he memorized a German/English pocket dictionary. Here his exceptional control of English has caused what is most likely a merely imaginative explanation. The same friend to whom he recounted his prison experience visited Eschmann's family in Germany and reports that they all spoke English easily. Had they all memorized a dictionary? If they had, that would have been at least a partial cause of their notable facility in English. The direction of causality, however, can run two ways: memorizing a dictionary indeed might be a cause of fluent English, but it is far more probable that this fluency has inspired the tale of a fictional "cause." Whether the tale is one more Aristotelian "embellishment" is hardly of pressing importance. Whatever the truth about what lies beneath his control of English, Eschmann seems never to have been at a loss for precise English terms to express his subtle thought. One happy consequence of this is that few editorial ameliorations of his text have been required.

In the fall of 1938 he was released from prison; popular wisdom had an explanation for this as well. According to a widely accepted account, certain classes of political prisoners were given an amnesty to celebrate the *Anschluss* of Austria by Hitler's Germany: Eschmann fell among their number. Although not impossible, this explanation seems improbable given the long lapse of time between the *Anschluss* in March of 1938 and the release of Eschmann months later, in autumn of that same year. The Hitler regime, after all, did not fail to maintain the proverbial efficiency of German bureaucracy. Here too the details are not of the first importance; Eschmann was indeed released, as many a victim of the regime was not. He spent some months recuperating in Bavaria and before the end of 1938 managed to find refuge in Canada. Leaving Europe was not without governmental obstacles of the sort he so often encountered: officials in Belgium refused to give him clearance to sail from a Belgian port. According to Shook's funeral homily, the Belgians alleged a health consideration because recently a dog had bitten him; French officials were less vigilant, and so he was cleared to sail from Le Havre. Against this explanation is the fact that in September of 1938 European powers and Britain had made their last concessions to Hitler at Munich; Belgium had mobilized her armed forces, but was attempting desperately to avoid any hint of violating neutrality. All of us who then were studying in that country witnessed a systematic assignment of Belgian troops that was designed to avoid fraternization across the defended frontiers: French-speaking Belgian soldiers were assigned to the German and Dutch frontiers, but Flemish-speaking regiments went to the French frontier. Belgian officials may have feared that helping a German citizen, lately out of prison, to leave from their shores, might provoke French objections. What better cover for a spy? A dog's bite may well have been an "official" cover for a spy's travel to a country likely to support England in a possible, even probable, war to come. Whatever their reasons were, the fact remains that the Belgians refused to give Eschmann clearance to sail from Belgium, but he did succeed in obtaining papers from officials in France. Except for brief visits to the United States and to Germany, the rest of Eschmann's life would unfold in Canada where he was to take out papers and become a citizen.

## E. Eschmann in Canada

Eschmann began his Canadian career with his fellow Dominicans in Ottawa. There the Dominican scholar, L.-M. Régis O.P., and his colleagues were working on a new edition of the *Summa theologiae* by Saint Thomas

Aquinas. Thomistic scholars will know that the "Piana" text which the Ottawa Dominicans presented in a modern edition, along with variants from the first (a second is planned) "Leonine" edition of that work, is a 1570 printing that had appeared with the blessing of Pope Saint Pius V, who was also a member of the Dominican Order. This eminently useful new edition appeared as the "Ottawa *Summa*" (1941) and is notable for two features which Eschmann will be seen below to have insisted upon as necessary for an understanding of Saint Thomas: first, a listing of parallel passages from other writings of Aquinas and, second, the identification of sources, including the anonymous references so common in medieval academic writing: *quidam dicit*, "someone says." Who was that "someone"? It is certain that Eschmann had a major share in providing that twofold research data, noted by Shook's list of Eschmann's Publications in the memorial notice mentioned above at note 5. Since the critical re-edition of the *Summa theologiae* projected by the "Leonine Commission" has not appeared as yet, no other version of that celebrated work now provides scholars with so much help; it is the edition of the great *Summa* that will be cited here. On at least one occasion in the course of that Ottawa project, Eschmann came with Régis to the Pontifical Institute of Mediaeval Studies in order to check references in our Library. This was Eschmann's first visit to Toronto.

During the 1939-1940 academic year Laval University in Québec invited Eschmann to join their Faculty of Philosophy. This arrangement, which must have seemed full of promise to both parties when it was proffered and accepted, came to an end by 1942, in part owing to academic dissent and in part owing to diplomatic difficulties into which Eschmann was once again to blunder. As for the latter, Eschmann made an effort to contact his father and brother through a friend in the United States, a country not yet at war with Germany, as Canada had been from September of 1939. Since he was technically an "enemy alien" in Canada, this attempt at communication through a neutral country, with citizens of a Germany at war with Canada, aroused the suspicions of the Royal Canadian Mounted Police which seem to have been shared by certain of his university associates in Québec. Coupled with the academic quarrel, to which more detailed reference must be made, this twofold difficulty rendered Eschmann's position at Laval impossible.

One result of that painful passage, which we may be excused for counting a happy one for the Pontifical Institute, was that Eschmann joined our teaching staff for the academic session 1942-1943. This appointment would last until his death. A second result would be less felicitous; his experience of a transfer to Hitler's Germany over a pungent book review had been matched in his Québec experience by an exchange of acrimonious publications. Within a few years, certainly by 1945, that dissent had resulted in bad blood between Eschmann and a Laval Dean.

The point at issue between them was the theory of "personalism" as proposed by the very eminent Jacques Maritain, but opposed in the name of the "common good" by influential personalities from Québec, Dean Charles De Koninck of Laval University and the Cardinal Archbishop of Québec included. Although protesting friendship for both De Koninck and for Maritain, Eschmann undertook to defend the position of Maritain, against objections by De Koninck, Dean of Philosophy at Laval,[7] in an article entitled "In Defense of Jacques Maritain" which he published in *The Modern Schoolman*.[8] Maritain, of course, (as De Koninck would not fail to remark) was more than competent to defend himself.

In that article Eschmann wrote, with a degree of obscurity, that he would not have responded to the De Koninck book had the same journal not carried, in an earlier issue, an article against Maritain by yet another controversialist who happened to be well-known to me. His reference was to Professor Jules Baisnée, S.S.,[9] whom I had known a few years earlier at The Catholic University of America in Washington, D.C. By an irony of history, Baisnée, a Sulpician priest, had lost an arm in the course of his service in the French Army during the First World War in which Eschmann had served as a German soldier. The most damaging effect of this academic squabble has been noted: for the rest of his life Eschmann was reluctant to publish,[10] reluctant even to deliver a paper at an academic

[7] Charles De Koninck, *De la primauté du bien commun contre les personnalistes. Le principe de l'ordre nouveau*, Préface de S.E. le Cardinal J.M. Rodericus Villeneuve, O.M.I. (Québec: Editions de l'Université Laval, Montréal: Editions Fides, 1943). This work was dedicated "au roi Léopold," and the Cardinal saw evidence, in the "personalism" at stake, of a "revival of the polycephalic monster of Pelagianism," p. XXII.

[8] *The Modern Schoolman* 22.4 (May 1945):183-208.

[9] Jules A. Baisnée, "Two Catholic Critiques of Personalism," *The Modern Schoolman* 22.2 (January 1945): 59-75.

[10] Of his few cis-Atlantic publications (they are nine) seven were with the Department of Publications of the Pontifical Institute. One of those nine occasioned an addition to the Eschmann saga. He had agreed to "give a paper" at a meeting of The American Catholic Philosophical Association but, having written the paper, he took to his bed; two Institute colleagues were brash enough to take the paper from Eschmann's desk and one of them read it at the conference and so it was published in the *Proceedings of the American Catholic Philosophical Association* 31 (1957) 25-33. It is reported reliably that the two colleagues were tactful enough after the event to pacify Eschmann's consequent wrath.

conference. That situation is a remote cause of this present edition.

In contrast with the turmoil of Eschmann's first years in Canada, although those years were surely less trying than his year of imprisonment in Germany, Eschmann's career at the Pontifical Institute was generally peaceful and rewarding. He was accepted by his peers as a valuable addition to the staff and, if one professorial function be set aside for the moment, his students agreed.

A number of Dickensian traits made Eschmann stand out among his associates. Our Librarian, for instance, was obliged to come to terms with two of his antinominian practices. The first of these was that, against regulations, Eschmann constantly smoked his pipe in the Reading Room of the Library; second, he did not always count it compatible with professorial dignity to sign for a book he might wish to borrow. Often (although, to be sure, not always) he simply took the books he wanted without signing for them. This did not mean that he accepted without extreme indignation the understandable response by the Library staff: they went through his quarters whenever he was absent from the campus in the hope of recovering books that seemed to have been lost, but which likely would be found on his shelves. Eschmann's smoking, alas, had more serious consequences than did his unrecorded borrowings of library books. His death would result from cancer and would come after lung surgery which, if it delayed his death, did not prevent it.

Student perspective on Eschmann's classroom teaching was favorable without qualification; his approach was like that of no other professor, but every idiosyncrasy was positive. His performance on the first day of term, for instance, has never faded from my memory. When his seminar ended Eschmann stood in the doorway, asked the name and shook the hand of each of us who had just heard his masterful introduction to the semester's work. During that same semester, in the autumn of 1948, the pioneer medievalist, Monsignor Martin Grabmann (several of whose books had been reviewed by Eschmann in *Angelicum*) died in Germany. On the day that word of Grabmann's death reached him, Eschmann spent the first ten minutes of his seminar on a sketch of Grabmann's work: "When a great scholar dies," he told us, "everyone in the republic of letters must take note of that passing." These concrete instances of his profoundly humane attitude reflected a consistent respect both for persons and for learning; Eschmann was marked by elegance as well as by erudition.

It has been mentioned, however, that Eschmann suffered from one serious limitation in his dealings with students: he was less successful as "supervisor" in directing a student in the writing of a doctoral dissertation than he was in the seminar room or in the lecture hall. He once protested to me when we were on staff together that he "could not evaluate what had not yet been written." This perspective led him to demand the complete, or nearly complete, draft of a dissertation before he would, or felt that he could, provide any help to a candidate. Since the Department of Philosophy turned over two of his students to me when his fatal illness overtook him, my knowledge of this detail rests on direct experience. In one of my two inherited cases, he had simply rejected, without a detailed critique—"This is unacceptable!"—the draft of a complete thesis; it had taken the student a full year, on his own and without direction, to produce that draft. In the other instance, after more than a year of work, the disheartened student had no more than a partial table of contents and a box full of primary texts, written on small sheets of paper. Those slips of paper, to be sure, became footnotes in his ultimate study; and both candidates, it is heartening to recall, succeeded in producing dissertations that were more than acceptable. Other students are said to have complained that he overrode their interpretations, insisting always on his own, often singular, perceptions.

If a diagnosis of this side of Eschmann may be ventured, perhaps his habitual benignity and his genuine concern for the development of embryo scholars were buried under his spontaneous involvement in the issues they aspired to handle: to demand less than what his own understanding indicated would have appeared to him a betrayal. His thesis direction was a project he approached *mit brennender Sorge*, and that "burning anxiety" was for the truth—naturally for the truth as he saw it. From all of this stemmed his "interference" with students' intentions. His unrealistic demand that a dissertation must be written in draft form at least before any intervention by a director, seems to have been a consequence of his own exceptional capacity to put his thoughts on paper. He seems to have over-estimated a beginner's ability by his demand that a full draft be contrived without direction, but simultaneously to have under-estimated the ability of talented young students to perceive, however imperfectly, solutions and goals that might not coincide with his own.

His fatal illness revealed a last aspect of Eschmann's character that must be recounted; he would not have wished the matter to be omitted. After the surgery by which he had lost a lung, Eschmann went for recuperation to a convalescent home, now called "Saint John's Rehabilitation Hospital," conducted then, as it is today, on Cummer Avenue in Toronto by Anglican nuns whose community is dedicated to "Saint John the Divine." On my visits to him there during his last months, he expressed repeatedly and in glowing terms, his admiration of those nuns and his gratitude for their devoted skill in the care they extended to him. This was in notable and welcome contrast to what he had led me to anticipate would be his attitude; Eschmann had more than once been bed-ridden in the infirmary on our campus with less threatening illnesses. There he had complained habitually that our nuns lacked the skills that marked the nursing sisters of Germany.

The day came when it was judged necessary to move him from the convalescent home to a more general medical facility; his cancer had spread to the esophagus. It was at Wellesley Hospital, in a room with the apocalyptic number "666," that Ignatius Theodore Eschmann O.P., on 11 April 1968, ended his impressive pilgrimage.

## F. Academic Views

It has been mentioned that this gentle and civilized scholar entertained many a personal, often an unpopular, position. The first course edited here exhibits a number of such positions. Chief among them is the strongly held and closely argued view that the "theological" works of Thomas Aquinas, as well as those of all other mediaeval theologians, ought not to be considered sources for the mining of "philosophical" positions, a project he will be seen to have dismissed more than once as "scissors-and-paste work." The lectures here edited were delivered under the aegis of the Department of Philosophy, a fact to which he adverted at least once, yet he protested from the beginning that they constitute theology. He offered no doctrinal resolution of this conundrum, but only a diagnosis of what he counted a prevalent ineptitude, a "modern" incapacity in reading medieval authors. President Shook, in his *Mediaeval Studies* memorial notice already alluded to, has made a percipient suggestion:

> His case argues that the currently-discussed problem of the proper relations between philosophy and theology will in the days ahead be more easily solved at the human than at the statutory level.[11]

By "modern" Eschmann will be seen to have intended especially the views of seventeenth- and eighteenth-century theologians, as well as those of their later followers. Equally important to him was the conviction that theology is a unitary discipline. He felt it right to reject, and frequently to express his rejection of, the "modern" division of theology into "dogmatic" and "moral" theology, to say nothing of "ascetic" theology, "pastoral" theology, and other such designations for "parts" of theology. Once more he ascribed responsibility for such divisions to the seventeenth century, but on this aspect extended the blame especially to the eighteenth century.

[11] Op. cit. p. VII.

These divisions were commonly, indeed all but universally, accepted in Catholic seminary and university departments of theology. As will be seen below, in another mood he found this division in certain authors as the twelfth century gave way to the thirteenth; his conception of "the modern" was somewhat elastic. That these divisions were in some way present even in the Angelicum of his day might be suggested by the course programmes recorded in the volumes of *Angelicum* for the years of his residence, first as student and then as professor. On this, to be sure, there are strong indications that at the Angelicum this was a division of labor rather than the programmatic division of theology itself to which he so strenuously objected; the terms he found so objectionable were not current there. In any event, his view was not calculated to be received with open arms by writers and teachers and administrators who had long since adopted those conventional divisions and on them had based their research projects and their course programmes.

Nor was he blind to parallel academic fissions in the middle ages: decretists against theologians, philosophers in the faculties of arts at war with "masters of the sacred page," the theory and fact of the *imperium*, "the empire," set against the theory and fact of the *sacerdotium*, "the priesthood": pope and bishops, priests, and deacons. The dialectic of this last opposition gave rise to outstanding courses offered by Eschmann (two of which I attended) on medieval political theory. Eschmann mentioned this opposition below in connection with Dante Alighieri as evidence that the great poet was "no Thomist"; indeed Eschmann concluded the second series of lectures presented here with a line from Dante that impugned a Pope as "the Prince of the new Pharisees." It does not seem excessive to characterize this contentious side of our old friend as "Eschmann the warrior," *Eschmannus bellator*.

In a more positive mode he insisted that in the moral life first importance be given to the virtue of prudence rather than to law on any plane. A human being, admitted by all biblical believers to have been created in the Divine image, is an infinitely diminished version of the freedom and intelligence of the Creator. There is more to morality than obedience to law in any form that law may take. That Eschmann was not opposed to obedience as such is clear to one who remembers his obedience in returning to the Germany Hitler had distorted. As the ultimate ground of ethical living, however, he insisted upon prudence rather than upon obedience. Indeed, he considered the theory and practice of giving primary place to law and obedience, rather than to prudence and responsible liberty, the source of the very partitioning of theology he so deplored. Since prudence presided so sympathetically and constructively over his thought, to "Eschmann the Warrior," *Eschmannus bellator*, must be added "the constructive

Eschmann," "Eschmann the builder," *Eschmannus aedificator*.

All this will be seen, enshrined in vigorous and academically impressive analyses of ancient and medieval texts, for Eschmann was an exemplary medievalist. He could read and evaluate medieval handwriting, he was not bewildered by manuscript variants, by the intricate structure and the unpredictable development of a given medieval book, by marginal notes and inter-linear glosses; his erudition allowed him to track down obscure citations and appeals to hitherto unidentified "authorities." His knowledge of the medieval university and of its programmes was professional.

Still, there was a degree of unreality in the energy with which Eschmann (and his opponents) went into the lists on such details as had provoked his troubles at Laval. A Louvain professor, M. le Chanoine Jacques Leclercq, in a short review of a book by Eschmann's primary Laval opponent, who sharpened his sword against the position of Maritain (so vigorously defended by Eschmann), included in his estimate some memorable observations that go well beyond the book under review, observations both witty and harsh, but not without penetration:

> ...Thus it is that certain well-meaning minds in the Church are no longer content to require the Thomistic orthodoxy recently added to the orthodoxy formerly called "Christian," but now add to it a "Maritain" orthodoxy.... If there are any minds that enjoy this sort of jousting and would like to keep score, let them first read the book of Monsieur De Koninck, the article of Father Eschmann, then the brochure of Monsieur De Koninck, then the principal works of Jacques Maritain, then those of Saint Thomas. After this they will be able to begin reflecting on what "the person" and "the common good" really are, on what deserves to be called "personalism," a complementary notion to that of "community," which it will be suitable to define as well, etc.[12]

[12] "...Ainsi quelques bons esprits dans l'Église ne se contentent plus d'exiger l'orthodoxie thomiste récemment ajoutée à l'orthodoxie autrefois appelée chrétienne, mais y ajoutent l'orthodoxie maritainiste.... S'il est des esprits qui aiment ce genre de joute et désirent marquer les points, qu'ils lisent d'abord le livre de M. De Koninck, ensuite l'article du P. Eschmann, ensuite la brochure de M. De Koninck, ensuite les principales oeuvres de Jacques Maritain, ensuite celles de saint Thomas. Après quoi ils pourront commencer à réfléchir à ce qu'il faut appeler personnalisme, notion complémentaire de celle de communauté, qu'il conviendrait aussi de définir, etc." Jacques Leclercq, *Revue philosophique de Louvain* 45 (1947): 278, 279.

It will be seen that Eschmann supported with formidable scholarship his own view of "Thomistic orthodoxy," especially against "modern scholastics." Whether one is entertained by academic jousting or not, it is most certainly worth our trouble to read sympathetically the texts Eschmann has left to us. The texts here edited, to one who followed a number of his courses (although these materials were not among them) evoke the memory of his voice, of his gestures, of his rhetorical expertise, of his honest and ingenious grounding of often unexpected assertions concerning the documents he expounded. A reader who has no such memories of Eschmann in the flesh will have the next-best experience: his very words in courses he had revised carefully across more than two decades of teaching in Toronto.

## G. Eschmann and Thomism

A particularity of Eschmann's terminology that at a point in the second set of lectures edited here he began to use in a systematic way the term "Thomasic" in place of the more usual "Thomist" which he had used before. To take one from among the many controversial positions which characterize the way he approached the *Summa theologiae*, the great *Summary of Theology* by Saint Thomas Aquinas, which is the flagship text of the "Thomasic" doctrine, Eschmann insisted on a detailed analysis of the "Prologues" with which the author introduced each "Part" of the work.

That complex *Summary* had been organized by its author into three major "Parts," each customarily indicated for reference by an upper-case Roman numeral. Thus the First of those Parts is designated by the upper-case Roman numeral "I". Since the Second Part is subdivided into two Parts, references to the Second Part become "I-II" and "II-II," that is, "The First Part of the Second Part" and "the Second Part of the Second Part." Like the First Part, the Third Part is not subdivided and so is indicated simply by "III." Arabic numerals that follow in standard citations indicate first the "Question" and then the "Article" within one of those "Parts." The more usual Roman numerals will be used in Eschmann's text, but the more economical Arabic numerals in the notes; thus *Summa theologia* I-II, 3, 1 in the text will become in the notes ST 1-2, 3, 1; the more simply divided *Summa contra gentiles* liber 1, caput 4 in the text will become SCG 1, 4 in the notes.

Eschmann was surely correct in judging that Saint Thomas had intended that a student read and weigh, even memorize, the Prologue to each Part—indeed, he will be seen to have given convincing reasons to think that medieval texts were intended universally to be memorized. He was right to think that a careful reader can hope to derive a preliminary vision of the path that the Common Doctor intended to follow from those Prologues, held in the reader's memory as one progresses through the text.

Long after Eschmann's death, Leonard E. Boyle O.P., one who for some years had been with him a Senior Fellow of the Pontifical Institute, presented a striking analysis to account for a number of puzzles posed by the *Summa theologiae* of Saint Thomas Aquinas, and in that analysis too the Prologues play an indispensable role.[13] Boyle (later the Prefect of the Apostolic Library of the Vatican) was less convinced than Eschmann had been that those celebrated Prologues unlock the meaning of what follows them, but he did make capital of the Prologue to the First Part which, in fact, bears on the whole tripartite work. Boyle interpreted the terms of the Prologue of Part I as referring literally to young Dominicans who were not destined to go through a university course in theology. Just such young Friars (the *fratres communes*, "the ordinary brothers," and the *novitii*, the "novices," of that Prologue) were the responsibility of Brother Thomas at Santa Sabina, the school of the Dominicans in Rome to which the Common Doctor had been assigned to oversee the Order's educational practices; he had been given authority even to revise the curriculum. In the view of Brother Thomas, much that had been written to help such beginners impeded rather than helped their study. Those faults Brother Thomas listed in that Prologue as "the multiplication of useless questions, articles, and arguments" and, in a negative way, that necessary matters were not presented according to the "order of discipline," but rather according to the "exposition of books" or their chance occurrence in "disputations," to say nothing of the "frequent repetition" which generated both "dislike and confusion" in the minds of those beginners. Hence, the great *Summa theologiae*, so esteemed by scholars through the centuries, was intended by its author to be a summary statement of what is necessary in theology for confessors and preachers, presented in a rational order based upon the requirements of students who were *not* to attend university theological courses.

Now Eschmann had been long in his tomb when Boyle proposed his striking views on how and why the *Summary of Theology* came to be. There is a certain common ground in the conviction held by both that the Prologues provide indispensable clues to what follows. A reservation on this harmony (one with which Boyle ended his study) is that, unlike Eschmann, the younger Dominican held that

[13] L.E. Boyle, "The Setting of the *Summa theologiae* of Saint Thomas," The Etienne Gilson Series 5 (Toronto: Pontifical Institute of Mediaeval Studies, 1982).

> the relationship between the parts of the *Summa* is not as clear as it might be in the various prefaces.... Thomas profitably could have been more forthright about precisely what he was up to.[14]

Eschmann more than once pronounced the various Prologues to be "keys" that open the mysteries of the *Summary of Theology*; Boyle thought them a bit mysterious and themselves in need of some unlocking. Both Eschmann and Boyle saw in Thomas Aquinas an original exponent of what the Church has proposed as theological instruction in a precise and communicable idiom, a language which all hands—Aquinas, Eschmann, and Boyle —"spoke" well.

The present project makes available from our Archives an edition of lectures which Eschmann gave on how Saint Thomas Aquinas O.P. (ca 1225-1274) analyzed the moral life of a Christian believer. There is evidence that Eschmann had re-worked his materials on this project several times and that his last revision can be dated to 1955-1956. The Prologue of Part I-II, and the text of Part I-II, Question 1, Articles 1-8, is the section of the *Summa theologiae* on which Eschmann based this course. This edition, therefore, is restricted to the 1955-1956 revision, found in the Eschmann papers under the archivist's designation "CLN 30," that is, "Class Notes, folder #30," supplemented especially on the Prologue, (which is treated very briefly in the basic source) with material from an earlier version now filed as "CLN 37," "Class Notes #37."

After this somewhat controversial course, materials will be added from a more irenic course on prudence, that "charioteer of the virtues," preserved in file "CLN 45." This selection of texts we owe to Professor Mark Jordan of Notre Dame University.

## H. Professor Jordan's Contribution

Almost ten years ago, while Professor Mark Jordan was a visiting Fellow at the Institute, he was invited to edit a volume of Eschmann's papers. This had been made possible by a "finding List" of the Eschmann Archives expertly contrived by Ms Sophia K. Jordan. Other pressing concerns occasioned Professor Jordan's withdrawal from the project on which he had expended much time and energy and in which he had demonstrated noteworthy expertise. Since no limitation of mine ought to be ascribed to Professor Jordan, the following remarks set out our respective parts in the present edition.

[14] Op. cit. p. 30.

In addition to Jordan's major contribution in choosing the materials to be edited (a choice which is here accepted), he has provided several pages on "Editing the Lectures" which include a number of eminently sound principles, generally followed, if with some expansions, in the present edition. Jordan provided as well a typed transcription of more than 250 pages of Eschmann's texts on the analysis of the Prologue and of the first eight Articles of the *Summa theologiae* I-II, 1. This transcription has been before my eyes at every step of the present edition of that portion of Eschmann's work. It has seemed right on a number of occasions to include phrases or sentences that Jordan had omitted, to omit lines he had included, to leave in Eschmann's words terms and phrases Jordan had reformulated or, at times, to reformulate them differently. In short, our two transcriptions of the first section on the Prologue and the first Question of I-II, generally, but by no means in all details, tend to coincide.

Last, Jordan proposed to show both the controversial and the constructive sides of Eschmann's teaching, visible in the two series of texts he selected. Here the author of the two series is termed alternately "Eschmann the warrior," *Eschmannus bellator*, and "Eschmann the builder," *Eschmannus aedificator*; the distinction, but not this terminology, is Jordan's. Jordan seems not to have reached the "constructive" materials on prudence, a course assigned the file heading "CLN 45," "Class Notes # 45," in the finding list and described by Jordan as "a straightforward exposition centered on the Thomistic doctrine of prudence" in which Eschmann seemed "to have abandoned the polemical construction" in favor of a more positive approach. It is true that the dominant air of Eschmann's presentation of prudence is significantly less bellicose than his presentation of the first series, but it will not require minute exegesis to catch echoes, and more than echoes, of Eschmann's impatience with academic Thomism and Thomists in his lectures on prudence. Indeed, he caught himself at it; in a hand-written addition to his own typescript, omitted here (as are the remarks that occasioned the addition), Eschmann noticed that he was indulging once more in polemics and remarked: "Here I am again at the job of criticizing. The cat doesn't seem to be able to quit chasing mice." In spite of all this, the general distinction between the polemic and the irenic Eschmann is well-founded in the two series of lectures.

In addition to his felicitous choice of materials, Jordan formulated under the heading "Editing the Lectures," a number of concrete guidelines for the edition he began. He felt that materials relevant only to the classroom ought to be excised. Instances that he noted are: discursive presentation, numerous citations and quotations, repetitions and summaries in view of examinations. Here and there Jordan felt that traces of Eschmann's background as a non-native English speaker needed amelioration. Nor ought a general reader be burdened with "blocks of Latin"; Eschmann rarely gave a text of Aquinas in English. All Latin must be given in English. All instances of objective error, for instance, typing errors, slips in spelling or in syntax, must be corrected. Professor Jordan explicitly, and in my view rightly, renounced any attempt at a "critical," or "diplomatic," or "archival," edition; edited in this way Eschmann's last expression of his views can be presented to a reader in a form as understandable as possible. The good sense of these prescriptions is obvious and the present edition honors them all. Final responsibility for the text presented here, however, is mine alone. Apart from my general responsibility, what follows in this Introduction is a number of additional editorial principles which strike me as appropriate. It may be noted finally that Eschmann's text gives no indication of where one day's lecturing ends and another begins; no effort has been made to identify such divisions, since they would be irrelevant to a reader.

## I. Additional Editorial Principles

A number of editorial decisions have been imposed by Eschmann's having (as is understandable in class lectures, generally speaking) omitted his references. With regard to Saint Thomas this, of course, is not the case; there Eschmann gave precise indications of where he was in the various Thomistic works. On other authors, however, it has been an editorial duty to identify, or to attempt the identification, of precisely what passage in a given author Eschmann wanted his students to read. Furthermore, in his references to the works of Saint Thomas himself Eschmann has used the Latin terms *Prima, Prima Secundae*, etc. in indicating the "Part" of the *Summa theologiae* at stake. It seems more in his spirit to use in his text the Roman numerals to indicate those "Parts" and. as noted above, in the notes to use the more economical Arabic numbers and un-Italicized letters.

No doubt when dealing with materials of the sort at stake here, Eschmann explained to his classes, perhaps in informal asides, the version of the medieval "Disputed Question" that appears in the *Summa theologiae*, the great *Summary of Theology*, by Saint Thomas Aquinas, on which these lectures are largely based. Since this is not given in the present materials, at least a brief exposition here of that now unfamiliar literary form seems desirable. This will permit reference to the various components of each "Question" by the precise technical terms of medieval university usage.

In this work Aquinas has structured each "Article" (a subdivision of a "Question") according to the conventional components of a medieval "Disputed Question," and thus each "Question" is composed of a series of such "Articles." For the sake of clarity, when the terms "Question," "Article," and "Argument" are used in this technical sense they will be capitalized, but not when used in their non-technical, general sense.

Faithful in this to the Aristotelian tradition, members of medieval universities were convinced that to understand any issue entails knowing what can be said on both the affirmative and the negative sides of a clearly formulated question. Hence, they began by posing a literal "Question" (introduced by the word "Whether" (in Latin, *Utrum* or *An*), a Question so formulated that it might be answered either by "yes" or by "no." This *aporia*, (a question from which there is literally "no escape" from answering "yes" or "no"), was followed immediately (in the format of Saint Thomas in his *Summa theologiae*) by a limited number of Arguments (in that work, usually between three and five), *against* the position that he intended to uphold. Thus Saint Thomas began with two strong Arguments for atheism in his celebrated Article on his "five ways" to demonstrate the reality of what believers call "God" under the *aporia*: "Whether there be a God?" Such negative Arguments were followed by the phrase "But to the contrary," *Sed contra*, which introduced, not a contrary argument but an "authoritative" assertion, an "Authority," that is, a relevant quotation from a respected source, calculated to put an opponent on his mettle. As Eschmann once said in my hearing, "The *Sed contra* is a projectile thrown at an opponent." There followed on this "projectile" the "Body of the Article," the *corpus articuli*, in which the Master set out succinctly his own position, his "Solution" or "Determination" of the issue. The Master's final duty was to "Respond," formally and by number, "To the first," "To the second," and so on, to each of the preliminary, negative Arguments, thus closing the dialectical circle opened by the *aporia*.

In the first set of lectures edited here Eschmann presumably read to his students the Latin of the major texts behind his analyses; in the second set of lectures he has often provided an English translation. My approach here has been to provide my own translation of any text he either left blank, presumably because he intended to read the Latin, or, more rarely, included the Latin in his written version. Where his translations are provided, they are presented; all are given in Latin in the notes. With very rare exceptions, in neither set of his class notes did Eschmann record all the references he made to various authors; it has been easy, of course, to identify those of Saint Thomas, but some others have posed difficulties. The Notes represent my best efforts to supply necessary information.

In my judgment another issue requires a statement of editorial principle on a most contentious issue. In the years when Eschmann had his last opportunity to edit his texts, the persuasion that "gender-exclusive" language ought to be avoided and "gender-inclusive" language adopted, was not on the horizon; at that time the term "politically correct" would hardly have been understood. In 1942, the very year of Eschmann's arrival on the Toronto, it was possible to find a woman, an author of stature who was notorious for her forthright address, introducing her own contribution to a collection entitled *This is My Best* in what are accounted now to be unacceptable terms (Italics are mine):

> Now what is a writer to say about a sample of *his* own work? If *he* takes one course, *he's* simpering. If *he* goes the opposite way, *he's* Saroyan. There seems to be left open for *him* only that most ignoble route, the middle of the road. I think that this story of mine is the nicest bit of writing, the most careful, that I have ever done.... It may be that I felt a certain *maternal* obligation to say a few words in its favor. Nobody else did.[15]

One must suppose that Dorothy Parker *rediviva*, "alive once more," would put all this somewhat differently. Now Eschmann was gentlemanly and kind; he treated women with respect and courtesy. Were he writing today it is hard to think that he would not wish to offend women by a mere choice of words. Nor is the observation that to adjust this custom is to falsify the history of an era. Apart from any "feminist" issue, his text reflects the Latin in which our human race, taken as a species, and the adult male of that species, are signified by two different words: *homo, hominis* signifies any member of the human race, female infants included; it has no overtones of sexual differentiation. Should a Latin speaker wish to insist on an adult male of our species a form of *vir, viri* must be used. In English, however, the single term "man" has served in the past for both sorts of referent. In addition, although Latin possesses distinct terms for the nominatives "he" or "she" or "it," and for the accusatives "him" or "her" or "it," often those terms need not be expressed by a Latin writer, whereas they may be required in an English translation. A Latin verb in the third person singular can convey without an expressed pronoun as subject what we express either by "he" or "she" or even by "it." If one must translate into English such a verb with respect to a human person, in that person and number, there is small alternative to saying "he" or "she"; occasionally the term "one" will serve. In the possessive case, the Latin genitive, *eius* does duty for "his," "hers," or even for "its"; we have no such gender-indeterminate term of possession in English. It may be remarked that not only Latin, but other ancient tongues as well made the distinction between the

[15] See the entry by Dorothy Parker in *This is my Best*, ed. Whit Burnett (New York: The Dial Press, 1942); for her words cited here, see p. 206.

gender-specific and the general use of terms for us; Greeks had *anêr, andros* for the first and *anthrôpos* for the second, Hebrews said either *ish* or *adam*.

In our time of heightened consciousness, grounded in grievances on the part of women against wrongs that every fair-minded person must deplore, writers have been led to employ a number of devices, not always felicitous, to avoid offending feminine sensibility. "He" and "she," "his" and "hers," "him" and "her," are at times used alternately with inevitably bizarre results. Another device, no less bizarre, is to say or to write "he/she," "his/hers," "him/her."

Since Eschmann would not have wished to offend women, but since his prose is careful and precise, the procedures used in editing his text are attempts to save whatever can be saved of his own words, but with adjustments that may smooth the way to acceptance. Wherever the sense Eschmann must be understood to have intended requires a gender-determined term, that term has been used without scruple. Thomas Aquinas is no more to be designated by "she" than Joan of Arc ought to be referred to as "he." Where both men and women are at issue, an indeterminate term has been preferred, but only where it distorts neither English usage nor the flow of the author's expression. On all other occasions, and they are relatively few, the Eschmann text is presented as Eschmann wrote it; at those points one may hope that women will not take umbrage. It is no doubt a futile hope that no reader will be annoyed by what seem to me minor and appropriate adjustments.

A parallel editorial adjustment of Eschmann's text has been made on another pair of terms. As was general usage in his time (it remains all but universal in ours as well) Eschmann used the linguistic and geographical terms "Arab" and "Arabic" to signify, for instance, Avicenna, who was a Persian who wrote in both Persian and in Arabic, and Averroes, a Moslem resident in Spain who wrote exclusively in Arabic, although some of his texts have survived only in Hebrew or Latin translation. More precise terms for such thinkers would be "Moslem" or "Islamic," terms preferred here to the terms "Arab" and "Arabic."

Apart from these questions of justifiable sensibility, wherever it seems right (for the sake of clarity for instance) to make an addition to Eschmann's text what is added will be within angled brackets, ⟨...⟩. All upper-case subheadings are editorial additions, intended to assist a reader in taking the stance of a student in Eschmann's lecture hall; it has been thought unnecessary to put these in brackets. Eschmann's own headings whenever they occur are in normal typeface. With these principles in place, we proceed to Eschmann's words.

# Part One

# *Eschmannus bellator*

# Saint Thomas Aquinas O.P., the *Summary of Theology* I-II: Prologue and Question 1, Articles 1-8

## ⟨A. Preliminaries⟩

The subject matter of this lecture course is the structure of the *Summa theologiae* Part II.[1] This Second Part is subdivided into a First and a Second Part, called respectively "The First Part of the Second Part" and the "Second Part of the Second Part," written summarily as "I-II" and "II-II." We shall pay special attention to I-II, and with this we shall have our hands full indeed.

Saint Thomas himself called this "Second Part" the "treatise on morals," the "moral treatise," *Tractatus moralium*, of the "Summation," of the *Summa theologiae*, at I, 83, 2, Response to the 3⟨rd preliminary argument⟩. Thus, the "Second Part" is theology for just the same reason, and just as much as, the rest of the work is theology.

There is in Saint Thomas no division of theology into "dogmatics" and "morals." This is a modern division which is now firmly established in our scholastic technique, our technique of teaching and learning, but which has absolutely nothing to do with Saint Thomas, is contrary to the spirit of Aquinas's great work, and is thoroughly unfit to be applied to the *Summa theologiae*. If a school intends to adjust teaching and learning "to the mind of Saint Thomas," if it wants to be faithful to Saint Thomas, and if, on the other hand, it continues teaching "dogmatics" and "morals," it is facing an intrinsically impossible task and, needless to say, intrinsic contradictions have a way of making themselves felt. Among all the Catholic schools of today, I know only one that does not conform to this nonsense.

[1] This material is from folder CLN 30, that is, "Classnotes number 30" in the terminology of the finding list referred to in the Introduction. The "Ottawa *Summa*" is the source for all references to the *Summa theologiae* of Saint Thomas, an edition on which (as mentioned in the Introduction) it seems that Eschmann worked, providing, if local tradition has this detail straight, the identification of anonymous references and the noting of parallel passages, two devices he held to be necessary for serious work on Aquinas.

This is the Dominican school, if and inasmuch as it is faithful to the Dominican Constitutions—which sometimes it is not! I, for my part, never learned Moral Theology according to one or another of those modern handbooks of which there are plenty, one like another. I learned theology out of this *Summa* by following the text in its entirety from start to finish. But this is a privilege which the great majority of our students do not enjoy.

The division into "dogmatics" and "morals" is of fairly recent date. It started in the seventeenth century and is a product of the peculiar situation of that century: the struggle of the Church in the midst of powers and tendencies that endeavor to reach autonomy[2] and to set themselves up against the unity of the Church. In a world of countless autonomies that were all striving for definition and assertion, theologians thought of nothing better than to set up their own autonomy. Hence the tendency to collect and synthesize everything belonging to *formal* dogma, in other words, a tendency to circumscribe and to limit the "deposit of faith," the *depositum fidei*, the treasury of faith as defined by competent ecclesiastical authority. This recourse to formal dogma already denotes the juridical[3] character which is so deeply impressed on modern theological science. For the main thing in "dogmatic theology" is not the understanding of faith, but the definition and the extrinsic, formal, juridical, certitude of the faith.

This juridical tendency was still more powerful with respect to the other branch of ecclesiastical studies, namely, with respect to morals. Here the tendency of the theologians was to describe the "treasury of laws" as distinguished from the "treasury of the articles of faith." Articles of faith on the one hand, and laws on the other hand, emerge slowly as two centers of ecclesiastical studies, the one as nucleus of "dogmatics," the other that of "morals." In the eighteenth century we witness a complete dismemberment of theology into two main pieces, dogmatics and morals, each an autonomous science, each using its own principles and its own methods. In all this a phenomenon that we might call "legalization" or "juridification" is all too visible. Everything is reduced in "dogma" to definition and in "morals" to law. The fundamental tendency of the jurist is to have some text on which he can put his finger, an "authentic" text emanating from competent authority and ready to put an end to all discussion and all

[2] The term our author used here is a Greek loan-word embodying two terms, one of which means "self" (*autos*), and the second "law" (*nomos*), hence, "autonomy" means "self-rule," in independence of other authority.

[3] "Juridical" like "autonomous" evokes "law," one Latin term for which is *ius, iuris*; "juridical" is not a favorable term in Eschmann's lexicon.

dissent.

In Saint Thomas the "treatise on morals," the *tractatus moralium*, is an integral part of theology. Speaking technically we should even say that it is a "potential part," a "powerful part," a *pars potentialis*, of theology, that is, a part in which the power, the *potentia*, the formative and constructive principle of the whole, is omnipresent. In other words, there is not a line in the Second Part that is not "theological." Take theology away from the Second Part? The operation would be comparable to removing light and color and perspective from a picture!

If the question is asked whether moral *philosophy*[4] might be learned or taught from the Second Part, the answer clearly is "No"! In order to do this one would have to cut out pieces from this work, declare them to be "philosophical" (a pretty arbitrary decree!) and put them together in a new unity. A science is not made up with scissors and paste. Now this lecture course is supposed to be lectures in "philosophy"; much as I should like to do philosophy, I refuse to work with scissors and paste. From this moment on, our subject is the text of the *Summa theologiae*; we just have to take this text as it is, and it is a theological text.

The method of cutting the *Summa theologiae* into pieces and then putting these dead parts together again, in the vain hope of obtaining something alive and organic, is a method often used, not only in philosophy, but also in theology. Just as it is wrong to find philosophy in Saint Thomas's *Summa*, so it is also wrong and vain to try to find in it modern dogmatics, that juridically minded "Dogmatic Theology" which we have inherited from the seventeenth and eighteenth centuries.

Once upon a time I attended a lecture (the subject was the first Article of the First Part of the Second Part, ⟨ST I-II 1, 1⟩) where the Professor "proved" from Holy Scripture the thesis of that Article: "All human actions are for the sake of an end," *omnes actiones humanae sunt propter finem*. He found some text where the tail of Tobias's dog is mentioned.[5]

[4] "Philosophy" is also a Greek loan-word constructed by the Greeks themselves from the terms for "I love," *phileō*, and for "wisdom," *sophia*, a construct traditionally ascribed to Pythagoras; see Cicero, *Tusculan Disputations* 5, 3, 8-9. In "scholastic" tradition, philosophy has been distinguished from theology in that the first must appeal exclusively to human intelligence, whereas the second examines the meaning and coherence of what is taken on faith.

[5] The text which the unnamed lecturer must have had in mind is Tobias 11:9 in which the Latin Vulgate text of the Bible describes the return of Tobias to his home and the welcome the dog manifested "with his tail"; what Eschmann's unnamed lecturer's point may have been in appealing to this text of course has been

To this day I do not know what it was all about, but the tendency was clear. This man was teaching theology and as a true modern "jurist-theologian" he had to contrive a "proof from Sacred Scripture," whatever the cost. No jurist can ever get along without appealing to an authoritative text, not because he finds there the intelligibility of his case, but because the text, being "authoritative," terminates any debate. I intend to bring out in this lecture course the "treatise on morals" of the *Summa theologiae* exactly as it was intended by the author.

## ⟨B. Reflections on the Proposed Project⟩

This lecture is inscribed "The Philosophy of the Human Act in Saint Thomas Aquinas" (a pretty large order which I cannot fulfill, nor do I intend to fulfill it!).

The first principle of the human act, the principle or cause determining its most essential structure, is its last end which is *beatitudo*, "beatitude." The very first consideration, therefore, which Saint Thomas in all his writings gives to the human act, is its end. To use a modern word, it is the "teleology"[6] of the human act and of human life with which the Thomistic doctrine of this subject begins. This matter is abundantly (and very completely) taken care of in the first five Questions of the I-II of the *Summa theologiae*. We shall read this text and I shall try to give a historico-systematic commentary on it.

The very first Question of I-II is generally acknowledged to be a very difficult treatise indeed. It is the cornerstone of the whole vast edifice of Part II. As everything in the *Summa theologiae*, so this treatise on beatitude had long matured in the mind of Aquinas. It is a definite statement and a statement proposed, not by way of a lengthy monographic study—an "Introduction to Moral Theology" as we should be tempted to write today —but by way of the questions and articles of a "summation," of a *summa*.

One of the more important consequences of this fact is that the expression of Saint Thomas is at the same time powerful and parsimonious. It is "powerful:" by this I mean that it contains virtually the whole II Part

---

lost. Unless memory deceives me, this very text was adduced by John Henry Newman as an instance of an *obiter dictum*, a "statement made in passing," that did not, in Newman's view, demand religious "faith."

[6] "Teleology" is another Greek loan-word, composed of the Greek terms for "end," *telos*, and *logos*, an extremely flexible term that can mean "concept," "term," "discussion of," or "study of."

which, in truth, is to be developed out of the propositions which we are to read. Such is the meaning of the analogy of the "cornerstone" applied to the intellectual organism of a doctrine; but second, the Thomistic diction is also "parsimonious," strict, close-fisted. Although giving a *full* account of what is in the writer's mind, and although giving this account in clear and understandable language, it refuses, nevertheless, to go into any details. Saint Thomas speaks here an even more abstract language than he does so often elsewhere.

The *Summa* was meant to be a textbook in school. In reading this book we must try always to conform to this very first, and important, condition. The articles are meant to be read slowly. The medieval professor had to read his text slowly: lighting conditions were poor, parchment expensive, ink not easily carried around, pens needed frequent sharpening. All this being so, medieval learning was mostly dependent upon memory as every biography of a medieval student tells us over and over again. Hence the articles of the *Summa* were meant to be memorized. I should like to stress this fact which, to my mind, is extremely important for everyone who wants to read this book. What is in our memory is, of course, not yet a truly "intellectual" possession of our mind, but it is ready to be remembered and so to become such a possession. The didactic skill ⟨visible in⟩ the *Summa* consists in this, that at the beginning of a given treatise principles and doctrines are proposed in the clearest and simplest way, but not with all their implications made explicit. The student is supposed to consider these doctrines, to understand them as far as possible, but also to hold them in the memory, ready to be used at any time. Everyone familiar with the *Summa* knows the almost endless repetition of certain principles, their use in different contexts, and of the new light which, consequently, is again and again thrown upon them. Thus the student will be able to fill in more and more details, penetrate more and more the virtuality of a given principle, and so more and more transform into formal, intellectual, possession that which first was only a material possession of memory. The transition from implicit to explicit knowledge is indeed the key to the extremely artful pedagogy of the *Summa*. This transition takes time: intellectual growth is as slow as, if not slower than, physical growth. The two virtues required for the accomplishment of fruitful work in the *Summa* are patience and persistence, doggedness.

I am not sure as to whether most Thomistic commentaries (mine included) may not sin against the very intention of the work. We sin, I venture to think, through an all too vivid intellectual curiosity. We are eager to make things explicit where the master teacher (which Saint Thomas really is), wants them to be—and for the time being to remain—implicit. An ideal commentator would confine his efforts to let the principles and propositions sink into the student's mind: he would simply aid the process. Given our natural laziness, that commentator would control the work of memorizing the text. One of the main parts of that job would be to keep both teacher and student from rushing on to premature, untimely, distinctness in the understanding of the text.

## ⟨C. THE PROLOGUE⟩[7]

> Since, as the Damascene states, the human being is said to be "made to the image of God" inasmuch as through "image" is signified what is intellectual, and free as to choice, and of itself endowed with power. After having spoken first of the Exemplar, namely, of God, and of those things which have proceeded from the divine power in accord with His will, it remains that we consider His image, that is, the human being as principle of that being's own works, as having free choice and power over that same being's own works.[8]

Let us repeat Saint Thomas's doctrine in our own words. The whole preceding Part of the *Summa*, Part I, which has treated of God and of the procession from God of creatures, is here characterized as a treatise of an "exemplar," of a model. And to this treatise, naturally, there now succeeds with Part II the treatise on one of those creatures which in a special way is modelled after that divine pattern. This is the human being who is an "image of God." The similitude between God and the human being (or rather that similitude which is called "image," a traditional theological notion) consists in the intellectual nature. Special stress is laid upon this: that

[7] Material from CLN 37, pp. 2-10.

[8] There is inconclusive evidence that Eschmann read longer Latin texts to his class and on a very few occasions provided English translations of them; his normal practice seems to have been to leave out both the Latin and the English from his meticulous class lecture notes, but presumably to bring the books from which he wished to cite. My practice has been to give his translations where he provided them, to translate all others in what seems to be his spirit, and to give the Latin in the notes, Here the Latin beneath my translation in the text is: "Quia, sicut Damascenus dicit, homo factus ad imaginem Dei dicitur, secundum quod per imaginem significatur intellectuale et arbitrio liberum et per se potestativum; postquam praedictum est de exemplari, scilicet de Deo, et de his quae processerunt ex divina potestate secundum eius voluntatem; restat ut consideremus de eius imagine, idest de homine, secundum quod et ipse est suorum operum principium, quasi liberum arbitrium habens et suorum operum potestatem." ST 1-2, Prologus; t. 2, p. 710 a, 4-15.

intellectuality enables a being to be the principle of that being's own actions. God is the principle of His works through His power as determined by His will. So too (and, of course, proportionally, ⟨analogically⟩) a human being is the principle of his or her own actions as having *liberum arbitrium* ⟨the freedom of discretionary, arbitrary, decision⟩ and *suorum operum potestatem,* ⟨the power over *whether* one acts, and over *what* one is going to do⟩. Thus the theme of this Part II is laid down: it is the human being as a free and responsible agent of his or of her own actions; in *this* the human being is an image of God.

We shall now have to proceed to a careful and proper explanation of our Prologue. Let us first of all establish our method, that is, the way by which we expect to obtain results in this investigation, to teach methods, to show, not what an orthodox opinion sounds like, but how to arrive at a well-established conclusion. Our present problem is the explanation of this text; how to go about it.

Here is how I think we ought to proceed. We have to find terms of comparison proper to this text. Everything, that belongs in any way to the "presuppositions" of this text, will be a "proper" term of comparison, helpful for the understanding of the meaning of what is being said. Everything, on the contrary, that lies outside those presuppositions, will be of no help in clearing up the text. Later or modern thought, for instance, problems and ways of understanding that have appeared at a later time, are certainly not "presuppositions" of this text. As long, therefore, and as far as we are dealing with the question of how to understand this text correctly all later problems and ways of thinking ought to be carefully kept out of the business. They are not terms of comparison "proper" to the text and cannot be expected to help in what is our first task: understanding the "letter," the *littera,* of our text.

They might be brought in later, that is, after the first task has been accomplished, but thus they would belong to a "discussion" of the doctrine presented here and of its implications—which can be undertaken only on the basis of a complete and accurate understanding of the text. That must come first. We ought not to expect Saint Thomas to solve *our* problems; strictly speaking we cannot expect anything of him but the statement and solution of *his own* problems.

Now, what are the presuppositions of our text and what are the proper objects of our comparative study?

⟨*a. Prologues*⟩

First of all, they are the "coordinated" texts in the *Summa* itself. Every Part of this work is introduced by a Prologue similar to the one we have just read in which the author stated his "intention," that is, the subject which he was going to treat and the principles of organization of his treatise. All those Prologues, taken together, constitute a sort of guidebook for those who travel through the vast construction of the *Summa*. At every point those travellers are informed as to where they are and how they might pass from one hall to another. Hence, we must study our Prologue in light of the others in order to see clearly what the real meaning of our text may be.

⟨*b. Parallel Texts*⟩

The second group of terms of comparison proper to our text is constituted by the so-called "parallel texts" in other works of the author. Parallel texts or passages are those in which the same doctrine is expressed. The notion of "parallel texts" is somewhat misleading inasmuch as it implies the analogy of one and the same plane on which lines lying evenly in the same direction are drawn. Often (this ought to be understood) the various expressions of one and the same thought in different works are not, in Saint Thomas, simple variations of one theme, equivalent and interchangeable one with the other, differing only verbally and in no way substantially. On the contrary, very often they are moments, or parts, of an intellectual development, a movement that grew constantly in volume as well as in depth. With the understanding that such may be the case, and that we must pay careful attention to this possibility, we may retain the traditional notion of parallel texts or passages, simply meaning: "passages which treat of the same point or doctrine." Such passages with respect to our present text should be taken into account: again, they belong to the presuppositions of this "letter," of this *littera*.

## ⟨D. The School as Context⟩

Thirdly, the opinions or positions of other thinkers who were known to the author of our text will have to be examined. They too belong to the presuppositions of the *littera*, ⟨of the *letter*⟩. No scholastic doctor or, for that matter, no writer at all is an isolated thinker, completely cut off from any contact with his predecessors or contemporaries. Least of all should we suppose a scholastic thinker to be such a lonely being since a "scholastic" is one who, by definition, moves within the framework of a tradition. To a scholastic, the cult of tradition is one of his main and essential interests. The relations of our text to tradition and to contemporary thought—"contemporary" with reference to Saint Thomas!—must be investigated. This investigation will bring to light the originality of our passage and this originality is perhaps its most outstanding characteristic.

*a. Coordinate Texts in the* Summa

It was customary for the author of the *Summa* to inform its readers at every new step about the fact as well as about the significance of what was being done. Thus the structure and the organization of the whole work were made manifest throughout. This announcement was laid down in the introductory passages found at the head of every Question or group of Questions. Every student of Saint Thomas ought to go through carefully all those passages (and saying "all" I mean *all*!) before using the *Summa*, in order to have a clear and detailed idea, not only of what is in this work, but also, and indeed foremost, an idea of its proper organization. Here we are concerned with those introductory passages that reveal to us the most general structural lines of the work. The passages thus to be considered are the Introductions to Part I, Question 2, to Part I-II, and to Part III. The first of these passages is the shortest, the most concise, and yet the fullest statement of the contents and structure of the *Summa*:

> Because, therefore, the principal intention of this sacred teaching is to hand on knowledge of God, and not only according to the way He is in Himself, but also according as He is the Principle of things, and their End, and especially the End of the rational creature, as is manifest from what has been said. Intending the exposition of this teaching we shall treat first of God; second, of the movement of the rational creature toward God; third, of Christ who, inasmuch as human, is for us a path for tending toward God.[9]

The three Parts of the *Summa*, thus should be inscribed: I Part "On God"; II Part "On the Motion of the Rational Creature Toward God"; "Part III, On Christ." As has been mentioned, The Part II (I-II and II-II) has been called by Saint Thomas himself "The Treatise on Moral Things." The Treatise on Moral Things is thus an integral part of Theology, that is, of the single science which has God for its object, that is, the knowledge of God. We can also say that the object of Part II is God inasmuch as He is the End of the rational creature. Let us conclude then that from this introduction to Part I we get two notifications of what is to be the content of the

[9] "Quia igitur principalis intentio huius sacrae doctrinae est Dei cognitionem tradere, et non solum secundum quod in se est, sed etiam secundum quod est principium rerum et finis earum, et specialiter rationalis creaturae, ut ex dictis est manifestum; ad huius doctrinae expositionem intendentes, primo tractabimus de Deo; secundo, de motu rationalis creaturae in Deum; tertio, de Christo, qui secundum quod homo, via est nobis tendendi in Deum." ST 1, 2; (Introductio), t. 1, p. 11a, ll. 20-31.

"Treatise on Moral Things:" (1) concerning the movement of the rational creature toward God and (2) on God inasmuch as He is the End of the rational creature. These two titles are, of course, equivalent; they affirm the same thing under different aspects.

Again, in the Prologue to Part III, Saint Thomas looks back to Part II and states what the content of the Treatise on Moral Matters has been by saying that it was "a consideration of the last End of human life, and of virtues and vices." Thus we add the third formula (a rather loose one) to the two already stated: "a consideration of the ultimate End of human life, and of virtues and of vices." A fourth formula is that of our Prologue to Part I of Part II, on the "image of God," that is, on the human being inasmuch as the human being too is the principle of that being's own working, as having free choice and power over that same being's own works.

Now doubtless all these formulas really indicate the same thing which, since it is a complex reality, can be viewed according to different aspects. There is always that movement of the rational creature toward God which is viewed (1) in its term, (2) in its principle, and (3) in its concrete movement or development which is achieved between the term and its principle.

This fundamental identity of all the various formulas by which the object of the Moral Treatise is characterized, at the present stage of our investigations is the only conclusion at which we can arrive. No other elements or facts, which could authorize us to go any farther in our conclusions, are as yet available to us. Nevertheless, let us observe that there is perhaps a special reason why at the beginning of the II Part Saint Thomas so forcefully insists on the human being's privilege of being, like God (and because of being in God's image) the principle of activity his or her own activity, possessing free choice and power over her or his own acts. The formula is very striking. Why this stress on the "principle" of human actions; why this manifest preoccupation, which even goes so far as to eliminate (at least from the surface of the text) an element which elsewhere is always in the foreground, namely, that God is the End of human life, the Term of the movement of the rational creature? To repeat: there is no contradiction between our text and the others. All those formulas which we have seen finally come to mean the same thing. Still, the question remains: is it possible that the peculiar accent of our text has a special meaning and significance?

*b. Parallel Texts in the Corpus*[10]

A second point of our comparative studies was to look into some parallel texts in other works of Aquinas. Here I submit to brief consideration the following passages: (1) a text at the beginning of the *Scriptum*, the "Writing," that is, of Saint Thomas's very first theological systematization in the form of the usual commentary on Peter Lombard's *Sentences*;[11] (2) the introduction to the Third Book of the *Summa contra gentiles*; and (3) the introduction to his *Exposition* of Aristotle's *Nicomachean Ethics*.

The text of the *Scriptum* is remarkable because it proves that Aquinas at the very beginning of his teaching and in his first systematic work already envisaged a division of theology which made it possible for him later to create theological ethics as a constitutive part of the whole of theology. There, at the beginning of his commenting on Book I, Distinction 2, he gives us to understand that, according to his mind, a theological system ought to contain two great parts, one of which treats of things inasmuch as they proceed from God and another which treats of things inasmuch as they return to God. There is a "first part," a *prima pars*, "On things according as they go forth," their *exitus*, from their Principle and a "second part," a *secunda pars*, "On things according as they return to their End."

It is easy to see that exactly this conception, the conception of a grandiose circular movement of procession and return (originally a neo-Platonic scheme) is to be the structural principle of the *Summa theologiae* and in

[10] Material from CLN 37, p. 7.

[11] Peter Lombard, first a professor of theology and then Bishop of Paris in the mid-twelfth century, composed *Four Books of Sentences*, that is, a collection in four books of "statements" by Church Fathers such as Augustine, Ambrose, Gregory the Great, etc. organized (as Eschmann will remark) in accord with the order of the Creeds and given short explanations by Peter Lombard himself. This work became the basic text for teaching theology in the universities and theologates of the religious orders in Europe, at least from the time of Alexander of Hales (first half of the thirteenth century) until the sixteenth century; having spent some years as a "bachelor of the Bible," an embryonic theologian was required to produce a "Writing," a *Scriptum*, on this work as a "bachelor of the *Sentences*" before proceeding to "incept" as a master in theology, that is, to give an inaugural lecture, an "inception," considered satisfactory by the "regent masters." The Latin text of the *Scriptum* on Lombard's work by Thomas is that of the edition, first by P. Mandonnet O.P., Vols. 1 and 2, then Vols. 3 and 4 by Maria Fabianus Moos O.P. (Paris: Lethielleux, 1929-1947); since the Fourth Book in this edition ends with Question 22, at the few points where Eschmann goes beyond that Question, recourse will be made to the (Paris) Vivès edition of the *Opera omnia* of Thomas.

that *Summa* it was to produce the "Treatise on Moral Matters," the *tractatus moralium*, as a constitutive part of theology. In the *Scriptum* this conception did not bear *this* fruit, and this for the simple reason that the *Scriptum* is a commentary and thus a work dependent upon the text which was to be explained. In fact, Peter Lombard's work did not, in his theological systematization, proceed according to the scheme of "going forth" and "return," *exitus, reditus.*

The *Summa contra gentiles*, a "summa against unbelievers,"[12] is the first theological synthesis which Aquinas undertook on his own, that is, no longer as a "commentator" who, as such, has to follow his text, but as an original thinker who relies on his own initiative and his own architectural plan. This work is substantially a "showing of the truth of the Catholic faith," a *manifestatio veritatis catholicae fidei*, yet with the specific purpose, not of simply teaching a doctrine, but of defending it against an attack or attacks coming from outside. The adversaries against whom the *Contra gentiles* is composed are the Greek and Islamic philosophers who especially reject, or would reject, Christian notions of God, of the Creator, and of God's Providence. This apologetic purpose shapes the organization of Aquinas's theology in this work. A good and clear résumé of this organization, at least insofar as the first three Books of the *Summa contra gentiles* are concerned, is found in Book 3, Chapter 1, toward the end of the Chapter, where Saint Thomas says that his First Book treats "Of the perfection of the divine nature," the second, "Of the perfection of the divine power" insofar as It is the Producer and the Lord of all things, and the third "Of the perfect divine authority and dignity," insofar as God is the End and the Ruler of all things.

This Third Book interests us particularly for it is often taken as the "treatise on morals" in the *Contra gentiles*, parallel to the II Part of the *Summa theologiae.* Yet the point of view of *Contra gentiles* ⟨Book⟩ 3 is re-

[12] The term "gentiles" in this title echoes the Hebrew Scriptures in so terming those who did not share the biblical faith of Jews, but here the Christian faith is the norm intended. It has long been proposed that the precise "gentiles" Aquinas had in view were Moslem theologians and philosophers, especially those in Spain. Although this can hardly be excluded (how could Thomas refuse to assist Christian missionaries faced with learned opposition?) there is no convincing evidence that this was his intent. His work is intelligible as simply a treatise on the hypothetical non-Christian receiving a knowledgeable indoctrination in Christianity, one in Eschmann's terms who "would object" on the grounds of Greek or Islamic thought. References to the *Summa contra gentiles* will be to the "manual edition" (Rome: Leonine Commission, 1934), rather than to the Commission's earlier folio edition of the work.

markably different from that of the II Part. This difference was stressed by Clement Suermont:

> In the *Contra gentiles* generally all moral questions are connected with the topic "God as final Cause or End of the intellectual creature" and are, therefore, treated under the aspect of God's Providence and leadership, while on the other hand, in the *Summa theologiae*, these are treated under the heading: The movement of the human being toward God, his last End.[13]

This remark, I think, is exact. Indeed, we have only to put Saint Thomas's own texts, one alongside the other, to see the difference:

> ...it remains in this Third Book to follow out, from His (God's) perfect authority or dignity in that He is the End and the Ruler of all things.[14]

and in the great *Summa*:

> ...it remains, that we consider His image, that is, the human being, insofar as that being is the principle....[15]

The structure of that Third Book (the topics treated therein) closely depends on the general idea as laid down in Chapter 1. It is particularly worthy of note that there is no treatise "On Human Acts," whereas the II Part in its totality is nothing but a treatise on human acts and on their "principle"—the human being.

In *Contra gentiles* 3 Saint Thomas proceeds in the following way. There is first a section (Chapters 2-24 inclusive) that explains the actions of all creatures in the neo-Platonic terms of an assimilation to God. Then the author goes on to a long treatise on beatitude, which is envisaged as the intended end of the divine government of rational creatures (Chapters 25-63). There are here, as might be expected, many elements later to be assumed in the synthesis of the *Summa theologiae*, but the point of view is different. When the *Contra gentiles* speaks of the role of the "end" in the human act, its reasonings are analogical. They serve to define and to illustrate God's action in the government of the universe rather than to dis-

13 Clemens Stephanus Suermont, *Tabulae schematicae...Summae Theologiae et Summae contra gentiles sancti Thomae Aquinatis* (Rome: Marietti, 1943).

14 "...restat in hoc Tertio Libro prosequi de perfecta auctoritate sive dignitate ipsius, secundum quod est rerum omnium finis et rector." SCG 3, 1; ed. cit. p. 227a, ca finem.

15 See full passage, note 8 above.

cuss the "human act" directly as does the II Part of the *Summa theologiae*. The long discussions about our beatitude are developed within a treatise which directly intends to clarify our knowledge of God's intentions with humans, that is, in other words, within a speculative treatise having as its object a better knowledge of God's Providence according to the end envisaged by that Providence.

After having so determined the "End," that is, the "final Cause" of Providence, the *Contra gentiles* continues with a treatise on that Providence Itself. This takes up the rest of the Book. Saint Thomas starts by considering divine Providence as extending to the universe in general (Chapters 64-110). Thereafter the special Providence of rational creatures comes up for discussion. There are two modalities of this Providence, namely, Law and grace. It is with these two treatises, on law (Chapter 111, then especially, Chapters 114-146) and grace (Chapters 147-163) that the *Summa contra gentiles* terminates.

In short then, and to resume, a great number of ethical questions are treated in the *Summa contra gentiles* 3 (note that Chapters 64-82 would correspond rather to *Summa theologiae* I, 103, 1 ⟨extending⟩ to I, 119, 2, than to anything in the II Part). Still, the reasons why they are treated, and the organic principles of the treatise, are always "God, End and Ruler," not "the movement of rational creatures toward God." It would be unjustifiable, I think, to speak of a "moral part" of the *Summa contra gentiles*. The moral part of a theological system is the originality of the *Summa theologiae* and the *Contra gentiles* must be explained on the basis of its own presuppositions and intentions. It is, (as I said—or rather, the author himself said) "a showing of the truth of the Catholic faith" against pagan philosophers. In the thought of those pagans one point, most directly contrary to Christian faith, was the negation of a personal God. *Contra gentiles* 3 deals with God's personal Providence and rectorship. Hence, on the very basis of this particular purpose of the work, the two *Summae* cannot in strictness be considered as corresponding efforts of their author. There is no absolute parallelism. Each one has its own organization imposed by the particular object of each. But, at any rate, the case of the *Contra gentiles* might teach us how a treatise on God the Exemplar might have looked. It could have been something like the *Contra gentiles*; it could not have been the II Part, which is a "treatise on moral realities," a treatise on human acts and acting, a treatise on virtues and vices.

Our third and last text is an *Exposition* by Aquinas of the *Nicomachean Ethics* of Aristotle. This work is prefaced by an Introduction, one of those great masterpieces of thought and of presentation that only Aquinas knew how to compose. The complete organism of the sciences is presented to us in a clear and simple way such as we shall not find anywhere else in Saint

Thomas's works. This, however, does not concern us here, where our point is to underscore the words by which Saint Thomas assigns a subject, *its* subject, to "ethics" or "moral philosophy:" the proper role of moral philosophy is to consider human operations inasmuch as they are ordered to each other and to the end. A few lines farther on Saint Thomas repeats, "The subject of moral philosophy is human operation ordered to the end or even, the human being, as acting voluntarily for the sake of the end." I translate *the* end, not *an* end, because the end intended here is, of course, the ultimate end. Only the ultimate end fulfills the pure notion of "end" inasmuch as "end" means something final, something absolutely and not merely relatively final.

This declaration and definition is very remarkable for two reasons. First, it is the very same formula we found in the Prologue of Part I-II. It is the same even in the point that, to his first definition, Saint Thomas added a second, alternative one, which reads clearly as a reminiscence of what was said in the I-II. Now this formula in the *Exposition of the Ethics* is couched with regard to the Aristotelian work. This is, in fact, what Aristotle thought the subject of Ethics to be. Hence, at least one of the reasons why the Part II, the moral Part, of the *Summary of Theology* opens with the striking formula to which I have drawn attention, is the very example formulated by Aristotle. Thus we meet Aristotle in the opening lines of Part II, even though he is not mentioned explicitly.

Second this definition at the beginning of the *Exposition* is remarkable because it gives us the exact formula by which the transformation of Aristotelian ethics into a sacred science, namely, theology or, more exactly "moral" theology, may be achieved. The point is to determine the general notion of "for the sake of the end."

If we add here the Christian determination of these words by saying "for the sake of the end of eternal beatitude," we are in the midst of moral theology. The Aristotelian ethics thus, inasmuch as it constitutes a science about the "human being acting for the sake of the end," without restricting this to a natural or earthly end, can be taken over in its entirety into moral theology. In its generality, then, the notion of "a human being acting for the sake of the end" is just as true in pagan moral philosophy as it is in Christian moral theology. Our Prologue to I-II is in large measure an "Aristotelian" piece of work; it marks Saint Thomas's readiness to incorporate into his *Summa theologiae* the deepest inspiration of Aristotelian ethical thinking, of Aristotelian humanism.

*c. Problems Raised by the Formulae*[16]

Here, however, a problem raises its head. How can the "object" or, to speak Thomistic language, the "subject" of Moral Philosophy be the same as that of the "Moral Part" in the *Summa theologiae* which is supposed to be, from beginning to end, moral "theology"? Here we touch on a point which, to the modern reader, is the most disconcerting point in the *Summa* of Saint Thomas. It is a point by which the modern reader, and mind you, the modern reader alone, the reader ever since (roughly speaking) the sixteenth century, is thrown off balance. We simply fail to understand this apparent confusion in Saint Thomas; the modern reader insists on distinct knowledge, distinct concepts, and what he finds in Saint Thomas is just the contrary. It is, at this point, an indistinct concept, embracing, as it were, both Philosophy *and* Theology; he finds a much broader basis for the "moral consideration," *consideratio moralis*, than a modern reader thinks can be admitted.

Now let me make a few notes with regard to this problem. I intend, however, to limit myself to, and to stress, that which falls within the boundaries of a "commentary." It is not my intention (nor am I even tempted) to state and to develop the problems of "moral theology," "moral philosophy," or of "Christian philosophy," as it is stated nowadays. Saint Thomas had the habit—a very disquieting habit for many modern interpreters—of stating and discussing *his own* problems, to state and to discuss them as he pleased; he did not intend to answer *our* problems. Our reading of Saint Thomas, therefore, cannot have for its primary object finding answers to *our* problems, but rather to know the answers to *his* problems.

Three things, I believe, ought to be remembered. The first of these is that, if we nowadays are faced with the problem of what is the object of moral theology? (in contradistinction to moral philosophy). The answer must be that theology is human activity under this formal aspect: that it supernaturally enables us to reach God as He is in Himself, the Object of our supernatural beatitude. The Object of moral theology is thus "God as God," God in His proper Reality of Godhead, as beatifying humans, not merely (as in philosophy) God as First Cause. If we put the accent on the supernatural order of human acts, which is mainly the order of the "theological" virtues, faith, hope, and charity, above all of charity, as J.M. Ramirez O.P. put it,

> The Godhead Itself is formally included in the very act of charity elicited with respect to God, whether because He is its proper and

[16] Material from CLN 30, pp. 6-10.

> formal Object since that virtue is formally "theological," or because charity is essentially a friendship with God Himself and therefore formally a communication in the very life of God; it also refers totally all virtues to God as to their proper End.... Whence it is the role of charity to order the totality of human activity toward eternal life.... For this reason this formation or ordering of the other virtues by charity constitutes them formally in the class of the strictly "theologically" moral.[17]

Second, all this is not only perfectly true, but also was acknowledged and (at least in equivalent terms) affirmed by Saint Thomas himself. Several texts might be quoted, but let me quote one or two mentioned by Ramirez.[18] In a text from his *Scriptum* Saint Thomas affirms at least virtually that moral theology belongs to the "superior reason," the *ratio superior*, whereas moral philosophy belongs to the "inferior reason," the *ratio inferior*. These two "reasons" are distinguished there:

> For the inferior reason, intending a choice, takes counsel from arguments grounded in temporal realities, as that something is "superabundant" or "diminished," "useful," or "respectable," and so for the other conditions which a moral philosopher treats. The superior reason, however, takes counsel from eternal and divine arguments, as "because it is against the command of God" or "it will produce an offense against Him," or something of that sort.[19]

[17] Jacobus M. Ramirez O.P., *De hominis beatitudine. Tractatus theologicus* (Madrid: Editio praeparata a Victorino Rodriguez O.P., Instituto de filosofía Luis Vives, 1972), in *Edición de las Obras completas de Santiago Ramirez O.P.*, [Consejo superior de investigaciones cientificas], 3.1: 62, no. 53, p. 63, no. 56, p. 66, no. 61; this enormous work hereafter cited as "Ramirez."

[18] The words of Ramirez to which Eschmann here referred are: "Obiectum (formale quod) Theologiae Moralis est moralitas supernaturalis, hoc est divina seu stricte theologica (i.e. solum cognoscibilis per revelationem); vel etiam Deus ut Deus, prout est finis actuum humanorum supernaturalium," Ramirez, p. 59; "Definitio essentialis theologiae moralis: scientia ordinis actuum humanorum in beatitudinem supernaturalem ex revelatione virtuali procedens," ibidem, p. 61; Eschmann here remarked "In opposition to this the definition of Moral Philosophy would be: Scientia ordinis humanorum actuum in beatitudinem naturalem procedens ex ratione humana" (texts cited in Eschmann's CLN 30, p. 7).

[19] "...ratio enim inferior consiliatur ad electionem tendens ex rationibus rerum temporalium, ut quod aliquid est superfluum vel diminutum, utile vel honestum, et sic de aliis conditionibus quas moralis Philosophus pertractat; superior vero consilium sumit ex rationibus aeternis et divinis, ut quia est contra praeceptum Dei,

That the term "moral theologian," as opposed to "moral philosopher," is not mentioned in this text is proof that to define th
e respective realms of moral philosophy and moral theology is not the object of the article from which I am quoting. With respect to sin, Saint Thomas states on a certain occasion offered to him in Part I-II, Question 71, Article 6, Response to the 5th Argument,

> ...sin is considered by theologian especially, *praecipue*, insofar as it is an offense against God, whereas by a moral philosopher inasmuch as it is contrary to reason.[20]

The most interesting word in this text is perhaps the "especially," *praecipue*, which, I believe, might be interpreted in this way: if you want to press the point and assign to each science its respective province, then here you have it! But, the medieval theologian did not hesitate to claim considerations "from reason," *ex ratione*, to be his domain too, just as a medieval pope had no qualms in vindicating as his own the domain of temporal things and of politics!

This leads us to a third remark. Saint Thomas, of course, did distinguish moral theology and moral philosophy, just as he carefully distinguished nature and grace, reason and faith; from a number of Thomistic texts is easy to build up a theory of this distinction. But is that the question? The question which occupies us here seems rather to be this: how does it come about that, at such an important and sensitive spot as the beginning of the Part II, the "Moral Part" of the *Summa theologiae*, Saint Thomas did not care to mention this distinction, but rather left the distinction hidden under an indistinct concept, namely, that of the "human being as principle of that being's own works, as possessing free choice and power over that same being's own works." This concept is evidently true in both the natural and in the supernatural orders.

The problem, I venture to think, is one of exegesis rather than of doctrine. Is it right for a commentator, if a certain lack of distinctness is found, to fill out the lacuna and present the doctrine as though it were distinct? Or ought a commentator to stress, and to consider carefully, that very fact? Personally I incline to the latter alternative. This very lack of distinctness belongs to the text over the essential features of which a com-

---

vel ejus offensionem parit, vel aliquid hujusmodi." *Sent*. Lib. 2, Dist. 24, Q. 2, A. 2; t. 2, p. 606.

20 "...a theologis consideratur peccatum praecipue secundum quod est offensa contra Deum; a philosopho autem morali, secundum quod contrariatur rationi." ST 1-2, 71, 6, Ad 5; t. 2, p. 1094b, ll. 27-31.

mentator has no power.

What is more, it might be the case (and very often is!) that exactly the *omission* is important and worthy of note. Here, in this Prologue, it is indeed very significant that Saint Thomas did not feel any urge to define either "moral theology" or "moral philosophy," and that his notion of the object of the "moral part" of the *Summa theologiae* comprises both indistinctly. This indeed gives the whole Part II its broad basis and its specific character. Part II can hardly be qualified as "moral theology" in the exclusive modern sense nor can it be qualified as "moral philosophy," again in the exclusive modern sense. Part II defies all attempts to fetter and to chain it to any narrow pattern. Part II is a scandal to both moral theologians and to moral philosophers of the modern age. It is a treatise on the total human being and on total humanity without ever insinuating however that humanity and Christianity should not be formally distinguished and still less that they be confused, that is, one be taken for the other. The essential definition of moral theology found in Ramirez is right; it is also Thomistic. Still, it does not seem capable of covering exactly the fullness of Part II of the *Summa theologiae.*

### ⟨E. DIFFICULTY OF DEFINITION⟩

This is the place to say a few words about "Christian Philosophy," more especially about "Christian Ethics" or, better, about "Christian Moral Philosophy." Abundant discussions among Thomists and other scholars have been going on for about fifteen years, but my suspicion is that these discussion are laboring under an ambiguity. If we try to define "Christian Philosophy" with clear-cut and distinct notions, I am afraid this will prove to be impossible for it is impossible to make specifically "Christian" what relies on nature and reason. This is not because reason and Christian faith are contradictory, but because they are diverse, irreducible to anything one. Nothing of divine revelation and authority enters, strictly speaking, the formal essence of philosophy, nor is theology constituted by any truth or knowledge whose last resource is human reason. Let us say, with perhaps a better formula, philosophy's sufficient foundation is, of itself, human reason.

Yet in spite of this, the defenders of Christian Philosophy have a good case,[21] especially with respect to the science of moral order. In my

[21] See CLN 38, p. 8; here the insight of L.K. Shook noted in the Introduction is apposite: "This problem of Christian theology and Christian philosophy is solved

view, the Part II of Saint Thomas is best described as "Christian Philosophy." It is neither pure and undiluted moral theology nor pure and undiluted moral philosophy in the technical senses of these terms. Still it implies no confusion of the two orders, natural and supernatural. Their intimate harmonization is the peculiar secret of the Part II. Saint Thomas worked out this enigma but never explicitly stated it.

There remains another problem: how is it possible that in a treatise on Christian humanity, Christ is not mentioned *ex professo*, "in a formal way"? Christ is the subject of Part III. Ought he not rather to occupy the Part II and only then a Part III, concerned with Christian morality which takes Christ as model, might be possible?

⟨*a. The Response of Suarez*⟩

One answer is to be found in the *Commentary* by Francisco Suárez S.J., at the beginning of his own treatise on the Incarnation. This was followed by the Salamanca thinkers, "Baroque Thomists," who learned a great deal from Suárez. Christ is God-Man. A composite, the elements of which, God (the first Element) and then man (the second element), were dealt with by Saint Thomas in a procedure suggested by Aristotle at the beginning of the *Politics*. A whole must be divided into its parts, and before dealing with a whole, the parts must be considered first.[22]

I am afraid that this answer by Suárez is more ingenious than true. It takes no account of the main structural idea of the whole *Summa theologiae* which is the "going forth," the *exitus*, of creatures from God and their "return," their *reditus*. It substitutes a rather static idea for the very dynamic procedure of the whole work. Christ becomes the object of theology and so theology as a science is destroyed since a science must have an intelligible essence as its object: Christ is not "an intelligible essence," but

---

better on the personal than on the abstract plane." Eschmann was, and worked, both as a theologian and as a philosopher who was a Christian.

[22] The text of Suárez to which Eschmann referred is: "...Est enim Christus Deus et homo, ex Deo et humana natura ineffabili modo compositus...idcirco oportuit de simplicibus extremis prius disputare, quam de illorum conjunctione tractaretur." *De incarnatione* in which Suárez considered the ST 3, 16, 1 and 2; in R.P. Francisci Suarez, *Opera omnia* (Paris: Vivès, 1856-1877), 17: 2b, 3a. The Aristotelian discussion referred to is: "As in other departments of science, so in politics, the compound should always be resolved into the simple elements or least parts of the whole. We must therefore look at the elements of which the state is composed, in order that we may see...whether any scientific result can be attained about each one of them." *Politics* 1, 1; 1252a 20-23.

a divine Person who became man by a divine decree.

⟨*b. The Response of Merkelbach*⟩

Another answer was given by Benedictus Henricus Merkelbach O.P.[23] The practical part of theology, that is, moral theology, treats first of the means of tending to God that are intrinsic to man and, moreover, necessary. It also treats of the sins by which we are estranged from God. The Part I and the Part II, the author points out, are "necessary" for the very constitution of theology. With them, theology is complete with respect to its essential parts. "But in the present order," the author continues, "God ordained by his free will other extrinsic means, special to humanity, that we might prosper in knowing and tending toward Him." Those means are (a) the Incarnate Word "Who shows the way of truth to us and leads us to the salvation of eternal life," and (b) the sacraments "by which we attain grace and salvation and which have their efficacy from Christ." This is the reason that the Part III had to be added to the system of the *Summa theologiae.*

This answer, I believe, is much better than the former one. It neither destroys nor neglects the great movement of the *Summa.* It fits into its main architectural law, namely, that law of the going forth of all creatures from God and their return to Him. It divides that return into two parts: the intrinsic and formally necessary principles and means of this return, Part II, and the incidental (that is, the historical) means for it, Part III. The Incarnation of the Word is a historical fact, deriving entirely from the free decision of God's will and mercy. Love of God, grace, virtues, and so on, are of intrinsic necessity for one who tends toward God, yet the Incarnation and the whole sacramental order are contingent facts. There is no intrinsic necessity for the Son of God to born among us, as Saint Thomas states energetically in his famous article on the motive for the Incarnation.[24]

⟨*c. The Response of Chenu*⟩

M.-D. Chenu O.P. stresses the original and profound idea of synthe-

[23] See Benedictus Henricus Merkelbach, *Summa theologiae moralis ad mentem D. Thomae...,* 3rd rev. ed. (Paris: Desclée de Brouwer, ca 1939), 3: 1, 2.

[24] "...convenientius dicitur incarnationis opus ordinatum a Deo in remedium contra peccatum, ita quod peccato non existente, incarnatio non fuisset. Quamvis potentia Dei ad hoc non limitetur; potuisset enim, etiam peccato non existente, Deus incarnari." ST 3, 1, 3, in corpore; 4: 2418a, ll. 19-25.

sizing abstract and necessary theory with concrete and contingent history.[25] Because in its roots Christianity is history, the problem for the scientific theologian is to integrate into a historical system this merely historical fact. Let us note that if, within the system of the *Summa*, the III Part on Christ follows the II Part on the human as such, this does not mean that Saint Thomas attempted to build up a system of Christian morals without Christ. The Anointed is living on every page and in a sense it is true to say that the "Image-formula" of the Prologue includes Christ who is the perfect Image of the Father and for us the Way and the Truth. For Saint Thomas, too, Christian morality is the "imitation of Christ."

Yet this remains provisionally hidden only to appear with great force in Part III. All of this proves the essential unity of the whole: the "Parts" do not treat different and specifically distinct sciences of a wider genus as is often affirmed (for instance, "dogmatics" and "morals") but rather the integral parts of the one species—Theology in the broad, Thomistic sense. Should one wish to characterize Moral Theology in contradistinction to Moral Philosophy, the answer must be that it, Moral Theology, is human activity under this formal aspect, that it is supernaturally enabled to reach God as He is in Himself, the Object of our supernatural beatitude.

## F. THE *SUMMA THEOLOGIAE* IN THE HISTORY OF THEOLOGY

The medieval reader[26] of the *Summa theologiae* must have felt the novelty of this work much more than we can realize today. On the whole, Saint Thomas' teaching and method was new. William of Tocco (a student of Thomas) referred to this impression: "In his lecturing he posed *new* issues, found *new* and clear methods of determining them, and he adduced *new* arguments in those determinations."[27] In a general sense Part I was a

[25] M.-D. Chenu O.P., "Le plan de la *Somme théologique*," *Revue thomiste* 45 (1939) 93-107. See also Chenu's *Toward understanding Saint Thomas*, tr. A.-M. Landry and D. Hughes, (Chicago: Regnery, 1964), pp. 310-322; this work is a translation of Chenu's *Introduction à l'étude de Saint Thomas d'Aquin* (Montréal: Institut d'études médiévales, and Paris: J. Vrin, 1950).

[26] Material from folder CLN 30, p. 10.

[27] "...Erat enim nouos in sua lectione mouens articulos, nouum modum et clarum determinandi inueniens, et nouas adducens in determinationibus rationes, ut nemo, qui ipsum audisset noua docere et nouis rationibus dubia diffinire, dubitaret quod eum Deus noui luminis radiis illustrasset." *Ystoria sancri Thome de Aquino de Guillaume de Toccoc (1323)*, Édition critique, introduction et notes, Claire le Brun-Gouanvic, Studies and Texts 127 (Toronto: PIMS, 1996), Capitvlvm XV, p. 122, ll.

novelty, but its great constructive lines were nevertheless traditional. From olden times theological constructions had treated in the first place God and the procession of creatures from God. Theological system had grown out of the Apostolic creed and the first two points had always been, as they still were in the *Summa* of Saint Thomas, "I believe in one God" and "Maker of heaven and earth."

The II Part is a novelty in a quite different and deeper sense.[28] Saint Thomas's creative genius is here at work more than in any other section of the *Summa*. Its other two Parts, I and III, had been constituted as parts of theological science long before Aquinas; all he had to do was to re-shape and re-organize them, whereas the II Part is his own. To[29] see this better we must cast a brief glance at a few of the earlier theological systematizations.

〈*a. The "Sentences" of Peter Lombard*〉

In the first place the so-called *Four Books of Sentences* produced by Peter Lombard (b. ca 1100, d. 1160) deserve attention since this work was the standard text in the theological schools at the time of Saint Thomas. Whatever the theologians' interpretations of the organization of the *Sentences* may be—it is known, for instance, that Saint Thomas found already in Peter Lombard's work the system ("procession from God," "return to God") for the plan of that work was nothing other than an enlargement of the creed—the first Book treats of God as One and of the Holy Trinity, of the attributes proper to each Person, and by which attributes there are relations between the world and the Creator: God's knowledge, omnipotence, will, and providence. The second Book passes on to "the Creator of heaven and earth" and systematizes the first Chapter of Genesis: the procession of creatures, that is, of angels, of the corporeal universe, and of humans, from God (Distinctions 1-20).

From Distinction 21 forward the focus is on the theology of the corruption of humanity and our estrangement from God: the sin of Adam ("original" sin), and since that fall, our sins ("actual" sins). In this connection an aspect of the theology of grace is also dealt with, namely with grace as the divine aid by which Adam could have persevered and proceeded to his end. Books three and four contain the doctrine of the "reduction" or "leading back" of all things, especially of human beings, to

---

19-23; available in older edition, *Fontes vitae S. Thomae Aquinatis* ed. D. Prümmer O.P. (Toulouse: Privat, 1911), p. 81.

[28] Material from Folder CLN 37, p. 12.

[29] Material from folder CLN 30, p. 11.

God. Christ is our Way back; hence "Christology" is the first topic to be treated at this point. The second topic is the doctrine of the sacraments, to which is added, again in conformity with the Creed, a part treating of the Last Things.

Now[30] the question is, where are moral matters in this scheme? An even more basic question is, where are moral matters in the various creeds that have come to us from the ancient Catholic tradition?

⟨*b. Remote Resources*⟩

There is no mention of moral matters, no article dealing with morals, in any of the early Creeds. This is a very remarkable fact, full of significance in itself, and also with respect to the further development of the science of theology. Far from giving rise to theological speculation, moral conduct was kept away from scientific efforts and enterprises during the first centuries of Christian history. True, the new religion made moral demands. One was not a Christian unless one lived and acted according to the new rules of Christian life, but it seems that the very urgency of those demands, and in those times, prevented their scientific elaboration. Rather, they were codified after the fashion of laws in a collection of prescriptions such as the *Didachê* or they became the object of pastoral exhortations, as in Saint Cyprian or Saint John Chrysostom. These were "moralists" to be sure, but they were such as men of action, as pastors, rather than as theologians.

There was also a deeply rooted aversion in almost all ancient Christian authors to making Christian morals an object of "science." The pagans had excelled in moral teaching but, in the eyes of Christians, theirs was the wisdom of this world; it did not, and could not, lead to salvation as Christians understood it. Knowledge of what ought to be done does not produce virtuous actions; on the contrary, it is liable to generate the pride that The Apostle denounces as the root of all sin (2 Tim 3:6). How could it be possible to deduce from any general moral principle Christ's passion and death on the cross, the ultimate rule of Christian life and the highest moral example of Christianity? All our Christian life is simply an answer to God's calling, for which there is no reason; it is a gratuitous and inexplicable fact.

No[31] pagan moralist taught humility; is not human reason incapable of saying one single word useful for our salvation? The student of the

[30] Material from CLN 37.

[31] This comment is hand-written with a sign for insertion on the reverse side of p. 13, CLN 37.

history of theology, above all of moral doctrine, must keep these objections in mind. They appear more or less clearly at the very beginning of the history of Christian theology and even today are far from being forgotten or eliminated from the Christian conscience.

What I should wish to emphasize is that intellectual consideration in Christianity was turned, not to morals, but to that other great domain of truth that is dogmatics. The "Symbols" (or "Creeds") in which our faith is articulated, and the catecheses based upon those Symbols, do not deal directly with morals. Now those catecheses constitute the original and primitive form of theology. The doctrinal efforts of the oldest thinkers in Christianity leave the issue of morals alone, not, of course, because they had no use for it, but because in their opinion it belonged, not to teaching, but to exhortation.

Let us turn once more to our Peter the Lombard. The very fact that he chose to adopt for his systematization the scheme of the Symbols, the Creeds, put him face to face with this alternative: either drop morals matters completely or make room for them within a scheme which originally had no place for them. Peter could not adopt the first alternative because in the twelfth century the situation was quite different from what it had been in ancient times. Moral matters had long since entered the domain of theological discussion, especially with Saint Augustine. They[32] had done so as well in the wake of that Gregorian movement which, counting all in all, is the greatest episode in the history of the Church and in the history of western civilization. This had happened also in consequence of a great renaissance of classical studies in the twelfth century; this had put into high relief the works of Cicero, of Seneca, and of others, in short, the works of the ancient Stoics with their considerable emphasis on moral matters. Once this second alternative was adopted, the whole work, from the viewpoint of systematization and structure, was bound to be a patchwork.

Peter found room for moral matters mainly in two places.[33] First, in his Second Book where, in the context of creation, he dealt with original grace and original sin, which entailed discussion of actual sin and its causes: will and intention, good and evil in our actions.

Second, at the beginning of Distinction 23 in his Third Book, Peter made a characteristic remark in a Christological context:

[32] This remark on the "Gregorian Reform" is hand-written, partly as an interlinear comment on CLN 30, p. 14, and partly on the reverse side of p. 13, with a sign for insertion.

[33] Material from CLN 30, p. 11, foot.

> Since it has been said above that Christ was "full of grace," it is not superfluous to inquire whether he had faith and hope as well as charity. For if he lacked these, he would seem not to have possessed the plenitude of graces. In order that this question might be the more clearly explained, something must be set out concerning each of them....[34]

There follows, in the fourteen Distinctions that complete this Book, chapters on virtues in general, on the three "theological" virtues, on "moral" virtues in general, on the "cardinal" virtues, on the "gifts" of the Holy Spirit, on the active and on the contemplative life, and on the ten commandments. In the course of these discussions the connection of these topics with the original Christological theme is more and more neglected. The run of Distinctions appears to be a "Treatise on Morals" presented as a long footnote, an appendix, to Christology,

The same artificial turn has been noted in the discussion of Book 2 where creation is taken as an occasion for discussing the various aspects of moral evil in human living. A love of such appendices seems to have been a main characteristic of Peter the Lombard; he was no master of synthesis and order! His basic error was to have thought that the scheme of the Creed can serve as a framework for the mass of moral teaching that had accumulated by the twelfth century when Peter wrote. This situation was to become even more hopeless during the thirteenth century after Aristotle had entered upon the scene.

Let[35] us look at a few of the post-Lombardian theological syntheses and inquire as to how they organize their theological material and especially how they deal with Peter Lombard's digressions and "footnotes," that is, whether and how they acknowledge and deal with the need for a better integration of moral discussions in the organization of theological science. Did they work for a constitution of moral theology that might have a definite place in the body of theological science as ethics—moral philosophy—has its place in the body of philosophy?

[34] "Cumque supra perhibitum sit, Christum plenum gratia fuisse, non est superfluum inquirere, utrum fidem et spem, sicut caritatem, habuerit: si enim his caruit, non videtur plenitudinem gratiarum habuisse.

Ut autem haec quaestio valeat apertius explicari, de his singulis aliqua in medium proferenda sunt...." *Sent.* Lib. 3, Dist. 23, Cap. 1; 3: 655, 155.

[35] Material from CLN 37, pp. 15a-15j, which constitutes a long *Einlage*, an "insertion," dated 1957, 1958.

⟨*c. Other Twelfth-Century Theologians*⟩

First, however, we ought to mention a contemporary of Peter Lombard who was in no way indebted to Peter's *Sentences*. This is Alan of Lille (ca 1128-1203) who invented a division of theology that is still with us today: "dogmatics" and "moral theology." There are, he says, two species of theology.[36] One is "rational" theology which provides knowledge of "heavenly" things, the other is "moral" which turns around morals or with shaping human beings, "informing" us on how to behave. The two, faith and morals, are merely juxtaposed in this remark of Alan. The unidentified author of an early gloss on the *Sentences* of Peter Lombard (the author has been identified wrongly as Peter of Poitiers) combined the "sign-reality," *signum-res*, he had found in Peter Lombard's work with that proposed by Alan:

> A summary of the divine Page consists of things that must be believed and things that must be done, that is, in the assertion of faith and in the confirmation of morals.... On these the Master ⟨Peter Lombard⟩ wrote in his work, but in a general way and in a specific way: in a general way on what things ought to be done, in a specific way on what things ought to be believed. Many dissent from him on what things ought to be believed, but few or none on what things ought to be done.[37]

The division of theology's subject into faith and morals seems to have had a special appeal to French theologians at the turn of the twelfth century, noteworthy among them Peter the Chanter[38] and Robert Courson.[39] Some

[36] "Le Traité d'Alain de Lille sur les Vertus, les Vices et les Dons du Saint-Esprit [*De virtutibus et vitiis*]," ed. Odon Lottin, *Mediaeval Studies* 12 (1950): 20-56; for Alain's text see p. 25 and following. It is, of course, difficult to reconcile this notice of so early an appearance of a division of theology into "moral" and "dogmatic" with Eschmann's more usual protests against a "seventeenth-century" distortion of theology's unity.

[37] The reference in Migne's *Patrology* is PL 211 789-1279; for the discussion of its ascription to Peter of Poitiers (d. 1205) by Dom Odon Lottin, see "Le Prologue des gloses sur les Sentences attribuées à Pierre de Poitiers," *Recherches de théologie ancienne et médiévale* 7 (1935): 70.

[38] See his *Verbum abbreviatum*, PL 205 23-370.

[39] See V.L. Kennedy, C.S.B. "Robert Courson on Penance," *Mediaeval Studies* 7 (1945) 291-336, especially p. 294: "...questiones morales et tam de fide quam de ceteris uirtutibus institutas pro posse nostro deo annuente prosequemur.... Morales siquidem questiones sunt que docent quid appetendum, quid fugiendum."

preferred to treat of virtue and the virtues, not after their Christology, but before: thus Master Hubertus,[40] Peter of Poitiers,[41] and Prevostin of Cremona.[42]

## ⟨G. Thirteenth-Century Developments⟩

### ⟨*a. William of Auxerre*⟩

One of the more outstanding works of theology in the early thirteenth century is the so-called *Summa aurea*, the *Golden Summa*, by William of Auxerre. Although it follows the structure of the *Sentences* of Peter Lombard, Christology precedes the treatment of virtues (which is very long and elaborate). "Having spoken of the Liberator of the human race (that is, of Christ), one must speak of those means through which He liberates us, namely, concerning the virtues,"[43] it gives much more weight and space to moral questions. This is a precious witness to the interest these matters had taken on in the minds of scholars and it must be noted that William counted the virtues to be "theological" rather than "moral"; after dealing with them he passes over to a treatise "On Precepts" with the following remark:

> After the theological questions one must approach moral questions by which we are instructed in our exterior doings and in singular cases.[44]

One can see that in the author's mind "moral" questions are "legal" questions: morality comes about by law. This author undoubtedly deserves

[40] See M. Grabmann, "Notes sur la *Somme théologique* de Magister Hubertus," *Recherches de théologie ancienne et médiévale* 1 (1929): 229-239; especially at 232.

[41] See P.S. Moore, *The Works of Peter of Poitiers. Master in Theology and Chancellor of Paris (1193-1205)* (Washington: Catholic University of America Press, 1936).

[42] See Martin Grabmann, *Geschichte der scholastischen Methode* (Freiburg i. B.: Herder, 1909-1911) 2: 557, n. 4.

[43] William of Auxerre, *Summa aurea*; printed editions were issued at Paris in 1500 and 1518; Venice, 1591. Modern editors have identified a mass of citations from William in the great *Summa fratris Alexandri*, that is, the English secular Master who joined the Franciscans and brought with him, not without controversy, the Chair he had held in Theology at the University of Paris.

[44] "Post quaestiones theologicas accedendum est ad quaestiones morales quibus instruimur in exterioribus operibus et casibus singularibus," William of Auxerre, *Summa aurea*; Eschmann has referred to fol. 80 of an early printing, but has not indicated which.

great credit in the history of scholastic moral doctrine since, among all the scholastics we have so far seen he has taken the greatest care to elaborate a moral system; ⟨yet his last word is that⟩ the characteristically moral quality of our life is due to law!

⟨*b. Franciscans*⟩

⟨*i. Alexander of Hales:*⟩ We enter upon a golden age of scholasticism when the Mendicant Friars, the Franciscans, start working in Paris. The first author to be considered is Alexander of Hales who entered the Franciscan Order in 1235 or 1236 and brought with him the Chair of Theology which he had occupied before his entry. If Roger Bacon O.F.M. is to be trusted, Alexander was the first in the University of Paris to make the *Sentences* of Peter Lombard the basic text of theology in his school.[45] In a gloss on the words of Peter Lombard which express one outstanding feature of Franciscan theology, namely, that it strives to keep close to the source of theology, the Bible, "The Old Law" and "The New Law,"

> Since the height of perfection consists in beatitude, this whole, complete, work is divided according to what they ⟨the two Laws⟩ do with respect to beatitude. The First Book deals with the One beatifying, the Second concerning what is susceptible of beatitude and of its opposite, the Third deals with the remote dispositions which lead to beatitude, the Fourth with the proximate dispositions, namely, with the sacraments. For the grace of precepts and virtues which are dealt with in the Third Book, are related more remotely to beatitude than is sacramental grace.[46]

[45] Alexander's *lectura scholaris* on the work of Peter Lombard was discovered in modern times and published (Quaracchi: S. Bonaventura, 1951-1954), in three volumes as *Glossa in quatuor libros Sententiarum Petri Lombardi*. The *Summa fratris Alexandri*, called also the *Summa theologica* (Quaracchi: S. Bonaventura, 1924-1948), has been considered mal-ascribed to Alexander, although he may have had some part in its formation. In any event, Book III, which is of interest here, is ascribed with great probability to another Franciscan, Johannes de Rupella. For the moment, we shall use the *Glossa*.

[46] "Cum summa perfectio consistat in beatitudine, dividitur hoc totale opus completum secundum se quae faciunt beatitudinem. Primus liber agit de beatificante, secundus de beatificabili et suo opposito, tertius agit de dispositionibus remotis quae ducunt in beatitudinem; quartus de dispositionibus propinquis, scilicet, de sacramentis. Gratia enim praeceptorum et virtutum, de quibus agitur in tertio libro, remotius se habent ad beatitudinem quam gratia sacramentalis...." Alexander of Hales, *Glossa in quatuor libros Sententiarum Petri Lombardi*, 1: 7.

Beatitude thus is made here the fundamental principle of a general division of the *Sentences* and of theology; there is no mention of Christ and Christology, which occupied the Third Book of Peter Lombard, whereas Alexander represented that Book as a treatise on precepts and virtues. In fact, however, in the text of the *Glossa* itself no account is taken of the original division: it deals with Christology just as Peter Lombard's original texts does. Alexander's division reads as though he wanted to suggest that what is now called "moral doctrine" belonged to the Old Law, whereas the "grace of the sacraments" is a matter for the New Law, a novelty introduced by Christ. The text above concluded,

> The former ⟨the grace of precepts and virtues⟩ under the ⟨Old⟩ Law did not remove the sword whereas the latter ⟨the grace of sacraments under the New Law⟩ has unlocked the Gate of Paradise.[47]

⟨*ii. John of Rochelle (de Rupella):*⟩ Our next author, Johannes Rupella O.F.M. (John of Rochelle), was the redactor of the First and Third Parts of the great Franciscan *Summa* named after Alexander the *Summa fratris Alexandri*. This was by far the most outstanding and the earliest great text of Augustinism and Franciscan theology in the thirteenth century; Saint Thomas knew this text and used it frequently. With John of Rupella for the first time we have a "moral part" as a division of a summary statement of theology. What had been a footnote in Peter Lombard is now promoted to the status of a constitutive part. The author's intention was a synthesis of moral doctrine and he began with the precepts and the laws: first law and then virtue. I know of no medieval text so diametrically opposed to the Prologue of the I-II Part, as this article by John Rupella, in the modern edition, Article number 280, p. 420. Which is prior, the precept or the virtue imposed by the precept? The author's answer is that the Law, or the precepts of the Law, are by nature prior to the virtues. But why?

> ...insofar as goods are due, they are ⟨the goods⟩ of the precepts; insofar as they are in fact voluntary goods, they are ⟨the goods⟩ of the virtues.[48]

[47] These words follow those of the last text cited: "...illa enim in Lege rumphaeam ⟨Gen 3:24⟩ non amovit, haec autem reseravit ianua paradisi." Ibidem, p. 7, ll. 11, 12.

[48] "[Ad obiecta]: 1, ...inquantum sunt bona debita, sunt ipsorum praeceptorum; in quantum vero bona voluntaria, sunt ipsarum virtutum. Sed prior est naturaliter conditio boni debiti quam boni voluntarie, quia prius accepit creatura naturaliter—

Remember Saint Thomas, saying at the beginning of his *Exposition of the Ethics* that a human being, voluntarily acting for the good or the end, is the subject of ethical consideration. Where Saint Thomas manifestly opts for the priority of the "good insofar as it is voluntary"; John of Rupella had taken the other option:

> The condition of the good that is due by nature is prior to the condition of the voluntary good.[49]

In Book 3, Part 2 of this work we have the main pre-Thomistic attempt at the construction of a moral teaching. The construction required a twofold effort: first, "moral theology" (in opposition to "moral philosophy") must be shown to be a part of the whole which is "theology"; second, it must be constructed. The first problem was solved by Rupella with the old distinction: "faith and morals," *fides et mores*, a distinction found for the first time, if I am not mistaken, in Alan of Lille. It is with this distinction that Rupella, at the precise place where Peter Lombard had entered into a long digression about virtues and precepts, inserts his own "moral theology" as a full-blown Part of the book.[50]

This insertion is difficult to understand from the point of view of the *Summa* of Alexander as well as on the basis of general considerations. The moral part of this *Summation* interrupts three general structural lines of the whole work which is built according to the scheme of Peter Lombard, that is, the scheme of the Creed. Moreover, to say what is obvious, connection by simple juxtaposition is not very artful. Here the *Summa Alexandrina*, "Alexander's Summation," reveals its general character as a work composed by several authors and patched together without a plan that had

---

unde ipsa est debitrix Deo tamquam principio—quam moveatur voluntarie in ipsum ut in finem...." *Alexandri de Hales ordinis minorum. Summa theologica* Pars 2, Inq. 3, Tr. 2, Sectio 1, Q. 1, Tit. 1, Art. 2, # 280, 4: 421. It may be remarked that a recent edition by J.G. Bougerol O.F.M. of *Jean de la Rochelle. Summa de anima* (Paris: J. Vrin, 1995), extends our knowledge of this influential scholastic beyond what was available to Eschmann.

[49] Continuation of the text cited, note 48.

[50] "Summa theologicae disciplinae in duo consistit, in fide et moribus. Expeditis inquisitionibus pertinentibus ad fidem, ut de Redemptor...procedendum est ad inquisitiones pertinentes ad mores. Ad informationem autem morum concurrunt necessario praecepta et leges, gratia et virtutes, dona, fructus et beatitudines, leges et praecepta, ut ostendentia debitum boni faciendi et mali vitandi; gratia et virtutes etc., ut praestantia facultatem faciendi et vitandi." *Summa fratris Alexandri* Liber 3, no. 48; 4: 313.

been elaborated previously and with care. The other problem, the structure of this moral part itself, was solved by Rupella in a way that deserves our most careful attention. Christian theological moral doctrine must start from the precepts because, he says, it is by them that "moral being," *esse morale*, is constituted; only thereafter can that doctrine turn to the virtues. This procedure in moral doctrine had been adopted already by William of Auxerre and Alexander of Hales. In John of Rupella, at any rate, it results from an examination of the natures of the two: precepts and virtues. Indeed at one point our author states his problem explicitly: "which is prior by nature, precepts or virtues?"[51] He answers with a well-considered argument that priority belongs to the precepts. For precepts are the manifestation of the creature's radical dependence with respect to God, the Creator, whereas virtues imply our human ordering to God as to our End, our *finis*. If the theologian considers both our coming forth from God as our creative Principle, and our returning to Him as to our End, then John assigns the precepts to the first motion and virtues to the second. Since God is naturally Creator before He is End, precepts naturally precede virtues.

However strange this reasoning may seem, let us consider it well and most of all, the conclusion. It means that the order of authority, that is, of One commanding and the other obeying, is the fundamental and central fact of Christian ethics. Virtue is essentially the obedient execution of precepts; virtue always and necessarily carries the element of obedience with it. Saint Thomas, of course, always treats precepts after virtues and the opposition between Thomistic ethics and the ethics of Rupella should be both evident and impressive. Saint Thomas explains the precepts by the virtues; Rupella explains the virtues by the precepts. Was Saint Thomas a follower of Rupella, we must ask, speaking about what is properly "ethical"? Does not Aquinas expose himself to missing the point completely and groping around in the dark? The precepts, according to Rupella, are the illuminating principles of moral life and teaching; if this is so, then this light was lacking to Saint Thomas for at least the first 89 Questions of the I-II!

Two points of history remain to be considered briefly; then we shall have a full picture of the situation in which Saint Thomas's Prologue was written and against which it clearly appears as a novelty. First, there are Saint Bonaventure and Saint Albert. How did they organize theology? What do they have to say concerning the division of theology into "faith,"

[51] "Dicendum quod lex sive praecepta legis naturaliter sunt priora virtutibus...." *Summa fratris Alexandri* Liber 3, no. 280; 4: 420.

*fides*, and "morals," *mores*, that is, into dogmatics and morals? There remains, second, a word to be said about the studies of the Aristotelian ethics in the first half of the thirteenth century. As the *Summa Alexandrina* shows, the problem of organizing theology was to an important extent the problem of making room for morals, a problem made acute for that period by the appearance of Aristotelian ethics. It is all the more surprising to see Saint Bonaventure and Saint Albert refusing explicitly, as it seems, to adopt a new scheme for their organization of theology.

For both, after their own academically required commentaries on the *Sentences*, wrote original theological systematizations. For Bonaventure this was his *Breviloquium*, his "short discourse," written before 1257 and for Albert it was his *Summa*, which seems to have been composed after the *Summa theologiae* of Thomas Aquinas. In these works the two authors were on their own, free to organize the theological material as they pleased; both chose the old and proven scheme and did so for definite reasons. It becomes clear that for them the traditional pattern was more than an old and venerable convention; it corresponded to their convictions. In their opinion, theology did not need division into two parts, one dogmatic, the other moral. Such a division was even incompatible with theology as they conceived it.

⟨*iii. Saint Bonaventure:*⟩ Saint Bonaventure clearly followed the old pattern of the Creed. To those who proposed a division into "faith and morals" he replied, No! His pattern was rather "Morals through faith," *mores per fidem*. Bonaventure even took over the Aristotelian description of ethics and applied it to theology as a whole. The main point in Saint Bonaventure is to conceive of theology as a "practical wisdom" through and through. This he did because he connected theology with Holy Scripture in the closest possible way and saw that Scripture is radically distinguished from all human teaching because it appeals, not to our intellect, but to our will.[52]

[52] "Progressus autem sacrae Scripturae non est coarctatus ad leges ratiocinationum, definitionum et divisionum iuxta morem aliarum scientiarum et non est coarctatus ad partem universitatis; sed potius...ad dandam homini viatori notitiam rerum sufficientem, secundum quod expedit ad salutem...describit *excellentiam finaliter salvandorum*,...describit *miseriam damnandorum*.... Scriptura...quae ideo scripta est, non solum ut credamus, verum etiam ut vitam possideamus aeternam...." *Breviloquium* Prologus, 3, 4.; pp. 4a, b, 5a.

⟨*c. Saint Albert*⟩

As for Albert, it will be enough to point to a few texts that are found in his work on the *Sentences*, texts that are fully confirmed by Albert's own *Summa*.[53] There Albert taught a doctrine fundamentally like that of Bonaventure. Hence Albert's *Summa*, written after that of Thomas and, we must assume, with knowledge of it, proceeds according to the traditional pattern. When Albert says that theology, properly speaking, is an affective science, that it is a science dealing with a truth inseparable from the notion of the Good, he clearly makes it impossible for theology to have a "moral part," a *pars moralis*, such as the theology of Saint Thomas contains as its II Part. This is roughly the situation which presented itself to Aquinas when he began his own construction of the *Summation of Theology*.

The opposition between the traditional notion or type of theology, and the new type to be created by Saint Thomas for which the Aristotelian canon is to be the rule, this opposition is very striking indeed. It all hinges, in Saint Thomas, around his appreciation of the human intellect, for Aquinas never hesitated to reject the fundamental assumption of Albert and Bonaventure that the will is the highest power of the human soul. There is hardly any proposition in Aquinas more fundamental than that intellect, *simply speaking, is higher than the will*.[54] With this thesis Aquinas is opposed to the entire crowd of the schoolmen around him, his own teacher Albert included! From this fundamental assumption it follows that theology must have two parts: since choice follows understanding, theology must have both a speculative and a practical part.[55] Theology must include a "moral part," a *pars moralis*.

## H. Remarks on the Structure of the First Five Questions of *Summa Theologiae* I-II, and Especially of the First Question

All this[56] change of theological order made by Saint Thomas has a much deeper sense. More than merely didactical change took place around the

[53] Albertus Magnus, *Super Sententiarum* Lib. 1, Dist. 1, A. 4; t. 25, pp. 18, 19.

[54] ST 1, 82, 3, in corpore. See, however, his reservation with respect to knowledge or love of what is "higher" than is the human person who knows or loves (ibidem, 2-2, 23, 2, Response to 1; 3: 1522b, ll. 30-45); here, incidentally, Brother Thomas made his celebrated observation that "Augustine was imbued with Platonic discourse."

[55] Ibidem, 1, 1, 4.

[56] Here one shifts from the material of CLN 37, p. 20, to that of CLN 30, p. 12.

middle of the thirteenth century and was brought to completion in the *Summa theologiae* by Aquinas. For what now comes to the fore is exactly, as Saint Thomas expressed it: the human being, principle of that being's own actions, possessed of free choice and power over that being's own acts...as we have seen the human characterized above. This "Thomistic human being" now takes out citizenship papers in the realm of theology; the doctrine centered on such a human has become worthy of constituting an integral part of the system of theology.

This is what I mean by speaking of the "humanism" of the *Summa theologise*. The characteristic of this Thomistic "humanism" is that it is both a full and a unique humanism. It is full because this human being of the Prologue is at the same time (though of course not under the same point of view), both a Christian and a human being. The scientific formula for this unity is hard to find and consequently the method followed in the II Part by Saint Thomas is one of his great secrets. We simply have to take the indistinct notion of the Prologue and leave it in its indistinctness.

Second, this human being of the Prologue is unique. No system like that of Saint Thomas had ever been achieved, nor was it to be repeated. The elements of Christianity and of humanity, strongly and artfully bound together in the Thomistic synthesis, were soon to part company. The very "commentators" on Saint Thomas themselves, who brought formal restrictions into the text of this Prologue are witnesses to this separation. They were unable to grasp the unique inner harmony of the Thomistic human being.

## I. THE STRUCTURE OF THE FIRST QUESTION:[57] ON THE ULTIMATE END OF THE HUMAN BEING, DIVIDED INTO EIGHT ARTICLES

Here, for the first time, there must be a consideration concerning the last end of human life and then, a consideration concerning those things through which a human being can arrive at this end, or deviate from It; for from the end it is necessary to derive the natures of those items which are ordered to the end.[58]

[57] Material from CLN 30, pp. 13-19.

[58] "De ultimo fine hominis in octo articulos divisa ubi primo considerandum occurrit de ultimo fine humanae vitae; et deinde de his per quae homo ad hunc finem pervenire potest, vel ab eo deviare; ex fine enim oportet accipere rationes eorum quae ordinantur ad finem." ST 1-2, 1, opening lines under the heading "Quaestio I"; t. 2, p. 710a, ll. 26-32.

In this matter we are to consider first the "last end" of human life and secondly, that by means of which we are able to advance toward that end, or (as Aquinas realistically added), perhaps stray from the path. His insight is that from the end of life alone we can learn both what that end is and also what, in fact, leads to that end. This preliminary ought to be understood in the presence of the Prologue Saint Thomas has provided for Question 6:

> Since, therefore, we arrive at beatitude through certain acts, it is consequently necessary to consider human acts in order that we might know by which acts one might arrive at beatitude, or by which one's feet might be shackled on the road.[59]

The first five Questions are thus a sort of foundation, of "first philosophy," of *proto-philosophia*, with respect to the whole II Part. This whole treatise of the II Part is about human acts. The preamble of such a treatise is the doctrine of beatitude, that is, about the end of those acts. Since, some lines further "it is set down that the ultimate end of human life is beatitude"[60] we might at once wonder as to what "it is set down," *ponitur*, means. It can be meant of the ancient philosophers or teachers who posit the last end to be happiness, as did Aristotle at the beginning of his *Nicomachean Ethics* (1, 7; 1097b 20, 21): "happiness...is the end at which all actions aim," and as was also the case with the whole of antiquity, with Saint Augustine for instance. Or it can be said of all human beings who universally hold happiness to be our last end. Aristotle said this as well:

> As far as the name goes, we may almost say that the great majority of humankind are agreed about this, for both the "many" and persons of refinement speak of it as "Happiness," *eudaimonia*.[61]

Now the precise referent in the text of Saint Thomas is of no great importance since the idea is clear that he divided his five introductory Questions in the following way: Question 1 will treat of the ultimate end in general and Questions 2 through 5 will treat beatitude, that is, happiness. The

[59] "Quia igitur ad beatitudinem per actus aliquos necesse est pervenire, oportet consequenter de humanis actibus considerare, ut sciamus quibus actibus perveniatur ad beatitudinem, vel impediatur beatitudinis via." ST 1-2, 6, Introd. De voluntario et involuntario, t. 2, p. 751b, ll. 28-33.

[60] "Et quia ultimus finis humanae vitae ponitur esse beatitudo...." Ibidem, Quaestio 1, Prologus; t. 2, p. 710a, l. 32-p. 710b, l. 1.

[61] *Nicomachean Ethics* 1, 4; 1095a 17-19.

reason for this division is the following distinction which we may make evident with Saint Thomas's own words in Question 1, Article 7: "It must be stated that we can speak in two ways of the ultimate end: in one way in accord with the formal notion, the *ratio*, of the ultimate end; in another mode in accord with that in which, *id in quo*, the formal notion, *ratio*, of the ultimate end is found."[62]

With respect to the "ultimate end" there is first, the "formal notion of ultimate end" in itself, that is, abstracted from every object or thing in which the ultimate end is found, and second, this very thing or object which is the ultimate end. We are free to find our ultimate end in several things. Let us say we find it in God or in earthly goods. According to this decision the "formal notion of ultimate end," *ratio ultimi finis*, is "found" somewhere, in some thing or in some object. That is the reason for distinguishing these two aspects and, at the same time, it is the reason for Saint Thomas to detach the first Question from the rest of the group.

The first Question thus deals with this "formal notion of ultimate end," that is, with the *ratio* or abstract formality of "being an ultimate end." One might ask whether there is such an end, what does that end mean, what is the function of the ultimate end as such with respect to human acts or to human life?...and so on. The second through the fifth Questions deal with the problem of where, in what things, is the "formal notion of ultimate end" concretely "materialized" (if I may use this very misleading English word). Leaving aside the construction of the group, Questions 2-5, of which we must speak in due time, let us now look at the contents of Question 1 and at the order of its Articles. Saint Thomas never gives the reason for going about a problem in the way he does; with him the phrase we find here is stereotypical:

> Concerning the first, eight questions are posed:
>
> First: Whether it belongs to a human being to act on account of an end?
>
> Second: Whether this is proper to a rational creature?
>
> Third: Whether the acts of a human being receive their species from the end?
>
> Fourth: Whether there be some last end of human life?
>
> Fifth: Whether there can be several last ends of one human being?

62 "Dicendum quod de ultimo fine possumus loqui dupliciter: uno modo, secundum rationem ultimi finis; alio modo, secundum id in quo finis ultimi ratio invenitur." ST 1-2, 1, 7, in corpore; t. 2, p. 717a ll. 15-19.

Sixth: Whether a human being orders all to an ultimate end?

Seventh: Whether the last end is the same for all human beings?

Eight: Whether all other creatures come together in that last end?[63]

Who asks these Questions? No ⟨single⟩ general answer can be given; each case must be investigated on its own merits. Most of the time, however, logic and history are combined in the Thomistic method of going about a problem. Let us see how things are in this case.

*a. The Logical Order of the Articles*

According to a great number of commentators (who are quoted by Ramirez),[64] this order would be the following:

I. On the end of human action in general, that is to say, insofar as it abstracts from the question of what is last: Articles 1-3.

II. On the last end according to the abstract formality of "the last," that is, as subordinating other ends to itself in the genus of final cause: Articles 4-8.

In accord with this division, the law of the movement of Thomistic reason in this case would be the well-known rule of proceeding from the general to the more particular. The idea of the first part would be (to put it in other words) "the metaphysics of final cause." Only after discussing this would Saint Thomas go on in Article 4 to treat his proper subject. This opinion about the intrinsic movement of Thomistic thought in this Question seems to prompt the commentators to begin their elucidations with a broad treatise on the metaphysics of final cause (as, for instance, John of Saint Thomas does). Thus the commentators supplement the treatise which is not found in Saint Thomas as though the Thomistic lucubrations were incomplete.

Ramirez himself proposes another logical division. The criticism which he bestows upon the former scheme is that these commentators

[63] "Circa primum quaeruntur octo. Primo: utrum hominis sit agere propter finem. Secundo: utrum hoc sit proprium rationalis naturae. Tertio: utrum actus hominis recipiant speciem a fine. Quarto: utrum sit aliquis ultimus finis humanae vitae. Quinto: utrum unius hominis possint esse plures ultimi fines. Sexto: utrum homo ordinet omnia in ultimum finem. Septimo: utrum idem sit finis ultimus omnium hominum. Octavo: utrum in illo ultimo fine omnes aliae creaturae conveniant." ST 1-2, 1, In octo articulos divisa; t. 2, p. 710b, ll. 4-20.

[64] Ramirez, loc. cit. pp. 163 ff.

make Saint Thomas divert at once from his initial purpose, namely, to treat the ultimate end. Saint Thomas never said he would treat the *end* as such; his purpose, clearly stated, was to treat of the *ultimate* end. Consequently we must assume that the question of the ultimate end is dealt with right from the beginning. Here is the scheme of Ramirez:

I. Articles 1-4 on the existence of an ultimate end of human life;
II. Articles 5-8 on the nature or essential conditions of that end.

Although Articles 1 and 4 might be in the relationship Ramirez points out, 2 and 3 have no relationship with 4; if Ramirez's hypothesis is true, those two must be considered an excursion, even an undue interruption of the reasoning. On this we might observe that it is true that Articles 1 and 4 could eventually be conceived as standing to each other in the relation which Ramirez points out, that is, Article 1 contains one premise of the argument developed in Article 4; but what about Articles 2 and 3? They have no relationship with the argument of Article 4 and must be considered as an excursion, even as an interruption of the reasoning.

The description Ramirez has given of Article 2 as a quasi-material consideration of the end is not easy to understand; the abstract and facile scheme of opposition between the "formal" and the "material" forces the dynamism of Saint Thomas onto the Procrustean bed of schematization. His thought is—or so it appears to me!—clothed in the ready-to-wear garment of common logic and the tailor, it seems to me, is too easily satisfied with the fit.

So too, Articles 5-8 do not give an impression of concern with the question, what is the ultimate end? The "essence" or "formal notion" of the ultimate end, the *ratio ultimi finis*, is that it is desired for itself, that it be the complete and completing good. Such a notion, to be sure, occurs in Articles 5, 6, and 7, but what is at issue there is not the "essential conditions of the ultimate end," but rather the unity of the ultimate end, first, in the life of an individual (Articles 5, 6) and second, in the cosmos (Article 8). Saint Thomas is a greater and more generous thinker than any of his commentators; that he cannot be chained by logic does not mean that he is illogical. He goes his own way and the structure of his Questions is commanded not by logic only, but also by history.

I should like to propose provisionally the following scheme which is suggested partly by logical and partly by historical considerations.

Articles 1-4, inclusive, speak of the teleology of the human act and in some way depend upon Aristotle; but note that the source is not the ethical side of Aristotle alone; his physical and metaphysical positions play a role and, although one has the impression that these Articles deal with Aristotelian problems, Aristotle is not the exclusive source.

Articles 5-8 speak of the teleology of human life and in some way depend upon the Augustinian tradition in theology and its problems.

My suggestion would be this:

The Teleology of the Human Act

Article 1: The existence of an end in every human act (explicitly stated in Article 1), Response to arguments 2 and 3.

Article 2: Human acting for an end as distinguished from the ways in which other beings act for ends.

Article 3: That the end gives an act its specific form and is the first identification of the human act as moral; the last word in the body of the Article proves that the author makes a division after the third Article.

The Teleology of Human Life

Article 4: The existence of an ultimate end in human life. Every human act must be either for the ultimate end, or for a proximate end that is itself part and parcel of a system of ends, of final causes, the principle of which is the ultimate end.

Articles 5 and 6: That ultimate end is one in every individual life; this is treated under two aspects, the second of which (in Article 6) seems almost to be psychological.

Article 7: The ultimate end is one in the life of all humanity.

Article 8: This supplementary Question argues that all creatures agree in tending toward an ultimate end.

Here a strictly "logical" scheme, such as that of Ramirez, is simply too narrow for the rich and abundant Thomistic text. It might fit a monograph on the subject, but Saint Thomas did not write monographs. Occasionally he repeats himself or (what is worse in a monograph) anticipates and takes for granted a thesis he will prove only later. Here, one Article assumes that God is the end of all humanity as well as of all other creatures, a thesis that has its place in another Question, where it will be carefully demonstrated. An architect of a *Summa* can do such things although they are not permissible in a monograph; the First Question of the I-II Part is a beautiful model of the technique proper to a *Summa*. What is its function from the standpoint of the construction of a moral doctrine or science? Saint Thomas is pursuing one problem, the all-important problem in every science, namely, the definition of its subject. Human life is the subject of moral science. Is not human life the infinite variety of what human beings do or do not do? How can infinite variety be defined, be reduced to one thing having one form, be made formally finite and delimited? Only the "formal notion of the ultimate end," the *ratio ultimi finis*, unifies and formally limits human life. By the same token, it makes that infinitely varied subject ready to be the subject of scientific investigation.

## J. THE SOURCES OF THE FIRST QUESTION

It will be useful first to say a few words about the sources of this Question. By this investigation, the object of Saint Thomas will become clearer and also why he took up and discussed *these* eight questions and no others. Merely abstract and logical considerations will be insufficient to render an exact account of either the presence or the order of his discussions. Saint Thomas has rarely if ever stated and discussed his problems in the thin and blue air of purely abstract considerations!

There are, as I have said, two main sources of this whole problem. One is Aristotle, mainly, but not exclusively, the Aristotle of the *Nicomachean Ethics.* The other source is Augustine, to be more specific, an Augustinian problem transmitted to the medieval schools by a few remarks in Peter Lombard's *Sentences* Book 2, Distinction 38. How shall we find those sources? How analyze a text as to its sources? A medieval text generally does not easily reveal them. Aristotle, for instance, is quoted many times in this Question, but the interesting part of the *Nicomachean Ethics,* that which is really the source of Saint Thomas in his discussion, is not quoted at all. The method must be indirect: one must know something of the topics discussed in the medieval schools in order to be able to compare texts and to discover their similarity. As for the Aristotle of his *Ethics,* his presence in these pages is easily discoverable. The beginning of the *Ethics* is written all over them in capital letters. As the teleological idea is Saint Thomas's starting-point so was it the prominent and characteristic feature of Aristotelian *Ethics.* The object of Question 1 is to prove that human actions and human life fall within a system, an order of ends, unified by the "formal notion of an ultimate end," a *ratio finis ultimi.* This is clear in the very beginning of Aristotle's work: "Every art and every investigation, and likewise every practical pursuit or undertaking, seems to aim at some good; hence it has been well said that the Good is That at which all things aim," *Nicomachean Ethics* 1, 1; 1049a 1-3.

But ends differ; there are as many ends as there are arts, sciences, and forms of action. All have ultimately one and the same End, an End sought for Its own sake while all others are chosen as means toward Its attainment; this must be the case for, if all our ends were but means to further ends, human endeavor would be an endless and vain process—Aristotle's "infinite regress." Knowledge of the true nature of the ultimate End, the final Goal, must evidently have great influence on the conduct of life. If we possess knowledge of It we shall be the more likely to do the right things in particular circumstances.

This argument has been called the argument upon which the whole system of the Aristotelian ethical doctrine rests and the same fundamental idea is the main inspiration of the II Part of the *Summa theologiae*. Hence it is that Aristotle is a primary and most important source for our first Question. Let me warn you, however, that neither is Aristotle the only source, nor is it (if I may so speak) the "Aristotelian Aristotle"; there is a "Thomistic Aristotle" who at times is hardly identical with the former one!

Now, what about the other source? For discovering that other, "Augustinian," source the so-called parallel texts in our editions are of great help. Particular attention must be paid to parallel places in the *Scriptum super Sententiis* by Saint Thomas himself for in that work he kept the closest contact with the school and the discussions of his time. *Sentences* Book 2, Distinction 38, is quoted as a parallel to Article 8 of the present Question 1. A study of the parallel passages of the *Scriptum* and of the whole context within which they appear in that work will convince us that the whole Question 1 of Part I-II, owes at least in part its origin to the topics discussed in the earlier work of Saint Thomas and also to Saint Albert's *Commentary on the Sentences*.

In a text from Augustine's *De trinitate* Book 11, Chapter 6 (a text quoted by Peter Lombard in *Sentences* Book 2, Distinction 38, Chapter 3), Saint Augustine speaks of the proper end of particular acts of the will, all connected with, and referred to, one general act by which we will to live "blessedly." Saint Augustine says, for instance, that one might wish to see a window, not to rest in that sight, but because through that window one might see a passer-by.[65] All these, and other such acts, have their own ends which, in turn, are referred to the end of that will by which we will to live in blessedness, and to attain to that life which is not referred to anything else, but suffices of itself to one who loves it:

> Those decisions, *voluntates*, ⟨that is, "decisions," the instances of moral willing by an individual⟩ are good and are bound to each other, if that final act of will to which all are referred is right. If, however, it is evil, all are evil. And so it is that the connected series of right

[65] *Petri Lombardi Libri IV Sententiarum* 2, Dist. 38, Cap. 3; t. 1, pp. 510, 511, marg. num. 353; Eschmann has here introduced and ascribed to Augustine (as cited by Peter Lombard) "the seeing of a scar in order to know a wound"; this illustration is not to be found in the short passage cited by Peter from Augustine's *De trinitate* 11, 6, 10.

> acts of will is a kind of road for those ascending to beatitude; but the entanglement of depraved and distorted willing is a bond by which the one who does this shall be bound so that one "shall be cast forth into exterior darkness" (Matt 8:12).[66]

The first part of this statement where it is said that all our individual particular wills form a system and an order under the one supreme will, namely, that by which we desire to live blessedly—this part is in accord, not only with the beginning of the Aristotelian *Ethics*, but also with the whole of ancient Greek and Latin ethics.

But something happened to the second part of the Augustinian text. Saint Augustine continues to speak of the volitions of one individual. Yet taken out of context (as it really is in Peter Lombard) this text speaking of the "end of right wills" might be understood, not of a series of the wills or volitions of one individual, but of the volitions of several individuals. Peter Lombard has committed this mistake; whether he is the first to have done so, I do not know, but he manifestly reads the Augustinian text as affirming something of several individuals, whereas Saint Augustine in truth had no such intention. That is the reason Peter Lombard introduced the text of Saint Augustine cited above in this way: "Now the question is posed, whether all good wills have one end only?" And after that quotation Peter concluded:

> It is clearly shown by these testimonies of these authorities that there are many right decisions, *voluntates*, among people of faith, *fidelibus*, decisions which have their own proper and diverse ends and, nevertheless, there is one and the same because all are referred to the one which is the "end of ends," of which we spoke a little while before and so, perhaps, it is with evil ones.[67]

In other words Saint Augustine's authoritative remark on our merely per-

[66] "...rectae sunt voluntates, et omnes sibimet religatae, si bona est illa, ad quam cunctae referuntur. Si autem prava est, pravae sunt omnes; et ideo rectarum voluntatum connexio, iter quoddam est ascendentium ad beatitudinem, quod certis velut passibus agitur; pravarum autem et distortarum voluntatum implicatio vinculum est quo alligabitur qui hoc agit, *ut projiciatur in tenebris exteriores*" (Matt. 22:13). Petri Lombardi, *Sent*. Lib. 2, Dist. 38, Cap. 3; 1: 511, marg. num. 353.

[67] "His auctoritatum testimoniis evidenter monstratur, plures in fidelibus rectas esse voluntates, proprios ac diversos fines habentes, et tamen unum eundemque, quia omnes referuntur ad unum, qui est finis finium, de quo paulo ante diximus; ita e converso forte est et in malis." *Sent*. Lib. 2, Dist. 38, Cap. 3; 1: 511; marg. num. 353.

sonal life has been transformed into an authority concerning the social life of the faithful and their radical unity.

How did the scholastics of the mid-thirteenth century take up this Augustinian-Lombardian problem? They discussed it under the terms of "the end of right wills" and "the end of evil wills," speaking mainly of one individual person, but neither explicitly excluding nor explicitly including the social problem. This social problem is for the first time (as far as I can see) explicitly stated in Saint Thomas, *Summa theologiae* Part I-II, Question 1, Article 7: "Whether there is one last end for all humans?" Saint Albert had written two Articles on this Augustinian-Lombardian text, Articles 3 and 4;[68] the same Question appears in Saint Thomas, *On the Sentences,* Book 2, Distinction 38, 1, 1, in preliminary Argument 5 and in the Response to Argument 5, proof enough (if any should be needed) that Thomas knew his teacher's text!

## ⟨K. DUBIUM⟩

Saint Bonaventure on the same text raised the issues of many good wills (in Question 3) and many evil (in Question 4) many evil wills. Even though understanding the Question as concerning one person, Bonaventure preferred to speak in the plural (he decided they do not have one end).[69] In both cases, as in Thomas's commentary on the *Sentences,* the questions are understood as pertaining to one person. Later we shall have to go further into the details of the opinions of these different doctors. We shall see that the group of Articles 5-8 in Question 1 is indeed a Thomistic discussion that engages both Saint Albert and Saint Bonaventure although neither one is even hinted at in the anonymous formula "some say," *quidam dicunt.* We see again that this group of Articles and consequently the order of the Articles in the whole Question can be fully understood only

[68] "Utrum sit unus finis bonarum voluntatum?" Albert, *In 2 Sent.* Dist. 38, E, Art. 3: t. 27, pp. 609a-611a. "Utrum malarum actionum sit unus finis?" Art. 4, ibidem, pp. 611b-612b.

[69] Bonaventure, *Liber II Sententiarum* Dist. 38, Art. 1. Quaest.3: "Utrum bonae voluntatis sit unus solus finis an possint esse plures.... Dicendum quod bonae voluntatis unus solus est finis principalis. Propter quod intelligendum quod plures fines statuere hoc potest esse tripliciter..."; Quaest. 4: "Utrum malae voluntates habeant unicum finem... Dicendum quod e contrario est in bonis voluntatibus et in malis. Nam bonarum voluntatum unicus est finis, sive bonae voluntates sint diversae diversitate numerali sive diversitate formali...." *S. Bonaventurae Opera theologica selecta* t. 2, pp. 919a-923b.

if it is compared to the discussions of the schools. For the moment, it will be enough to have provided some evidence that the last group of Articles —and mind you Articles 5-8 are a unit—is based on a text of Saint Augustine as transmitted by Peter Lombard. The purely speculative commentators are unable to integrate this group into a clear and neat scheme. Even Ramirez's idea is thoroughly unsatisfactory. This shows that the history of a given theme is of some value, indeed, for understanding—and I mean *understanding*—Saint Thomas.

## L. THE EXPOSITION OF ARTICLE 1

Repeated[70] reading, slow reading, ruminative reading—this is the first and foremost condition of understanding a text, of assimilating it; one reading is by no means enough. In what follows then, I shall assume that you have already read the text many times.

Note the slightly different statements of the problem at hand, or better, the different ways in which the author clarifies this problem. In the introduction to the Question he writes, "Whether to act on account of an end be an essential characteristic of the human being?" Then, in the beginning of the Article, "Whether to act on account of an end befits the human being?" Then, in the conclusions of the second and third arguments to the contrary, "Therefore, a human being does not do all things on account of an end." There are thus almost two different problems: first, whether final causality has any place in the matter of human acts and second, whether every human act is for the sake of an end. The main problem is the second. It corresponds to the conclusion of the body of the Article: "it must be that all human acts are for the sake of an end." The meaning of "all" is manifestly "distributive," that is, "all" is to be taken in its strictly universal application, No exceptions! This is clear from the way in which the same conclusion is formulated in reply to the second argument: "Therefore, whatever a human being does, it is true to say that a human being acts on account of an end."

The suggestion of this first Article (as also of the second and fourth) comes right out of Aristotle's *Nicomachean Ethics*:

> Every art, every teaching, and likewise every action, every choice, are seen to seek some good. Therefore, they have defined "good" as "that which all seek." A certain difference of "ends," however, is seen: some of them are indeed operations, some, however, are certain

[70] CLN 30, pp. 20, 21.

> items beyond those operations.[71]

In his *Exposition* ⟨of that work by Aristotle⟩ Saint Thomas explains the first words as embracing the whole of human activity, activity rooted in speculative reason as well as in practical reason, the acts of both "Art" and of "Prudence." It is in order to avoid having to explain this—in order to avoid having to gloss the whole opening of the *Ethics* ⟨here⟩—that Saint Thomas chooses in the "But to the contrary," the *Sed contra,* a quotation from Aristotle's *Physics* (2, 9; 200a 34) rather than from the *Ethics.* Sometimes, to be sure, the texts in the *Sed contra* give us a fairly good indication of the sources for a given Article. How this rule can be misleading is shown in our present "But to the contrary." That the *Ethics* provides the real inspiration for this Thomistic doctrine is proved beyond doubt by the second argument where Aristotle is quoted. Of course, the quotation is not literal; in fact, it is pretty considerably transformed so as to fit better with the author's intention. The second argument, and the answer to it, show most clearly how Saint Thomas at once takes Aristotle as his source of inspiration, but also most definitely transforms the whole spirit of Aristotelian ethics.

The body of the Article contains two clearly distinguishable parts. The first goes to "It is thus clear..., *Manifestum est autem....*"[72] This part explains the notion of human act and lays the foundation, develops the first premise, of the proof of the conclusion. The second part presents this proof—or rather, presents its second premise. I begin with the first part:

> I answer that, of actions which are performed by a human being, those alone are said to be "human" which are proper to a human being insofar as human. For a human being differs from other creatures, which are irrational, in this that the human is the lord his ⟨or her⟩ own acts. Whence it is that those actions alone are called properly "human" over which a human being is dominant. A human being, however, is dominant over acts through reason and will, whence too, free choice is said to be "the faculty of will and of reason." Those actions, therefore, are said to be properly "human" which proceed from a deliberate will. If, however, other actions

[71] "Omnis ars et omnis doctrina, similiter autem et actus et electio bonum quoddam appetere videtur. Ideo bene enuntiaverunt bonum quod omnia appetunt. Differentia vero quaedam videtur finium. Hi quidem enim sunt operationes, hi vero praeter has opera quaedam." *Nicomachean Ethics* 1, 1; 1094a 1-6; "Versio antiqua, p. 1.

[72] ST 1-2, 1, 1; t. 2, 711a 43.

belong to a human being, they can indeed be pronounced "acts of a human," but not properly "human," since they would not be the acts of a human insofar as human.[73]

The first part is a very simple and straightforward way of getting at the notion of the "human act." It is a procedure almost like that used by Socrates with carpenters and shoemakers.[74] What is a "human act?" Doubtless an act in which a human being acts *as* a human being. It would not be too difficult to get this answer out of anyone. Thomas, however, gradually develops this answer. There are many definitions of the human act, definitions proceeding analytically from the merely nominal to the real. At the same time the major premise of an argument is being established. This argument will be ⟨implicitly⟩ the following ⟨syllogism⟩:

> "Human actions" are those that proceed from a "deliberative will";[75]
>
> But, all actions of a deliberative will proceed from it according to the abstract formality of its object, that is, the end (the good);
>
> Therefore, it must be that all human actions are for the sake of an end.

The second part of the body of the Article contains the statement as well as the proof of that reasoning which constitutes the content of the whole Article. The text ⟨a syllogism also⟩ reads:

> It is manifest, however, that all actions which proceed from any

[73] "Respondeo. Dicendum quod actionum quae ab homine aguntur, illae solae proprie dicuntur humanae, quae sunt propriae hominis inquantum est homo. Differt autem homo ab aliis irrationabilibus creaturis in hoc quod est suorum actuum dominus. Unde illae solae actiones vocantur proprie humanae, quarum homo est dominus. Est autem homo dominus suorum actuum per rationem et voluntatem, unde et liberum arbitrium esse dicitur 'facultas voluntatis et rationis.' Illae ergo actiones proprie humanae dicuntur, quae ex voluntate deliberata procedunt. Si quae autem aliae actiones homini conveniant, possunt dici quidem hominis actiones; sed non proprie humanae, cum non sint hominis inquantum est homo." Ibidem, p. 711a, 26-43.

[74] Eschmann's reference is obscure; he perhaps here refers to Plato, *Apology* 22 D-E, in which Socrates questioned craftsmen and found them skillful, each in *a* craft, but also found them ready to pronounce on other matters of which they knew nothing, showing by this that they were less wise than was Socrates who recognized his own ignorance.

[75] This expression is an echo of the Aristotelian "desiderative reason or ratiocinative desire" of *Nicomachean Ethics* 6, 2; 1139b 5, 6.

power are caused by it in accord with the formal notion, *rationem*, of its object;

Now, the object of the will is the end and the good;

Hence, it is necessary that all human acts be for the sake of an end.

The proposition[76] is not new to a reader of the *Summa*; the metaphysics of "the good," especially its definition "that which all things desire" (Aristotle, *Nicomachean Ethics* 1, 1; 1094a 3, cited by Saint Thomas at I Part I, Question 5, Article 1; 1: 27a), a Question and Article which are meant to be an introduction to the doctrine of the goodness of God. The metaphysics of the will had been treated in Question 19 of the same Part I, especially at Article 1 on "Whether there be a will in God?" (t. 1, pp. 130b, 131a) and then again on various problems concerning the Trinity. Thus, the Holy Spirit proceeds "through the mode of will and of love," for love is the fundamental act of will. One must note that scholastic speculation on the will originates and has its proper setting in discussions of the Holy Spirit, in this work, at Questions 36-39. Thus, at Question 37, Article 1, "Whether 'love' be the proper name of the Holy Spirit" (pp. 233a-234b) is one of the most important documents of Thomistic teaching on the will.

Again, this doctrine comes to the fore in the teaching of Saint Thomas on the angels and note that this whole teaching proceeds *theologically*: will in God, will in angels, will as a faculty belonging with intellect, as belonging to an intellectual being, "...will follows upon intellect," (Question 19, Article 1, body of the Article, p. 131a, l. 6) is the most fundamental Thomistic proposition with respect to the will. Will is investigated first as it appears in God, secondly as it appears in different beings according to the "going forth of things from their Principle."

Within the doctrine on angels, precisely Question 60 "On the love and delight of the angels" (t. 1, pp. 361b ff.) is noteworthy in our context. Question 63 is also important for it brings up for the first time the issue of an "evil will": "On the malice of angels with respect to their guilt" (t. 1, pp. 379b ff.). Two Questions are devoted to the human will, 82 and 83, in the context of the "going forth from ⟨our⟩ Principle," that is, our creation by the Holy One. These are introduced by two others: 80 "On appetitive powers in general" and 81 "On sensuality" (t. 1, pp. 495a-500b).

[76] CLN 30, a handwritten insert, marked by Eschmann "zu S. 21," "to page 21"; his words "The proposition" clearly refer to the proposition functioning as the major premise of his syllogism, that is, "...all actions that proceed from a power are caused by it in accord with the formal notion of its object."

This goes to show that, whereas one who had read Part I is indeed well prepared to take the statement in Article 1, a reader without the preparation of reading Part I, yet would plunge into Part I-II, would drown in no time! The statement in the latter portion of our Article is an abbreviation, a resumé, of a doctrine which is assumed to be known, although by the way, it will be explained more fully in many an Article to come. These six short lines, however, are in truth the supporting pillar of the whole edifice of the Part I-II and II-II. Every word of that Part is contained *virtually* in them. Again, they are nothing but a more formal statement of that "definition of the object" which we found in the Prologue.

Hence[77] it is that we cannot pay too careful attention to every line that we read here. The "body" of the first Article lays down two conclusions. The first part of our Article presents the definition of the "human act," for the expression seems to be ambiguous and it is the first ask of philosophy and theology to remove this ambiguity. The human act is the *free* act; it is the act in which a human person, the individual human being, is committed, ⟨and it manifests⟩ the proper dignity of a person endowed with autonomy.

An ambiguity comes to the fore with actions produced without liberty. Saint Thomas's examples are just examples, perhaps the most typical examples, but today (especially after Freud and his teaching on the conscious and unconscious motivations of acting) we might be inclined to find those examples naive. I think we should regard them just as examples, most forcefully (in a didactic way) clarifying the issue. Saint Thomas knew the unconscious also: He knows "the concupiscence that transcends the limits of reason."[78] Still, it is not the "nocturnal" aspect of human acting with which he is concerned here; this is rather the luminous aspect, the only one from which a moral treatise may correctly proceed. What ethics would look like if our thinking, not only proceeded from the night of the unconscious, but also principally[79] remained there, we may see in

[77] Here Eschmann has added to his typed "page 22" five closely handwritten pages marked in red pencil "zu S. 22, alpha, beta," ("to page 22, a, b,") and so on through "epsilon"; two other pages (from which the opening sentence has been borrowed) are not marked for insertion and seem to be a first draft of the five here presented.

[78] "...concupiscientia autem quae transcendit limites rationis...." ST 1-2, 82, 3, Response to the First argument; 2: 1165a, ll. 9, 10.

[79] The word "principally" is written clearly and the term makes sense; still, rather than giving the game to Freud, Eschmann may have had in mind "by principle," i.e., that a Freudian explanation were given "on the principles" of Freud.

Freudianism. Still, as Saint Thomas had said (I-II, 1, 1, Arg. 3),

> A human being does many things apart from deliberation, concerning which at times there is no thinking, as when someone moves a foot or a hand, paying attention to something else, or strokes the beard. Therefore, a human being does not do everything for the sake of an end."[80]

Thus are actions produced without liberty. There are actions (for instance, seeing) which need no concourse of liberty, and passions (a difficult notion!) are considered by Saint Thomas as just such "actions." All our sensitive activity, even as such, insofar as it a human's sensitive activity, is affected by a *human* modality: cats and dogs do not see as we see! Still, this human modification does not constitute a "human act" for in the expression "human act" the qualification "human" must be taken in a more rigorous sense and this Article in its first part elaborates this rigorous sense.

It is thus with the "act proceeding from reason and will" that we are dealing. Note the variants of the formula "acts of which a human being is master," "act proceeding from a deliberate will," and the formulation which reaches still another degree of philosophical rigor, "deliberation of reason which is the proper principle of human acts." It is with what we call the "free act" that we are concerned in this Part of the *Summa*. Now this part of the Article is pretty clear even to a student who has not read the foregoing part of the *Summa theologiae*, but to such a reader the final part of our Article is, I presume, pretty dark. It is a summary of a doctrine that has been developed amply in Saint Thomas. Ever since Kant—if not long before, in Franciscan "voluntarism"—the starting-point of philosophizing about the will has been to set forth an irreducible opposition between the will and nature. Will is not nature; will is free, that is, undetermined; nature is necessary and determined. If one has this radical, irreducible opposition in view, one can never understand Saint Thomas. In Saint Thomas the will is rooted in intellectual nature, and as such is naturally determined: "The will is naturally determined to one common (intellectual notion) which is the Good (common and universal)." To paraphrase this in order to bring out its meaning more clearly, the will is endowed with, has the fortunate or happy natural endowment of a constitutional determi-

[80] "Sed multa homo agit absque deliberatione, de quibus etiam quandoque nihil cogitat; sicut cum aliquis movet pedem vel manum aliis intentus, vel fricat barbam. Non ergo homo omnia agit propter finem." ST 1-2, 1, 1, Arg. 3; t. 2, p. 711a, ll. 14-19.

nation of *nature*, of a spiritual nature whose very spirituality does not (as in Scotism) eliminate nature and everything natural, but specifies and qualifies this nature of the will. Modern philosophy, and popular thinking sees in "will" a purely gratuitous origin of activity, an activity coming from nowhere other than from the will itself. Our liberty, therefore, Sartre concludes, is *absurdity*. It is, under this supposition of nominalistic will, like everything which is "nothing but," a thing which has no connection whatever, an absolutely detached, an absolutely lonely will, is sheer absurdity for Saint Thomas too! One can understand that with this notion of liberty, Sartre is invaded by an anxiety which knows no bounds.

Saint Thomas's philosophy of the will starts with a characteristic determination which is the source of indetermination, that is, the source of liberty. This determination, however, is not being bound to any concrete or particular object (not even to God). The will is bound to "the good in its universality," to "universal good": this "good" is "being in its universality," it is being as referred to will. Being in reference to intellect is "the true." In this way must we understand the proposition "The object of the will is the good"; the will's nature is here defined as an intellectual, spiritual nature. At first it would seem that, in declaring the will to be a nature, a determination, and that therefore boundaries are drawn around the will, the will is confined and restrained. It is sufficient to keep in mind this "universal good" (all and every good *inasmuch as* it is good) to see that it is wrong to identify here "determination" with the imagery of boundaries. On the contrary, the infinite openness of the will is here not restricted, but *founded*, made possible.

The metaphysical background of this is best presented in Part I, Question 19, Article 1. (Unfortunately for beginners in philosophy in the twentieth century, this Article is complete in answering its question, but economic, thrifty, in its presentation; I shall paraphrase it.)

An axiom belonging to the general ontology of acting presides over this elaboration. Every nature, every form, is the origin of an inclination by which this nature, this being, is enabled to tend towards its proper existential perfection and to repose in it once it has been attained. This inclination is specified by the nature, that is, by the form of the being. ⟨Here⟩ we are dealing with intellectual beings. An intentional possession of the natures of beings is the specific principle of an intellectual inclination. To the special capacity of the *receptivity* which we find in intellection, there corresponds a tendential capacity, a power to tend to, and this power, like the intellect, is ⟨a power⟩ of a spiritual nature: it is will. Hence ⟨arises⟩ the immanent activity of both intellect and will together. In a word, the "agent" who is an intellectual agent, establishes an integral communion with being. By intellect an agent interiorizes being, brings being within the self, assimilates that being to the self of the agent.

However, at the term of this intellectual interiorization, when being is in the intellect, the intellect, as it were, is deprived of its own interiority; whence there arises (once more "as it were") an appeal for restitution. That restitution is accomplished by the agent's turning, through will, to the being known as that being is in itself. In other words, the intellectual agent first becomes, through the assimilative intentionality of intellection, *other than itself*; then through the will, ⟨through⟩ the intentionality of love, the agent becomes an agent according to the perfection of the *agent's own being*.

We[81] are now faced with the question, what is the objectivity of the objects of volition? If you do not mind the word, what is their "volibility"? ⟨What is their capacity to be willed?⟩ Saint Thomas answers, "The object (meaning of course, the formal nature of the object, the *ratio obiecti*, of the will is 'the end' and 'the good'."[82] The most remarkable thing here is the formula which puts together the "end," *finis*, and the "good," *bonum*, and gives the end the first and more prominent place. The reader of the *Summa theologiae* is quite familiar with the formula "the object of the will is the good," *obiectum voluntatis est bonum* (that is to say, "the universal good," "the good in general"). That reader is also familiar with the doctrine "the 'good' has (or implies) the notion of 'end'," for instance, at I, 5, 4.

This formula, "the object of the will is 'the end' *and* 'the good'" is not strictly a surprise, but it has a characteristic worthy of note. The formula means neither that the object is this or that end, nor the other way round: this or that end is the object of the will. No concrete end is the formal object of the will, not even That Which is our last End is truly "formal" and the meaning ⟨of the expression⟩ is *formal*. Finality is the object of the will, here understood as "the order of an end," *ordo finis*. The will is a faculty ordained to end: whatever it tends to it tends to in the context of a finalized,[83] a teleological, order. The fact that Saint Thomas (again with Aristotle) stresses the teleological aspect of the question is significant.

[81] Here we return to p. 22 of CLN 30 after the inserted pages of handwriting designated by Eschmann for insertion there and identified with the Greek letters from alpha to epsilon.

[82] "Obiectum voluntatis est finis et bonum," body of the Art., t. 2, p. 711a, ll. 46, 47; Eschmann has here shifted to a handwritten supplement which he assigned to his typed "page 22."

[83] Here "finalized" does not carry the colloquial English "meaning" of "having been brought to completion," but rather the scholastic meaning of realities ordered to each other as "means to ends."

Historically this significance will appear in its proper perspective if we consider that certain pre-Thomistic works elaborate a moral doctrine by unfolding the idea of the good, for instance, Saint Albert's *Summa de bono* the very title of which indicates the starting point and direction of the work. Compare Albert and Thomas on that score! In Saint Thomas the very plan of the *Summa*, "the going forth-the return," the *exitus-reditus*, stresses the end; this present stress on the end was already contained in the *Summa contra gentiles* Book Three, Chapter nine:

> Now the object of the will is the end and the good. Hence, moral matters are assigned their species from the end.... Since, therefore, "good" and "evil" are pronounced in accord with a universal order to an end, or the privation of that order, it must be that in moral matters the primary differentiating notes are the good and the evil. Now, in a single general class there must be a single primary measure. The measure of moral matters is necessarily reason; therefore, it is from the *end* of reason that certain things in morals are pronounced "good" or "evil."[84]

Here you can see that the accent on "the end" is quite purposeful in the "treatise on morals." "End" or the "Order of the end" carries of itself the morally decisive notions of the moral good and evil which, again with the idea of the end, are susceptible of an immediate elaboration by bringing out the idea of "measure," of "reason." The notion "end of reason" in the *Against the Gentiles* is especially noteworthy. I wonder whether Albert would have been able, with his starting-point ("the good"), to put together such a short outline of Ethics in such an elegant way!

This text from the *Summa contra gentiles* is noteworthy also because it shows that, and ⟨shows⟩ how, the thesis of the present Article of Part I-II is a thesis in *moral doctrine*. Here, of course, it is an assertion about the nature of the will which Saint Thomas sets forth. The object of the will, "the end and the good," and the fact that therefore "all human acts are on account of an end," these are natural data of the will. We could, therefore, speak correctly of a physics or, if you prefer, a psychology of the will. Morality is founded upon this psychology. Morality is not a predicate

[84] "Voluntatis autem obiectum est finis et bonum. Unde a fine speciem moralia sortiuntur: ...Quia igitur bonum et malum dicuntur secundum universalem ordinem ad finem, vel privationem ordinis, oportet quod in moralibus primae differentiae sint bonum et malum. Unius autem generis oportet esse unam mensuram primam. Moralium autem mensura est ratio. Oportet igitur quod a fine rationis dicantur aliqua in moralibus bona vel mala." SCG 3, 9; p 234a.

which we attribute to the acts of the will by having recourse to some principle outside; rather morality, that is, moral good and moral evil in actions, result *immediately* from this: "All human acts are on account of an end." Saint Thomas therefore says in his *Summa contra gentiles*: "...the object of the will is the end and the good" (a statement in physics, or in psychology) and "Hence moral matters are assigned their species from the end" (a statement in ethics). The inference is correct because a human act *is* immediately and intrinsically, by itself, inasmuch as it is a human act, a *moral* act, that is, either good or bad: "Moral acts are the same as human acts" (Article 3). Here we are in ethics, not in an ethically neutral, nor even in an ethically irrelevant field. Modern scholastic ethics deviates considerably from Saint Thomas at this very fundamental point. In sixteenth- and seventeenth-century theologians, even of the Thomist school, the human act is one thing, the moral act another. They would say that here, in this Article, Saint Thomas deals with the physics of the human act, but not with its ethics. The point, to my mind, is that for Saint Thomas the word *ratio* has a different meaning than it has with the moderns. Saint Thomas does not use the word *ratio* in a meaning which would in fact turn out to be *non-ratio*. Sin does not come from *ratio* but from *non-ratio*, the negation or privation of *ratio*. Thomas is, therefore, able to conclude

> That, therefore, in moral matters which is assigned its species from an end which is in accord with reason, is said to be according to its species good; that, however, which is assigned its species from a end contrary to the end of reason, is said to be evil according to its species.[85]

In other words then, in the very definition of the human act, "an act proceeding from reason (and from the will)," the order according to reason which is the constitutive element of the moral order is included: "reason," *ratio*, is "of itself," *per se* "right reason," *recta ratio*. In his early *Scriptum super Sententiis* 2, 24, 3, Thomas had put this sharply:

> ...a corrupt reason is not reason, just as a false syllogism is not properly a syllogism, and thus the rule of human acts is not any "reason" you like, but "right reason" and thus The Philosopher in the Third Book of his *Ethics*, Chapter 6 and in the Ninth Book, Chapter 4, (1115b 10-13; 1166a 13,14) says that the virtuous human is the

[85] "Quod igitur in moralibus sortitur speciem a fine qui est secundum rationem, dicitur secundum speciem suam bonum: quod vero sortitur speciem a fine contrario fini rationis, dicitur secundum speciem suam malum." Ibidem.

measure of the others.[86]

The notions of "reason" and of "right reason" are often so close together in Thomas that the simple term "reason" can stand for "right reason." For Saint Thomas "reason" is never considered a merely functional process without attention to its object; the study of reason presupposes the study of the object. That object is truth; the object of thought is truth. Hence we cannot study a "non-right reason" since, by definition, such a "reason" is one that does not arrive at truth; the concept is practically an antinomy. If "reason" is not "right" it does not and cannot arrive at truth; if it cannot arrive at truth, how can it still be designated "reason"? It is the objectivism of Thomas's thinking that makes him speak about reason in a way which may seem naive to modern thinkers. On the other hand, the ability of modern thinkers to speak of reason in a subjective, that is, objectless or object-stripped, fashion would have been unintelligible to Saint Thomas.

In[87] modern ethics things are different at this very fundamental point. There we sin "with reason," our sins come from a lot of "reasoning" —only this reasoning is fallacious. When moderns read the formula "an act proceeding from reason" they think of a morally neutral reason, a reason that can do every trick, fabricate every sophism. Thus they need something over and above reason in order to constitute the moral order over and above the human order. The principle of modern ethics (and here I speak of Catholic "Thomistic" ethics) is a profound irrationalism, or anti-rationalism, a deep-rooted skepticism against reason. Modern Catholic ethics is rooted in a criticism of reason of the kind we find, for example, in Luther. Modern Catholic ethics is affected at its root by this specific kind of anti-rationalism which originated as opposition against Nominalism, against Nominalistic scholasticism and has nothing to do with Saint Thomas. In order to understand Thomas we have to eliminate the anti-ra-

[86] "...corrupta ratio non est ratio, sicut falsus syllogismus proprie non est syllogismus; et ideo regula humanorum actuum non est ratio quaelibet, sed ratio recta; et ideo Philosophus in III *Ethicorum*, Caput vi, et IX, Caput iv, dicit quod homo virtuosus est mensura aliorum. Unde ex hoc non sequitur quod in ratione non sit peccatum, sed quod non sit in ratione recta." *Sent.* 2, Dist. 24, Art. 3, Ad 3; 2: 624. Eschmann's discussion of this text until the end of the paragraph ("to speak of reason in a subjective...unintelligible to Saint Thomas") is taken from his handwritten insertion marked "epsilon."

[87] At this point we return to the narrow, handwritten sheet marked for insertion at page 22, typed and designated "d," leaving the full-size, handwritten sheets, designated by the lower-case Greek letters from "alpha" to "epsilon," also marked for insertion at typed page 22.

tionalism which is to be found deep down in our minds too; our "kerygmatic" theology, which sounds so pious to our ears, is full of it. In Saint Thomas the word "reason" has a meaning which in our everyday language appears in the word "reasonable," if not in our word "reason"! Sin is not "reasonable," although some sinners might put up a clever barrage of sophistry, of "rationalizing."

⟨*a. Arguments and Responses*⟩[88]

Father Ramirez, who is very keen and not infrequently successful in analyzing the logic of Saint Thomas's proceedings, gives the following account of the order of the three *negative* arguments which we find at the beginning of Article 1. The problem of that Article is "Whether it be a property of the human being to act for the sake of an end?" In this formulation there are three terms: (1) "human being," (2) "to act," and (3) "for the sake of an end"; or (to put these three in a different order according to their importance with respect to the problem: (1) "for the sake of an end," (2) "to act," and (3) "human being." It is at once clear that in stating the problem, as he does at the beginning of the Article, Saint Thomas follows a scheme in accordance with the second ordering. Hence the first argument concerns the end; it is an argument taken from the very metaphysics of final cause and states the impossibility, or inner contradiction, in such a cause.

The second argument concerns acting for an end; as the objection shows, not every human act seems to be an instance of acting for the sake of an end.

The third argument concerns whether a human being might not be doing something, yet not be acting for an end.[89] I think that this very ingenious finding of Ramirez is worth noticing as an example of how, at least in this case, Saint Thomas seems to have worked out these arguments. A similar procedure might be found elsewhere but, of course, not everywhere. Each case must be, and deserves to be, studied on its own merits. Saint Thomas is a great master in playing the instrument of his methods. One thing, however, is clear and may always be presupposed: the arguments are not just thrown down pell-mell. They are set in a neat and orderly fashion. There is a reason why number one is number one and not two! Saint Thomas proceeds in a reasonable way, his writing is a "human act" which, as we learn here, is always for an end.

[88] At this point our text returns to the typed materials of CLN 30, at page 24.

[89] Ramirez, loc. cit.; t. 3, pp. 181-206; pp. 247-279, no. 285-372.

⟨*b. The First Argument and the Master's Reply*⟩

The first argument, as we stated, concerns the metaphysics of final causality. There seems to be a contradiction in the very concept of "final cause," on the assumption that the end is a cause. For "cause" means a beginning and thus the "final cause" would also be in the beginning, which seems contradictory indeed.

Saint Thomas's answer as you can see is very short. It is true, he says, that every cause is a beginning, a "principle," a *principium*: "a cause is prior to its own effect" (at least according to the ⟨non-chronological⟩ order of nature and of perfection). But let us consider two intimately connected processes, that of final and that of efficient causality; according to Thomas there is neither efficient causality without final causality nor the reverse. As for efficient causality, the effect produced by it is its end, its ultimate termination, the product that comes into existence at the very end of the whole process. That end, thus considered, is called the "end effected," the *finis effectus*, or (to use the word Thomas uses here), "the end in execution," *finis in executione*. This end cannot be a cause since it is an effect, but the very notion of final causality implies that the agent, that is, the efficient cause, leaps, as it were, over the whole process of efficient causality to its end in order to start from that end. This end, then, must exist in some way. As yet it cannot exist as a physical reality; some other mode of reality must be found in order to explain its existence. The answer is that at the very first moment the end has an "intentional" reality in the mind, in the will, in the intelligence of the agent. Thus the "end in intention," *finis in intentione*, is the final cause as Saint Thomas says very briefly:

> To the first ⟨argument⟩ it must be stated that the end, although it be last in execution, is nonetheless first in the intention of the agent. And in this modality it has the nature of "cause."[90]

I cannot help thinking again that the brevity of this passage is purposeful. It is not the fact that the Thomistic metaphysics of final cause had been explained earlier in the *Summa theologiae*; there is no Question or Article in the Pars I on this subject. The implicit supposition is again that the reader keep this in mind, holding it ready to be referred to and more distinctly understood, on other occasions. As you can imagine, this is the time and place where commentators go to town on the metaphysics of teleol-

[90] "Ad primum ergo. Dicendum quod finis, etsi sit postremus in executione, est tamen primus in intentione agentis. Et hoc modo habet rationem causae." ST 1-2, 1, 1, Ad 1; t. 1, p. 711a, ll. 50-53.

ogy. They do so indeed and have a really good time, visiting all the shows, and all the acrobatics for which they ever can get a ticket. Well, I assume we might as well for once break our rule and accompany them just as far as to see where they are going; we shall not have any very extensive peek at the shows themselves.

The discussions seem to center around three points.

First, What does "intention" mean here? The word, as used here, might have two meanings. It might mean the intention of the will. There is indeed an act of the will which might be called the "intention of the end," *intentio finis*, which Saint Thomas treats below in Question 12. This act, as the name implies, "intends," that is, "stretches out," as it were, toward the end; it is the determination of the will to will the end. This act of will *effects* the whole order of execution, that is, the order of seeking out the appropriate means and of actually using those means to attain the end. In this case the "end in intention" would designate the order of intention, that is, the act of will whose object is the end, in contradistinction to other acts which belong to the order of execution and the object of which is whatever is "for an end," that is, the means ⟨to achieve the end intended⟩. Now the intention of the end, that is, the very act of aiming at the end, and the act of the will, is the *efficient cause* of all the other acts following upon it by which we are concerned with the order of execution, that is, with the means leading to the desired end. Yet on the other hand, this very act of aiming, the "intention," depends upon the end as on its "final cause." The "end in intention" is thus the final cause of the "act of intention" while this "act of intention" is the efficient cause of the other acts following upon it such as the choice of means and so on. "To the will it pertains to move the other powers by reason of the end"[91] Saint Thomas says below, Question 9, Article 3, in the body of the Article.

But the word "intention" as used here (so the commentators say) might have still another meaning. It might refer, not to the end "as intended by the will," but insofar as it is in the "apprehension or intellection" of intellect. In other words, what might be meant is the "end known," the "end of intellect," which as such has an intelligible or intentional being, *esse intentionale*, in the mind. According to this understanding, the end in intention would be opposed to the extra-mental, natural, and (in this sense) *real* being which the thing that is the end has outside our minds. Understood this way, the formula would mean that the end exercises final causality insofar as it is apprehended, or known, by the

[91] "...ad voluntatem pertinet movere alias potentias ex ratione finis." Ibidem, 1: 770a, ll. 18, 19.

agent. Here we approach the well-known principle "Nothing willed unless known first," *nihil volitum nisi praecognitum*. The end "as known beforehand" would be the thing Saint Thomas holds here to be the final cause in question.

There[92] is, doubtless, an epistemological problem in the background of this "intention of the will." Yet consider carefully that this is a problem as to the very essential terms ⟨of that sort of reality⟩ to which the will belongs. It is a problem of the origin of practical knowledge, of moral knowledge. Saint Thomas has taken great care to emphasize the Aristotelian principle "Of whatever sort anything is, such its end is seen to be"; applied here, "Such and such is the human being, such and such an end will appear desirable to the human being."

In other words, in explaining practical knowledge, or in explaining the epistemological aspect of the "intention of the will," account will have to be taken of the personal quality of the knowing subject, of the whole background of the individual subject—education, character, etc.—in short, of all that is meant by these words "Of whatever sort anything is." Now it may seem to an impartial observer (and perhaps not too far from the truth) that Cajetan,[93] by shifting the emphasis of the problem to the intentional being a thing has in the intellect, did indeed disarrange, jumble up, the original data of the problem. The net effect of his operation, we might say, was that intellectualization or rationalization which is a striking feature of so many later interpretations of Thomistic morals. There is little doubt but that here we are at the roots of the whole story.

Looking at our present text I am inclined to say that Saint Thomas has in mind, not the intention of the intellect of Cajetan, but the intention of the will. The reason for this is he opposes to the "end in intention" the "end in execution," not the "end in the reality" or the "external end." Thus, the meaning of that proposition which we are analyzing is "the end has the nature of 'cause' insofar as it is in the intention of the *will*."

But[94] this brings up the old hard question that was formulated as the second point—the "second show" which the commentators are running here—the question (as it is called) of the "formal constituent of the

[92] Here Eschmann has directed us to leave the typed text of CLN 30, page 26, and to go to the handwritten reverse side of that page as well as to the reverse of the page following, page 27.

[93] "Cajetan," that is, "Cajetanus," "The Man from Gaeta," nickname of Thomas de Vio O.P. (1469-1534), was one of the classic commentators on the thought of Saint Thomas Aquinas and thus one of Eschmann's *bêtes noires*.

[94] Here Eschmann returns us to CLN 30, the middle of page 26.

final cause." If you oppose the intentional being of the end, or of the good, to its real and natural being, and if you say that the end has the nature of "cause" insofar as it *is* intentionally, then it seems that this very intentional being, but not the real being, is the formal constituent of the final cause. It is what makes a real being, or a good, to be an "end." Thus, for example, not real and natural health would stir our desire to be healthy and to do everything required for that goal, but rather the *idea* of health which we have in the mind. What the commentators want to investigate at this point is the relation of our apprehension of the end to the exercise of final causality. Is the apprehended, intentional, being a necessary condition for final causality, the adequate and formal reason for its being the extra-mental and objective good, as Cajetan most prominently contends? Or is the intentional being the very formal reason why we desire the end, as Capreolus[95] seems to think when he says, "Knowledge of the object is for the will itself the formal reason for acting." Finally, should a way between these two opinions be sought, a way which Bañez[96] seems to have found?[97] Bañez seems to have been the man who, within the Thomistic tradition was most prominent in opposing the interpretation of Cajetan. His opposition, however, is neither absolute nor categorical, for he grants that Cajetan is right in certain cases, as in this case, for instance: I intend to be healthy; I do not intend "health as it is in the mind, but as it is in reality." I want to have real health; what I want is not an idea of health. The point here is, as Bañez notes very intelligently, that if we analyze this ("I want to be in a state of health") we find that the following judgment is at the bottom of this desire: "The state of health is convenient to me" that is, it is a good and an end for me. Now here the subject of this judgment is something real, something extramental. The intentional being of this reality outside the intellect (the state of health) is nothing but

[95] John Capreolus O.P. (ca 1380-1444) known as "The Prince of Thomists," native of Languedoc, important in reviving the prestige of Aquinas after a relative eclipse, an eclipse owing especially to the succession Henry of Ghent, John Duns Scotus O.F.M., Durandus of Saint-Pourçain O.P., and William of Ockham O.F.M.

[96] Domingo Bañez O.P. (1528-1604), studied at Salamanca, later taught at Avila and Valladolid among other places, returned to Salamanca where in 1580 he held the chief Chair in theology; conspicuous in the controversy on grace in which he opposed the notion of a divine "midway knowledge," *scientia media*, proposed by the Jesuit theologian, Luis de Molina S.J. (1535-1600); considered by modern experts (v.g. Gilson as well as by Eschmann) to be the best of the "classical commentators."

[97] At this point Eschmann directs a return to the handwritten supplement on the reverse side of his typed page 27.

a "condition without which not" of this reality's status as an end and a good for me. "Nothing willed unless known"! In this case, therefore, and by metaphysical analysis or description, Cajetan's position is proved to be legitimate and justifiable.

There is another case in which Cajetan's thesis is not justifiable.

> Someone wishes...to pursue a moral good. From this it is certain that this individual apprehends that good, judging by synderesis[98] that it is appropriate for one to lead one's life in accord with law and the rule of reason. Hence, that judgment is already a measure and rule to which the will intends to be conformed and proportioned, and hence it is reason giving the act of the will an end and the means necessary for such conformity.[99]

Let[100] me paraphrase. Suppose that, being a bad boy, I want to convert to a good and honest life. I want to conform my life from now on to the law of God and the rule of reason. Well now, this "conformity" is nothing real of the sort that health, or a good meal is, which I might desire. I judge in virtue of the habit of the primary moral principles, "synderesis," that it is fitting for me, that it is good and proper end for me, to conform my life to law and to the rule of reason. While, therefore, in the first case my state of health, something real and extra-mental, was the measure and rule of my desire, here this same measure and rule is a being of reason, namely, the judgment of synderesis that I must conform my life to law and to reason, and Bañez concludes:

> The reason for the aforesaid difference, why the apprehension itself

[98] "Synderesis" is a technical term, current in mediaeval speculation thanks to Saint Jerome who used it in the Prologue of his commentary on the Prophet Ezekiel, to designate human knowledge of the first principles of morality; apparently a corruption of the Greek term *suneidesis*, "conscience"; medievals used it for the basic habitual grasp of natural law rather than for the here-and-now decision of "conscience."

[99] "Vult aliquis...prosequi bonum honestum. Tunc certum est quod finem apprehendit, iudicans per synderesim sibi convenire agere vitam secundum legem et regulam rationis. Unde iam iudicium illud est mensura et regula cui voluntas intendit conformari et proportionari, ac proinde est ratio finalizans actum voluntatis et media ad talem conformitatem necessaria." Domingo Bañez, *Commentarios ineditos a la Prima secundae de Santo Tomas*, ed. Vicente Beltrán de Heredia (Madrid: CSIC/Ministerio de Educación Nacional, 1942), 1: 45.

[100] Eschmann here sent the reader to two typed pages, each designated as "appendix to (discussion)," p. 26.

> of the end should be sometimes a condition only, sometimes the reason giving an end, has been sufficiently suggested in the examples themselves. For when a good intended consists in agreement and conformity with such a judgment, that judgment is already a rule and a measure. When, however, the nature of the good intended does not consist in conformity of this sort, but something is sought which in some other way is fitting for a human being thanks to its own real essential being outside the intellect of a human, without dependence on the dictate of reason, then a judgment of fittingness of this sort cannot be a reason of measuring and giving an end, but is a mere condition and, as it were, an application of the end, in order that it provide an end for that act of such an agent.[101]

In other words, the two cases are quite different. In one, I desire an apple, a steak, or a bath. (Incidentally, this example of the bath, taken from Averroes,[102] is Cajetan's crowning example. He always quotes it when he discusses this problem: "a bath, according to Averroes, *In Metaphysics* 12, is an external end...." This text of Averroes is doubtless the true constructive principle of that disciple of the Paduan Averroists who was Cajetan.) In one case I desire to conform my life to law and to reason; in the other case the apple and the bath are fitting for me, not because I judge them to be such, but because they are such even before I start formulating any judgment about them. In the other case, the good of virtuous living, the *bonum honestum*, are good for me *because* reason judges it to be so. This judgment of reason, this principle of synderesis, is the very measure and rule for the measure and rule for the "good life" being a good and an end for me. This judgment of reason is, of course, a reality of reason, not something extra-mental. In this case, therefore, the intentional being of the

[101] "Ratio praedictae differentiae, quare ipsa apprehensio finis aliquando sit sola conditio, aliquando ratio finalizandi, satis insinuata est in ipsismet exemplis. Quando enim bonum intentum consistit in convenientia et conformitate cum tali iudicio, iam iudicium illud est regula et mensura. Quando vero ratio boni intenti non consistit in huiusmodi conformitate, sed appetitur aliquid, quod alias convenit homini ex propria et reali quiditate extra intellectum hominis, sine dependentia a dictamine rationis, tunc iudicium huiusmodi convenientiae non potest esse ratio mensurandi aut finalizandi, sed mera conditio et quasi applicatio finis ut finalizet actionem talis agentis." Bañez, op. cit., 1: 45.

[102] Ibn Rushd, "Averroes" for the Latins, (1126-1198) is "The Commentator" on Aristotle; this example of the bath, *In Metaphysicam* 12, commentum 36, is frequently encountered in scholastic authors; this is to be found in Averroes, *In Metaphysicam* 12, commentum 36, Iuntas edition, t. 8, fol. 318v I-K.

end in my mind is more than a mere "condition without which not"; it is the very "reason providing an end," a *ratio finalizans*. Thus is Saint Thomas's principle, "an end, insofar as it is in the intention, has the nature of end," is now verifiable according to its obvious and full meaning.

If Bañez is right (and I am inclined to think so) he has hit upon the very central point in Thomistic Ethics: is nature or right reason the rule of our actions? If Cajetan is right, then nature must be the rule of our actions and, what is more, that conformity between the bath of Averroes and the one desiring it, is a physical conformity for the evaluation of which speculative reason is competent. This means (or, let us speak more cautiously) this *could* mean the reduction of ethics to speculative reason. It *could* mean (once again, we speak with caution) the extinction or at least the incorrect evaluation of practical reason, which, followed through to all its consequences, would destroy the moral life as conceived by Saint Thomas. There is, as you can see, hardly any decision more fundamental in ethical thinking than the one which we meet at the beginning: was Averroes right or wrong in saying "A bath, according to its being in the soul effects desire; according to its external being, however, it is an end." Restricted to the bath, to apples, to steaks, and things of that sort, he is right, but such things do not interest ethics. In matters truly relevant to ethics, according to Bañez, he is wrong.

To[103] finish, there is still a third major problem in the context of our Response to the First preliminary Argument. In what does final causality as such consist? How is it distinguished from efficient causality? One word is often used to describe both causalities, namely, the Latin word *movere*, "to move"; the end moves, *finis movet*, but the agent also moves, *agens movet*; as we read a while ago "the will moves the other powers," *voluntas movet alias potentias*. Clearly this "to move" cannot have the same meaning in regard both to the motion of a final cause and the motion of an efficient cause. What is their difference?

The present problem has not been stated explicitly by Saint Thomas here, but rather in its more appropriate context, Part I-II, Question 26, Articles 2 and 3, where he dealt with love and there gives the clearest indications of how the problem could be solved in a Thomistic way. Still, there are a few texts apart from that, first among them the famous Aristotelian definition of "end" (so commonplace in Saint Thomas that it is not worth our while to give references for it): "the end is that on account of which something comes to be"; in Latin, which is significant here: *finis est id cuius gratia aliquid fit*. The end is that for (or even "through") which

[103] Here we return to CLN 30, typed pages 27, 28.

something is being done. Thus final causality is nothing but the attractiveness which certain things have for us. In his *Disputed questions on Truth* 22, 2, Saint Thomas has been explicit on the difference: "As the influence of an efficient cause is to act, so the influence of the final cause is to be the object of appetite and desire."[104] As the efficient cause requires a verb in the active voice, so a final cause can be expressed only by a verb in the passive voice. In short, the influence of an efficient cause is *acting*; to *be* desired, to *be* longed for, is the influence of a final cause. "The causality of the end, however, consists in this: that on its account, other things are desired";[105] or again: "An end is a good loved and desired by some one. Hence, it is manifest that every agent, whatever it may be, in any action whatever, acts out of some love."[106] If we compare this latter text with the axiom of the present Article of Question 1 we conclude that the two, the "on account of an end" and the "love," are one and the same; to act on account of an end is to act out of love of that end.

This is the way John of Saint Thomas[107] arrived at a solution of the problem. In his own words "Metaphorical motion by which the end is said truly to cause, is first, love of an end as passively dependent on what is the object of appetite, not as actively elicited by the will."[108] When we say "the end moves" this means that the end causes in us a love for it. In one respect this love depends in the sense of "efficient cause," but not in the sense of "final cause," on our will which is indeed the efficient cause of the act of loving; in another respect, namely, insofar as love is a passion, it depends upon the end. In this passive dependence we have the proper result of final causality. The "moving" of the will is not physical, efficient, movement, but is metaphysical, or moral, or "movement" by an object of appetite. Here is where the text of I-II, Question 26, Article 2,

[104] "Sicut influere cause efficientis est agere, ita influere causae finalis est appeti et desiderari." *De veritate* 22, 2; Leonine ed. t. 23, 3: 616, l. 47—617, l. 1.

[105] "Causalitas autem finis in hoc consistit quod propter ipsum alia desiderantur." SCG 1, 75; p. 71b.

[106] "Finis autem est bonum desideratum et amatum unicuique." ST 1-2, 28, 6, in corpore; t. 2, p. 870a, ll. 13, 14.

[107] John of Saint Thomas O.P. (1589-1644), born in Lisbon, studied at Coimbra and Louvain, taught at Alcalá; he opposed the Thomism espoused by Francisco de Suárez S.J. and Gabriel Vázquez S.J., and was the author of a commentary on the *Summa theologiae* termed *Cursus theologicus*.

[108] "Metaphorica motio, qua finis dicitur causare secundum veritatem, est primus amor finis ut passive pendens ab appetibili, non ut active elicitus a voluntate." John of Saint Thomas, *Cursus philosophicus* t. 2, pp. 276, 277.

comes in:

> Thus too, the object of appetite itself first gives to the appetite a certain adaptation to itself which is, in fact, a kind of "pleased with," ⟨a state of "being pleased by"⟩, *complacentia*, in the object of appetite from which follows "motion" to what is desired.... The first mutation in the appetite by the object of appetite is, therefore, named "love," which is nothing other than a "being pleased with" the appetible; and from this "being pleased with" there follows a "motion" in the appetite, which is "desire," and finally quiet, which is "joy." Thus, therefore, since love consists in a certain mutation of appetite by the appetible, it is manifest that love is a passion....[109]

Saint Thomas here uses language that is entirely metaphorical. He speaks of a "certain shared pleasing," "a certain adaptation," a "certain mutation" which "what is sought" causes and in which final causality would properly consist. Where intellect is concerned, we speak of "information," the introduction of form, and even from the point of view of language everything is clear and like light. Where will is concerned, however, everything is obscure, even in point of language; the will is by its essence a blind, lightless power.

Yet some clarity is thrown upon the matter by these different considerations. The end, the desired object, exercises true causality, yet not efficient causality, which latter is the type of causality we always think of when the word is mentioned. Efficient causality moves physically, the final cause moves metaphorically, as an object, morally. The efficient cause unfolds its efficiency in action, in physical motion, physical contact and power; to the final cause there corresponds (and in it also consists), rather a re-action, a passion. Final causality consists in this emotion provoked in us by the charm and attractiveness of the desired object, in this rather mysterious change in our appetitive faculty, *immutatio appetitus*, in this "adaptation with," *coaptatio*, and sympathy, in the "weight" which, as it were, the object "deposits" in us: "My weight" says Saint Augustine, "is

[109] "Sic etiam ipsum appetibile dat appetitui primo quidem quandam coaptationem ad ipsum, quae est quaedam complacentia appetibilis ex qua sequitur motus ad appetibile... Prima ergo immutatio appetitus ab appetibili vocatur amor, qui nihil est aliud quam complacentia appetibilis; et ex hac complacentia sequitur motus in appetibile, qui est desiderium; et ultimo quies, quae est gaudium. Sic ergo cum amor consistit in quadam immutatione appetitus ab appetibili, manifestum est quod amor est passio...." ST 1-2, 26, 2; t. 2, p. 858b, ll. 86-54.

my love."[110] All this is difficult to explain because here we are in the midst of the metaphysics of will where light is essentially lacking.

⟨*c. The Master's Reply to the Second Argument*⟩

The second argument and its answer are not without difficulties, especially if one should look at the commentaries. I venture to think that here some commentators have made a mountain out of a mole-hill. Not patient enough to inspect the text as it stands, they have thought far ahead. Let us see this.

The major premise of the argument is this: "That which is the *last* end cannot be for the sake of an end. This is self-evident from the very definition of 'last end'."

The minor premise: "But, in some cases, actions are the ultimate end as is clear from the Philosopher in *Ethics* 1."[111]

This proposition is not a quotation from the *Ethics*, but at best is a conclusion suggested by the *Ethics*. In *Summa theologiae* Part I, Question 103, Article 2, Argument 2,[112] Saint Thomas indeed quotes the *Ethics* text, which here he might have had in mind: "The Philosopher says in *Ethics* 1 that of ends some are operations, some or works, that is, things effected." There is most of the time a distinction in Saint Thomas's saying "as is clear, *patet*, through The Philosopher" and "as The Philosopher says, *dicit*." In the second formula he quotes, ⟨but in⟩ the first he presents a conclusion drawn from Aristotle's text. Aristotle did not speak of the "ultimate end," but simply contrasted "immanent" and "transient" actions, the ones remaining in the agent and perfecting that agent, like vision, thinking, and so on, the others producing something outside the agent, a building, and so on. These latter actions, the actions of "art," of "technique," are not for the perfection of the agent, but for the perfection of the work produced. Some actions have the end in themselves, their sufficient reason in themselves, and cannot be referred to anything else. Because they have their sufficient reason in themselves, they, at least, are not "for the sake of an end."

[110] "pondus meum amor meus" (*Confessionum* 13, 9, 10). Augustine saw the literal weight of each of the "four elements" stipulated by the physics of his day as moved, each to its "proper place" by its intrinsic "weight": earth beneath water, air above water, and fire above all; for a partly spiritual being such as a human being, Augustine saw a parallel between the role of our spiritual loves and the role of physical weight in the material world.

[111] *Ethica* 1, 2; 1094a 4.

[112] ST, 1, 103, 2; t. 1, p. 615b ll. 19-24.

The same objection is stated in the ⟨earlier⟩ *Summa contra gentiles* 3, 2, near the end:

> There are some actions, however, which seem not to be on account of an end such as playful ones, and contemplative ones, and actions that come to pass apart from attention, such as stroking the beard and things of that kind; from these one can think that there might be acting *not* on account of an end.[113]

As you see, here in the *Summa theologiae*, the objection of the *Summa contra gentiles* is split into two; moreover, here the reasoning of that earlier work is given a depth it did not possess in the former work. We are faced here with the affirmation that an action is really the ultimate end and that nothing else is above it in the order of final causes.

That Aristotle had held this, and that to him this truly "last action" and "last end" of human life, to which everything else was ordained, was the *theoria*, the "contemplation" of the philosophical mind, is beyond doubt. Hence one may think, not without reason, that here the very last word of Aristotelian ethics stands in crisis. If, as Aristotle assumes, the action of contemplation, of *theoria*, is the ultimate end, having no further point of reference, then how can it be true that every human act is for an end? If, on the other hand, as the body of the Article proves, every human action is for an end, what about the theory in which the *Nicomachean Ethics* Book 10,[114] finds its culminating point? Saint Thomas answers: Let us, for the sake of argument, assume that a human action be the last end (in his words: "...*if* some human action were the last end..."). Saint Thomas could not have made it more evident that he there speaks hypothetically; whether there is or can be such an action is simply left open, neither approved nor disapproved. You have, however, already granted that it is a "human" action. Consequently, it must proceed from a deliberate will; it must be voluntary, else it would not be "human." Such an action might either be the act of the will itself: to will, to intend, and so on; or it might be an action dependent upon the will, "commanded by the will" as Saint Thomas says here, not speaking technically for "command," *imperium*, is not properly an act of will, but of reason as we shall seen farther on in Question 17. (Incidentally, here note that the famous principle "Thomas

[113] "Sunt autem aliquae actiones quae non videntur esse propter finem, sicut actiones ludicrae et contemplatoriae et actiones quae absque attentione fiunt, sicut confricatio barbae et huiusmodi: ex quibus aliquis opinari potest quod sit aliquod agens non propter finem." SCG 3, 2; p. 228b.

[114] *Nicomachean Ethics* 10, 7; 1177a 12-18.

speaks most formally, *formalissime*," suffers some exceptions!) If speaking or walking is to be a "human act" then it must depend upon a "deliberate will." Those actions are acts of other faculties, but to be "human acts" they must be commanded by the will, done willingly.

Our first question will now be, can the act itself of the will, merely considered as an exercise of will-power, be an ultimate end? A second question is, can the act of another power, considered as a "human act," that is, as an act posited voluntarily, be an ultimate end?

To the first question, the answer must be "no." The will is a driving power, the supreme motive power in the dynamism of human life. An act of will from which everything else is excluded, an act without any object, is impossible. I cannot exercise *mere* will power any more than I can exercise my visual power without seeing *something*. Furthermore, that object of willing must be an end for the will always aims at that something. In other words, the will exercises motion toward the object, whatever that object may be, as toward an end, exercises its actuality for that end, on account of that end. Hence it is impossible that "willing itself," *ipsum velle*, the will's own actuality considered as having no other object, be the ultimate end or (which means the same) the "primary object of appetite," the *primum appetibile*, the first and foremost desirable thing. The same fundamental and very important insight into the nature of the will appears also in Question 2, Article 4, and in Question 3, Article 4.[115]

Now the second question: the answer is that, at this point, the question is left open. In the text we find again the hypothesis: "...if a human act, as such *qua*, were the ultimate end...." It is enough to see here that if there were such an act, for example the act of intellect, as a human act it will be for an end, dependent on the will. It would be an "act commanded by the will" and perhaps, "elicited by the intellect." Hence the conclusion, "Whatever a human being may do" ("*as* human" of course) "it is true to say that the human being must act for an end, even in performing the action which is the ultimate end."[116] The principle "All human acts are for the sake of an end" is absolute and universal; it suffers no exceptions. Here the commentators are much concerned with two more questions. First, is the conditional on which Saint Thomas here insists true or not? *Is* any human act the last end? If we state the question about the human act it must be denied. No human act is the last end, but every human act is

115 ST 1-2, 2, 4; t. 2, p. 721a l.10-b 52; ST 1-2, 3, 4; t. 2, p. 729b, l.11-p. 730b, l. 42.

116 "Quidquid ergo homo faciat, verum est dicere quod homo agat propter finem, etiam agendo actionem quae est ultimus finis." Ad secundum; ST 1-2, 1, 1; t. 2, p. 711b, ll. 20-23.

for an end. Still, if we state the question simply in this way—"Is any act the last end?"—it must be answered with a distinction: "objectively" or "subjectively?" Since in Thomistic doctrine the question is about the act of the intellect in the beatific vision, then "objectively," that is, the object of the beatific vision, is the highest good, God. On the other hand, if we speak of the "subjective end," the act by which we possess the object of beatitude, then an act, but not a *human*, act might be the last end, and consequently, not for an end. In this lies the proper importance of this "Answer to the second argument": there is no human act which is the last end. Human life is not a final thing! The Christian idea that we are but pilgrims and strangers in this life, finds here somehow its philosophical expression. Our last end is not to live a morally good life! The last act, the eternal act of the beatific vision which we are to perform (if we may call it "an act performed") is no longer a "human act." It transcends the essential conditions of the human act; no longer *for* an end, it *is* the end.

The second question with which the commentators have been concerned at this point is a "Scotistic" problem; John Duns Scotus was to maintain that this last act is an act of will, and not an act of intellect. There is no point at this moment, however, of our commentary to go into this; ⟨Thomas had died long before Duns appeared⟩.

⟨*d. The Master's Reply to the Third Argument*⟩

The[117] third negative argument and its reply are the most interesting from the point of view of modern psychology, deeply interested as it is in these unconscious happenings found in the depth of our souls. Saint Thomas speaks indeed of such unconscious happenings; the negative argument is quite explicit in this regard: "One does many things without deliberation about which one sometimes thinks not at all, as when someone moves a foot, or a hand, while intent on other things, or strokes the beard...."[118] In *Psychopathology of Everyday Life* Freud has paid careful attention to these actions. He calls them "chance actions" but, owing to his theory of psychoanalysis, prefers the name "symptomatic actions" or "symptomatic expressions." Freud gives a somewhat more detailed enumeration of such actions. One group is formed by actions occurring habitually, regularly under certain circumstances, such as playing with the watch-chain, fingering one's beard. They can, Freud says, almost serve as

[117] Here we shift to handwritten pages that face Eschmann's typed page 31.

[118] "Sed multa homo agit absque deliberatione, de quibus etiam quandoque nihil cogitat; sicut cum aliquis movet pedem vel manum aliis intentus, vel fricat barbam." ST 1-2, 1, 1, Argument 3; t. 2, p. 711a, ll. 14-18.

a characteristic of the person concerned. They are related to the numerous "tic" movements. In another group, namely of isolated actions of this kind, Freud places playing with one's cane, the scribbling with one's pencil, the jingling of coins in one's pocket, kneading dough, and other actions of the same order. Clinical experiences led Freud to assume that these actions were not senseless and sometimes they are not even harmless:

> ...these playful occupations during psychic treatment regularly conceal sense and meaning to which other expression is denied.... Every change in the customary attire, every little negligence, such as an unfastened button, every trace of exposure, means to express something that the wearer of the apparel does not wish to say directly, usually he is entirely unconscious of it.[119]

In other words, these actions have an affective teleology. They are at once the effect and the sign of an interior state, but their relation eludes the consciousness. Psychoanalysis undertakes the task of establishing and interpreting their symbolism through the associative method, that is, a method which, by eliciting from the analyzed person a number of spontaneous associations, brings to light an identical theme common to all these associated elements and so is able to reveal the meaning of these actions. Here we are not directly interested in the method of psychoanalysis; our point is the teleology of these actions. Freud says they have a *meaning*; in Thomistic terms, they have an *end*, they are elements found in a teleological order. the principle of which is not reason. In affirming this unconscious teleology, Freud is indeed in agreement with Saint Thomas. I do not say that anything like Freud's symbolism and his method of psychoanalysis is present in the mind of Saint Thomas. Still, both thinkers are in agreement on this precise point: they deny that these actions are merely chance events in our psychic life; they are meaningful!

Indeed, how does Saint Thomas solve the problem of this third ⟨negative⟩ Argument? His phrase is *quasi finem imaginatum*, normally translated "as it were an imagined end." Does "as it were" translate *quasi*? We now are meeting for the second time a term difficult to interpret. I am of the opinion that we ought not to translate *quasi* by the terms "as it were," nor "as an imagined end," nor "so to speak," nor "it is as though...." The author had no hesitation over how to explain the teleology of these unconscious actions and the proof is in the parallel text from the *Summa contra gentiles* Book 3, Chapter 2, which has already been cited: "actions that

[119] Sigmund Freud, *The Psychopathology of Everyday Life*, tr. Alan Tyson, ed. James Strachey (New York: Norton & Co., 1965), p. 194.

come to pass apart from attention, such as a stroking the beard and things of that kind."[120] There Saint Thomas speaks of

> ...actions...which come to pass without attention are not from the intellect, but from some sudden imagination or natural principle, such as the disorder of a humor exciting an itch is the cause of stroking the beard, which comes to pass apart from the attention of intellect. Yet these do tend to some end, although ⟨to an end⟩ outside the order of intellect.[121]

Looking (perhaps too exclusively) at the one example of a seemingly "chance" action, the stroking of the beard, Saint Thomas (a) explains this action by a physiological stimulus—an itching caused, as he says in accordance with ancient physicians, by a "disorder," an imbalance of the "humors"; (b) he is enabled to point to an "end" of such an action: the removal of an itch, the restoration of the balance of the humors. He is also enabled (c) to say that all this, although it is a psychic happening, comes to pass "outside the order of intellect," that is, in the unconscious region of the soul.

This is also the authentic teaching of our present passage, "authentic" because supported by another text (as above), but also by another from the work under scrutiny: Part I, Question 78, Article 4. There we appeal to Saint Thomas's psychology of the "interior senses" in order to explain his expression "imagined end." "Fantasy" or "imagination" he explains is "as it were, a kind of store-room of forms, gathered through sense."[122] Those past sensations leave a trace in our psychic life and so become the material for the "cogitative power" which works to a certain extent on those sensitive data, "collating" them as the expression has it. This doctrine is of Islamic origin (Avicenna seems to be its main source) and for it Thomas seems to rely mainly on Albert. The main thing to remember here is that we are, in all of this, in the sub-rational and subconscious region of the soul. We are, in a way, on the threshold of reason,

[120] See text last cited above, note 107; Saint Thomas repeated this illustration on several occasions a the reader will have noticed, occasions unnecessary to list here.

[121] "Actiones autem quae fiunt sine attentione, non sunt ab intellectu, sed ab aliqua subita imaginatione vel naturali principio: sicut inordinatio humoris pruritum excitantis est causa confricatione barbae, quae fit sine attentione intellectus. Et haec ad aliquem finem tendunt, licet praeter ordinem intellectus." SCG 3, 2; p. 228, ll. 34-42.

[122] "...phantasia, sive imaginatio, quasi thesaurus quidam formarumn per sensum acceptarum." ST 1, 78, 4 in corpore; t. 1, p. 478a ll. 26-28.

but have not gone through the door!

In order to understand this doctrine and, let me add, in order not to be scandalized by its meagerness, as modern psychologists (and sometimes also the moralists) would be tempted to be scandalized, we should keep in mind carefully what the intention of Saint Thomas's doctrine is at this point. It is to elaborate the formal aspect of the human act, that is, what finally, definitely, essentially, and rigorously constitutes an act as "human" and "moral," that is, good or bad. For there is no third thing, no human act in an individual case, in the existential order, that could be morally indifferent or neutral. We are looking at the concrete thing, but under an abstract point of view, namely, with the question: "What is it 'formally'?" In ethical doctrine this is indeed the very first question. Modern doctrine directs its main, if not often its exclusive, attention to the material side of the human act. This is done to such an extent that the question may be allowed, "Whether certain authors are even aware that there is more to the human act than what comes to the fore when it is considered under the aspect of 'material cause' only?"

Now, no one can say on the first page everything that may be in one's mind! Saint Thomas's intention here is philosophical and formal; he achieved his goal. He is going to stay with this essential, but abstract, consideration for the first 21 Questions. Only from Question 22 forward to Question 48 will he turn to the fact that the human act is the vital expression of a rational animal, the accent falling then on the "animal." The abstraction under which Saint Thomas works at first, especially in Questions 6 through 21, does not imply a *negation* of the other, the mammalian aspect. What is abstract is not necessarily false. On the contrary, there is indeed no concrete human act which would be nothing but pure reason, pure spiritual volition; we are not angels! The doctrine of the unity of soul and body makes the existence of such absolutely pure acts a metaphysical impossibility and a vain and dangerous assumption. Our body is implicated in all our spiritual activity; the question is not how to eliminate it, but how to integrate it into a completely human order.

## M. The Exposition of Article 2

The inner logical connection between Article 1 and Article 2 is easy to perceive, ⟨but the inner structure of Article 2 is not⟩. Article 1 established that every human act is for an end and Article 2 now deals with the mode of this "acting for an end"; it goes one step deeper into the topic by defining more thoroughly the subject of the Moral Part which is, as we have found, "human action ordered to an end." If we are asked to present its conclusion in one short sentence we should do it in this way: the mode of acting for an end in rational natures is that they move themselves toward an end in a way very different from that of any other agent acting for an end. Of primary importance in the sequence of Article 2 ⟨that is, why Article 2 follows Article 1⟩ is that part of its conclusion ⟨the conclusion of Article 2⟩ concerns the ⟨more limited⟩ mode of acting found in rational natures only, whereas of secondary importance is the more general assertion that every agent acts for an end.

Now a curious thing is that the Article, if read as it lies and without any logical prejudice, offers a quite different picture. Its construction is quite different from what one might expect it to be. In reality, as every reader can easily be convinced, the two parts of the conclusion are in an inverted order: the primary lies with what, on a logical analysis, is secondary. The first, and more emphatic, statement of the Article as it lies is that every agent whatsoever acts for an end and only the second place is occupied by what we should expect to be the main thing, namely, that the rational agent has a proper and unique way of acting for an end. In short, the ⟨relative importance of the two themes of the⟩ Article is turned upside down. What on a logical reading is primary ⟨because more general⟩, in fact is secondary. If, as our logic and our monographic method would seem to require, the main thesis were concerned with the proper and specific mode by which rational beings act for an end, the ⟨preliminary, negative⟩ Arguments ought to have been constructed in such a way that their conclusion would be "Therefore, a rational nature does not act on account of an end, as directing itself to an end."

As you see the actual conclusions of all those Arguments are quite different: they argue that not all irrational creatures act for an end. Consequently, the main thesis which the author himself had in mind is that they *do* act for an end. The main intention of the text, of the *littera,* is to show and to prove the principle of teleology to be valid for *every* agent. The text of Saint Thomas here is constructed differently than a "monographic study" would have been. If a student presented a paper on the contents of these two Articles in monographic form, but followed Saint Thomas in every detail, the paper would be exposed to criticism for not having followed in a straight a clear line: ⟨first, the general statement, "all agents act for an end" and second, the subordinate statement, "therefore, human agents act for an end"⟩. This is the point I wish to make. This Article is a splendid and typical example of the proper and inimitable method of writing Articles in a *Summa,* in a *Summary,* as here, a method thoroughly strange to our minds and to our way of proceeding. One who writes a *Summa* builds each Article as a self-sufficient whole, like a gothic architect building a chapel *in* a cathedral. This method gives more liberty, but what is more, it obeys different formal, structural rules. The sequence in this case of Articles 1 and 2 cannot be *entirely* subsumed under the rules of an alien method (although, of course, in part it can be). In a modern treatise or monograph the only, and all-dominant, rule is the inner logic and uninterrupted procedure of reasoning and the author of a *Summa* does not really sin against this logic. His topic here is, in fact, universal teleology, with an eye on the teleology proper to an intelligent agent, not the proper teleology of the latter, with an eye on universal teleology.

I insist on this point with a purpose. Every one of you may be obliged to teach branches of Thomistic philosophy—metaphysics, psychology, ethics, or whatever it may be. In our time you will be urged to do this, not only on the basis of the text of Saint Thomas, but also by reading and explaining that text. You must be aware that such reading implies a great deal of technical explanation and my purpose is to make you aware of the fact that a medieval text has its own technique which, if not known, exposes us to misunderstanding. My personal view is that setting out Thomist *doctrine*—building up in your own modern and understandable way a body of teaching thoroughly informed by Thomistic principles and theses is one thing—and reading the *text* of Saint Thomas with your students is another thing. If there is a workable combination of the two, I have never found it!

With respect to this Article 2, its *historical background* must also be taken into account. The fact of universal teleology, the principle that "Every agent acts for an end" is one of the cornerstones of Thomistic metaphysics and theology; Saint Thomas repeats it unceasingly and sometimes dwells on it for page after page; the "parallel places" are more numerous than the editors indicate. The main one for us would be the *Summa contra gentiles* 3, 1-2.[123] It is there that we best can study the true historical setting of this principle, the great discussion between Christian and Greek-Islamic philosophy. The greatest and most important theme of Christian philosophy, the doctrine of divine intelligence and will, of creation and providence, belong to that discussion and are decided by the principle, every agent acts for an end. The material of our two Articles is treated in the two Chapters, 1 and 2, of the *Summa contra gentiles*, but the way in which this doctrine was treated there is very different from what it is here. After having proposed in Chapter 1 the object of the whole Third Book as divine government, especially with regard to rational natures, Saint Thomas at once started to treat in Chapter 2 of the principle: "Every agent acts for an end." He thus started with the more general truth and mentions the

[123] Pp. 226a-228b.

particular one of *human* acting for an end within that universal context. Thus the doctrine of the two Articles of the *Summa theologiae* was announced in Chapter 1 of the earlier work, but inversely: first the universal rule, and then its application to human acts whereas, in Article 1 of the *Summa theologiae* I-II, the same issue is approached more directly and shows a more emphatic tendency toward the inductive, toward a more analytic procedure as against the deductive, synthetic procedure of the *Summa contra gentiles*. This difference of method can be shown in many other examples.

*a. The Body of the Article*

The first conclusion of the Article is clearly stated at the beginning: "It is necessary that all agents act for an end." The demonstration proceeds by showing the absurdity which would follow the negation of this principle. A demonstration *a priori* (that is, "from the cause," properly and strictly speaking) of course cannot be given for any "first principle" in philosophy. Such a demonstration would have to be based upon the cause on which the final cause depends; now the final cause is the very first cause, it is the "cause of causes," the *causa causarum*. By definition no cause can be prior to it; other causes can be demonstrated by pointing to the final cause, but the final cause itself cannot be demonstrated in that way.

Neither can there be a demonstration *a posteriori* (that is, "from the effects") of this principle of final causality, for every cause posterior to the final cause depends upon that final cause. A demonstration from effects would clearly commit us to the vice of circular argumentation, the "vicious circle." Saint Thomas, therefore, appeals to the "reduction to absurdity," the *reductio ad absurdum*. As he put this in his *Commentary on the Metaphysics*, "It must be known that, although in certain cases, the end may be last in being, still in causality, it is always prior; whence it is named 'the cause of causes' because it is the cause of causality in all causes."[124] "The first among all causes is the final cause"; the proof of this, or rather, the simple analysis of the contents of this proposition, is here given a sort of ascending investigation, beginning with matter, ascending to form, and then transcending the genus of inner, or essential causes, considers the extrinsic or existential causes, first the agent (or efficient cause) and from it reaches up to the final cause. This is the usual manner of Thomistic demonstration in this matter as you can see from the few texts mentioned as

[124] "Sciendum autem est, quod licet finis sit ultimus in esse in quibusdam, in causalitate tamen est prior semper. Unde dicitur causa causarum, quia est causa causalitatis in omnibus causis." *In Metaphysicam Aristotelis* Liber 5, Lectio 3; no. 782, p. 259b.

"parallel places" and in many others as well. In his *Commentary on the Metaphysics* Saint Thomas proposes the same proof by descending from the final cause to the efficient and then to the formal and material causes:

> ...For it is the cause of efficient causality.... The efficient is then the cause of the causality of the matter and the form. For by its motion it makes the matter to be receptive of the form and of the form to be in the matter.[125]

The source of this doctrine on the "order of causes" is the passage in Aristotle's *Metaphysics* to be sure, but Saint Thomas has done a great deal to render the doctrine more precise.

Saint Thomas always maintained that this principle of final causality was acknowledged and taught by all the greater philosophers. To him, the only ones who had contradicted it were the ancient physicists, Leucippus, Democritus, and Empedocles, philosophers who, as Saint Thomas says (following Aristotle) "babble when they speak about principles."[126] The question with neo-Platonists and Islamic thinkers was not about the principle itself, but about its application, as we shall see later. Saint Thomas distinguished the following modes of acting for an end. Something by its action or motion tends to an end in two ways: ⟨1⟩ as moving itself to the end ⟨as does a⟩ human; or ⟨2⟩ as moved by another to the end in two ways: ⟨a⟩ to an apprehended end ⟨as does⟩ an animal; ⟨b⟩ to an end not apprehended ⟨as does⟩ a natural, inanimate thing.

On the basis of this doctrine scholastics later than Saint Thomas elaborated the following notions and distinctions:

(1) To act for an end *by direction and choice* or *freely*. In this case the agent possesses both the efficient principle of positing the act, namely, free will (for indeed one might not posit the act) and the essential notion of

[125] "Est enim causa causalitatis efficientis, ut iam dictum est. Efficientis autem est causa causalitatis et materiae et formae. Nam facit per suum motum materiam esse susceptivam formae, et formam inesse materiae." Ibidem.

[126] "Sicut enim pueri de novo loqui incipientes imperfecte et balbutiendo loquuntur, ita philosophia priorum philosophorum nova existens, visa est balbutiendo et imperfecte de omnibus loqui circa principia..." (1, 17; no. 272, p. 93b). Aristotle was here the source for what Aquinas knew about Empedocles and, in *Metaphysics* 12, 6; 1072a 7, for Leucippus; for Democritus, the same work 8, 2; 1042b 9-12. In his SCG 3, 2, p. 228b, at the end of the Chapter, Saint Thomas accounted for the errors of the "ancient naturalists" by the fact that they excluded final causality from the realities they examined: "...antiquorum Naturalium error, qui ponebant omnia fieri ex necessitate materiae, causam finalem a rebus penitus subtrahentes."

acting for an end (or, more simply, the notion of an end). This latter means that by practical knowledge the agent knows that the end is an end, and also that the act to be posited is proportionate to the end and might lead to that end. This knowledge must be "practical"; a speculative, metaphysical, knowledge of final causality is, of course, not required for acting.

(2) To act for an end *elicitively*, that is, to act or rather to tend toward an end, not only on the basis of an intrinsic principle of action (appetite), but also out of a certain "knowledge" of the end; this knowledge need not be formal, but may be only material, as is the case with brute animals.

(3) To act for an end *in the order of execution*. This is acting for an end without any knowledge, but still on the basis of an intrinsic efficient principle of the action, namely, nature, which is also called "natural appetite." In truth, there is a further distinction in this regard in that the principle may be either ⟨a⟩ "natural" with the result that the motion is permanent and connatural (an unsupported stone falls) or ⟨b⟩ "unnatural" with the result that the motion is violent, forced, outside nature, or even against nature (as when a stone is thrown).

We learn from a very profound text of Saint Thomas, *On Truth* Question 23, Article 1, that for him, the principle of distinguishing these different modes of acting for an end is the very notion of "acting for an end" or "acting from a tendency toward an end." This differentiation comes from the different ways in which final causality functions; in other words, the different ways in which the "motion" of "end-cause" is receivable and received in an agent is according to the various natures of the various agents. The division which Saint Thomas establishes follows this rule for divisions: "Division comes to pass in accord with the formal nature of the whole that is divided." Here is the principle of this division as formulated by Saint Thomas:

> Now since one reality must be ordered to another reality through something which it possesses in itself, inasmuch as one thing possesses something differently in itself, in accord with that, this ⟨reality⟩ is ordered differently to that other ⟨reality⟩.[127]

The intellectual nature is capable, in virtue of its immateriality, of receiv-

[127] "Cum enim res habeat ad rem aliam ordinari per aliquid quod in se habet, secundum quod diversimode in se aliquid habet, secundum hoc diversimode ad aliud ordinatur." *De veritate*, Quaestio 23, Articulus 1, in corpore; t. 22, p. 653, ll. 140-143.

ing another reality as other, *aliud ut aliud*; it is therefore capable also of receiving by knowledge the end as end, that is, the "nature of that end." It knows in a practical way the very finality of the end. This implies a judgment about the attractiveness of the end, its desirability, and moreover, a judgment about the order of the means to that end, a judgment about their proportion.

In the sensitive and cognitive agents, that is, in brute animals, there is an "imitation," a "similitude," of liberty which is often deceptive; the end is "known," not formally, but materially: a thing appears as good and convenient and, accordingly, the motion towards the end in such beings will be natural and instinctive.

In agents in which there is no knowledge that motion toward the end will be purely natural. It will be received in the natural appetite which, however, is not a potency, but simply the nature of the being conceived as inclined toward something else which is its perfection.

Such is Saint Thomas's doctrine about the different modes of acting for an end; it has all but innumerable parallels in Thomistic works. In accordance with the general tenor of this Article Saint Thomas does no more at this point than simply to elaborate a division of the different modes of acting for an end.

*b. The Replies to Preliminary, Negative Arguments*

In accordance with the problem that has been stated, and in accord with the somewhat surprising way in which it was stated, Saint Thomas was preoccupied in all his Responses, not with the second point of the Body of the Article (the diverse ways of acting for an end), but rather with his first point (every agent acts for an end). Mere logic might have dictated the opposite, namely, the diverse ways of moving toward an end; had this been a merely logical continuation of the doctrine, objections could have been found easily against the *human* mode of acting for an end. Saint Thomas could have pointed to many facts in the world of brute animals which often have a very deceptive way of acting for an end; often they act just as we do, if not better. As someone has said, the distance between this human and that human is often greater than the distance between this human and that animal!

To the First Argument:

The text of this Response is noteworthy for the following reason (a reason I am surprised not to have found in any of the commentators). Here, acting at the command of another appears in a rather unfavorable light. Saint Thomas opposes it to acting for a known end, which is human acting in the full and proper sense. In the Thomistic scheme, acting on command clearly is put on the same level as that acting which is found in irrational creatures.

What about obedience? What about the virtue of obedience? I think the answer is this. Analyzing an act done on command we find that its proper reason is not that which is commanded, but the command itself. "If obedience be taken strictly," Saint Thomas will say later, "it concerns by its intention the formal notion of a precept...."[128] I obey, not because the *contents* of the command, the material object and the end of the act commanded, are known to me in their full teleological context. Inspecting only *what* is commanded, I do not know its ultimate *Why*? If I did, the command would be superfluous; I would determine the act for myself. I obey, formally speaking, because the command is expressed by a competent superior to whom, in virtue of some form of justice, I owe obedience. This act of obedience is a human act in the full sense, an act through which one acts through oneself and with knowledge of the end—in this case, the very formal notion of precept, the fact that the act is commanded by some legitimate authority. Such is the case, at least for the virtue of obedience in which the formal notion of action is a special good, namely, the order of authority or power to which I am subjected. This order is a good, a value, in itself; without it, human social life would be impossible.

Looking at *what* is commanded, at the *matter* of the act which I carry out, the picture changes. This "end of the action," which is secondary if the act be taken formally as an "act of obedience," is not known to me, or need not be known fully and in its ultimate reasons. I need not know the exigencies of the "common good." Under this material aspect an act done on command is not a fully "human act"; it is incomplete as human action. Therefore, Saint Thomas affirms, with regard to human law (the only law in which there is an element of coercion) that the virtuous and the just are in some sense not subject to the law *as coercive*, whereas the evil are under the coercive law.

Now law, according to Saint Thomas, is a pedagogical institution: "the Law was not set in place for the just!" (1 Timothy 1:9). The present text of the first Response is in perfect harmony with this theory. When Saint Thomas says here, "...for instance, when one acts at the command of another, or is moved, another giving the impulse," the second part of this proposition is the explanation, the more precise determination, of the first part. Saint Thomas has in mind, not simply acting under the direction of the law, but an acting under its compulsion which, as we have learned from his *Summa theologiae* I-II, 96, loc. cit., behooves, ⟨is for the good of⟩,

[128] "Sic ergo, si obedientia proprie accipiatur, secundum quod respicit per intentionem formalem rationem praecepti...." ST 2-2, 104, 2, Ad 1; t. 3, p. 196b, ll. 33-35.

evil and imperfect people. Through compulsion these are forced to act well. It is to be hoped that, by repeatedly doing so, a good habit, that is, an intrinsic principle of good acting, will be formed in them.

To sum up: when the question is asked "Is acting under command 'human' acting?" the answer must be given with several distinctions. (a) When the command is coercive, that is, given with the sanction of a penalty, it is not fully a human action. The coercive command is given only on account of either the actual or potential evil-doers.[129] A human being acting under the impulse of passion does not act as a human being ought to act; ⟨under passion⟩ assimilated to brute animals, and eventually, through punishment, disposed of as one disposes of a beast.[130] (b) When the command is directive only (a case which Saint Thomas does not consider here) then we must make a distinction.

The act of obedience has its own good and its own end; obedience itself, given the distinction between superiors and inferiors, is an act of justice, that is, of doing what is due to the superior. But when the same act is considered with regard to that which is done it participates in the relative imperfection of the condition of the one who obeys. What is done in obedience to a precept is done in the first place "because it is commanded," not "because it is good."

To the Second and Third Arguments:

The Responses to the Second and Third Arguments both bring out the fact that the universal teleology which we know to be a metaphysical law binding all agents can be explained only by the existence of a rational agent. That agent is either the one who acts (as in rational creatures) or some other agent, over and above the one acting for an end, as is the case for all "natural" agents. This leads to the conclusion that, to use a formula familiar to Saint Thomas in other places, for instance *On Power* 1, 5; 3, 15, "the work of nature is a work of intelligence." The Responses to 2 and to 3, therefore, illustrate the "Fifth Way," *Summa theologiae* I, 2, 3, to demonstrate that there is, and must be, what "all call 'God'" by appeal to an extra-mundane Intelligence to account for the intelligent activity of agents, the natures of which are irrational.

The end is the principle of any order, and every order is the work of

[129] "Dicendum quod homines bene dispositi melius inducuntur ad virtutem monitionibus voluntariis quam coactione; sed quidam male dispositi non inducuntur ad virtutem nisi cogantur." ST 1-2, 96, 1; Ad 1; t. 2, p. 1231a ll. 37-42.

[130] "Dicendum quod homo peccando ab ordine rationis recedit; et ideo decidit a dignitate humana...hominem peccatorem occidere potest esse bonum, sicut occidere bestiam...." ST 2-2, 64, 2, Ad 3; t. 3, p. 1757b, ll. 35-37, 49, 50.

intelligence or reason: "To order is proper to reason," *rationis est ordinare.* In an intelligent agent, insofar as that agent acts intelligently, there is no difficulty in admitting that those acts are part of an order. Yet the actions of irrational creatures are also part of an order, which order is not their own doing. It is imposed upon them by an ordering intelligence outside them.

To the Second Argument:

> It must be stated that to order to an end belongs to that which directs itself toward an end. To that which is directed toward an end by another, it belongs to be directed toward an end. This can be characteristic of an irrational nature, but by some one who possesses reason.[131]

It is fundamentally the same doctrine which is presented in the "To the Third Argument," except that there a further step is taken. There we learn what the essential structure of a teleological order is: it is an order of universal and particular causes. There are two senses of "universal" or "general" in the philosophy of Saint Thomas as we might best learn from Saint Thomas himself, among other places, in his *Summa theologiae* II-II, 58, 6:

> It must be stated that something is said to be "general" in two ways. In one way through predication, as "animal" is "general" as to a human and to a horse. And it is necessary that "general" in this mode be the same essentially with respect to those to which it is general because a general class belongs to the essence of its special class and falls in its definition. In another mode something is said to be "general" with respect to its power, as a universal cause is "general" with respect to all its effects, as the sun is with respect to all bodies which are illumined or changed through its power....[132]

[131] "Ad secundum. Dicendum quod ordinare in finem est eius quod seipsum agit in finem. Eius vero quod ab alio agitur in finem, est ordinari in finem. Quod potest esse irrationalis naturae, sed ab aliquo rationem habente." ST 1-2, 1, 1, Ad 1; t. 2, p. 712b, ll. 12-17.

[132] "Dicendum quod generale dicitur aliquid dupliciter. Uno modo, per praedicationem, sicut animal est generale ad hominem et equum et ad alia huiusmodi. Et hoc modo generale oportet quod sit idem essentialiter cum his ad quae est generale, quia genus pertinet ad essentiam speciei et cadit in definitione eius. Alio modo, dicitur aliquid generale secundum virtutem, sicut causa universalis est generalis ad omnes suos effectus, ut sol ad omnia corpora, quae illuminantur vel immutantur per virtutem ipsius...." ST 2-2, 58, 6, in corpore; t. 3, p. 1723a-1723b, ll. 50-7.

In other words, there is logical universality and a causal universality. There is a universality of general class, of *genus*, with respect to its special classes, *species*, and the universality of a cause with respect to its effects. Now the structure of a teleological order is commanded by its principle which is a universal cause, namely, its universal good, that good which is either the cause of all other goods, or a certain series or group of goods. To illustrate such a teleological order Saint Thomas here uses the example of a "common good," that is, the good of a city. The common good is a comprehensive and total good, a universal good of a definite kind: it comprises all the particular goods which may fall within its orbit; it is their end and, therefore, "the ruler of a city moves by his command all the particular services, *officia*, of the city."

Order in nature rests, in the last analysis, on three facts: (1) the universal good, that is, the cause of all goods, or that through which all goods are good; and (2) this universal good is the object of one will, namely, of the divine Will, the absolutely universal Good is, indeed, God Himself; and (3) that all created goods are parts of that universal good, not material or formal parts, but parts of a system of final and efficient causes. Every particular efficient or final cause is part (in an analogical sense) of a universal efficient or final cause because, and ⟨is such⟩ inasmuch as, the particular cause depends in its causality on the universal cause.

Saint Thomas here stresses a point which is familiar to readers of the *Summa theologiae* as well as to everyone who has even a slight acquaintance with his thought. His own words are clearer than any explanation ever could be. One thing, however, must be stated in the Response to the Third Argument: there are two notions introduced, the "universal good" and the "good in general," *in universali*; these are by no means the same. "Universal good" designates as cause, a supreme final cause. "Good in general" belongs to what Saint Thomas calls "generality" or "universality of predication." "Good in general" is an abstract notion; from all things that are good we abstract the notion of "being good" and this is the "good in general." It is the most general *predicate* "good." It indicates a formal notion, not a universal cause.

Now, as we know from the first Article, the object of the will is the "end" and "the good"; this proposition here receives further precision. The object of the will is the end and the logically universal good, the "formal" *bonum in universali*. The will intends whatever it intends because it is "good," that is to say, one can attribute to what is willed the predicate "good." Saint Thomas does not mean by this to give the human will an abstract notion as the object of its intentions since no one intends to have an abstract notion, but rather a real good, ⟨a good reality⟩. The "universal good" is, therefore, not the material, but the formal, object of a human will. It answers the question, why does our will become active?, not the question, as to what does it become active? This difference between the formal "good in general," *bonum in universali,* and the material "universal good," *bonum universale,* is very important for the correct understanding of this Response to the Third Argument and will play an important role in our understanding of Question 2, Article 8.

## N. THE EXPOSITION OF ARTICLE 3

This Article carries the title "Whether the acts of a human being, *actus hominis,* receive their species from their end." Now the titles of the Articles, as they appear in our editions, are not from Saint Thomas, or to be more precise, they are not found in the manuscripts. Those titles have been inserted by later editors. Here the editor manifestly takes his title from the Introduction; strictly speaking ("pedantically speaking"!) the title is wrong. It ought to be, not "acts of a human being," but "human acts," just as the beginning of the Article indicates. Of course the mistake goes back to Saint Thomas himself who, in listing the Articles of this Question, had written what would be questioned in the third Article. It slipped his mind that in the first Article of this Question he was to establish a terminology, in the light of which this title would not be quite correct. "Even good Homer sometimes nods," *aliquando etiam dormitat bonus Homerus.*[133] There are not many places where you will discover Saint Thomas not to have been on the alert; this is one, but it does not really matter.

The Article is very simple and clear if only we take care of reading its text as it stands and keep in mind that its statements, in the mind of Saint Thomas, are complete as they stand here, in their proper place. Of course they are not complete in every respect; further precision and development will be given in due time ⟨which will be⟩ later in the *Summa theologiae.* The commentators here are generally rather impatient and indiscreet in that they try to involve in this simple problem all the questions to which Saint Thomas himself assigned places later in the Part I-II. The "parallel places" as given by editors from olden times are already an indication of the way this Article is generally treated by the commentators.

133 Here Eschmann (as well as Homer and Aquinas) has nodded; citing from memory presumably, Eschmann referred to Quintus Horatius Flaccus, *Ars poetica,* l. 359: "Indignor, quandoque bonus dormitat Homerus," "I take it amiss that sometimes good Homer nods." As Eschmann has remarked of the present "nodding" by Aquinas (or perhaps by his scribe) the slip does not matter.

Those references are not absolutely out of place and indeed they can be helpful, but they, and many more, ought to be placed on the margin of this or that specific development in the Body or in the Responses ⟨of this Article⟩. There is no place parallel to this Article in any of his works, no place where he would have treated the same problem with the same limitations; they are due to the place in which it is dealt with here.

What is the problem? Let us study the places which are always revealing. Such places are, first of all, the Arguments for those "Arguments to the contrary," in a Thomistic Article are less "objections" than the means of elaborating a clear "state of the question."

> Now the end is an extrinsic cause;
> but everything possesses species from some intrinsic principle;
> therefore, human acts do not receive their species from the end.[134]

In the first Article we learned that every human act is for an end, is done for an end, proceeds from the will intending an end. The first and also the second Article discussed the two extrinsic causes of the human act, namely, the efficient and the final cause. These ⟨extrinsic⟩ causes concern directly the *existence* of what they cause. What about the formal, essential, and intrinsic causes of this act, the cause determining its *essence*? The question to which Saint Thomas now proceeds is, what is the essence of a human act expressed by its formal and specifying cause? Or better and more precisely, is the end not only the "final" but also the "formal" principle with regard to the human act? The transition from Articles 1 and 2 to Article 3 is thus perfectly clear and simple. It is the first task of a science to have a clear definition of its subject, which in more ordinary terms means that everyone who speaks of a thing in the first place should know and be clear on what is talked about. A definition of the "moral part," of the *pars moralis*, is the proper subject of this third Article.

The second Argument brings nothing new on the problem of the state of the question. You will notice that the "objection" is already known to a reader of the Part I-II, for it is almost the same as in Article 1; it is good to remember that we are reading a *Summa*, not a monograph!

The third Argument is the most serious one. With every act we perform we can intend an indefinite number of ends. By doing one and the same thing, for instance, by bringing about a human person's death, a Judge intends to preserve justice and the ordinary killer intends ven-

[134] "Finis enim est causa extrinsica. Sed unumquodque habet speciem ab aliquo principio intrinseco. Ergo actus humani non recipiunt speciem a fine." ST 1-2, 1, 3, Argument 1; t. 2, p. 712b, ll. 46-49.

geance, or something else. Is not killing a person merely *what* you do and not what you *intend* to do?

From this Argument it is clear beyond any doubt that Saint Thomas, in this place, speaks of the end which, in a given concrete act, the human will intends. There is, in Thomistic philosophy, a distinction between the "end of the operation," ⟨"of the work"⟩, the *finis operis*, and the "end of the operator," ⟨"of the agent"⟩, the *finis operantis*. The first, the end of the operation, is the end which a given work has in itself; the end of the operator is the intention which an agent pursues in doing that work, which intention might or might not coincide with the end of the operation. It is clear that, if this distinction between the two "ends" should be brought into the discussion at this moment, then our text indicates clearly that we are now discussing the end of the operator, or simply the intention. The point which Saint Thomas wants to make seems to be, so far, that the intention specifies a human act.

The conclusion, or rather the several formulation of the conclusion confirm this impression. At the end of the Body of the Article Saint Thomas says indeed,

> ...moral acts are given their species in the proper sense from the end, for "moral acts" and "human acts" are the same.[135]

This identification of the human with the moral acts, which a reader encounters here for the first time, is worthy of note. A human act is by that very fact a moral act. It belongs at once to the genus, the general class, of "the moral," the *genus moris*, and because the Article treats of the specification of human acts it treats at the same time of the specification of this general class. Hence what we learn with regard to the statement of the problem is that the intention of the end is the specifying principle in the order of morality.

Something else is at the moment of even greater importance in this formulation of the thesis. Saint Thomas says that human acts, or moral acts, "gain their species in a proper sense from the end." What this "in a proper sense" may mean is made clear a few lines before where he had said that the principle of human acts, as such, is the end; the question is therefore stated with respect to human acts as such. Now human acts are such insofar as they proceed from a deliberate will. Consequently, what we are looking for is not everything which might have something to do with the specification of human acts (and there are a few such things), but

[135] "...actus morales proprie speciem sortiuntur ex fine; nam idem sunt actus morales et actus humani." ST 1-2, 1, 3, in corpore; t. 2, p. 713a, ll.44-47.

that which specifies human acts as such. That something is the intention, the end for which one acts. It is not said that this intention will suffice for judging the moral quality of an act and still less is it said that the intention sanctifies everything else, that the end justifies the means, or something like that. Here we are not up to a complete discussion of the whole problem of the moral specification of our acts; that discussion comes later, see below, Questions 18-20, especially Question 18, Article 6, which again takes up the problem of the present Article. What we are up to here is an initial and fundamental statement on this matter, namely, that "human acts" (or moral acts) gain their species in a proper sense from the end.

This brings us to the historical background of the problem. Saint Thomas gives a hint in the "But on the contrary" with the Augustinian text which he quotes: "according as the end is culpable or laudable, according to this are our works culpable or laudable" (*On the Morals of the Church and of the Manichees*, Book 2, Chapter 13).[136] The text is cleverly chosen since it simply stresses the specific importance of the end for our doings without touching on any of the problems which this Augustinian thesis has raised.

If you wish to have some notion of these problems, read Peter Lombard's *Sententiarum* Liber 2, Distinctiones 36-40 and Saint Thomas's remarks on those texts. In them we find some questions whose affinity to our present problem is at once manifest, for instance, Distinction 38, Question 1, Article 5: "Whether a will must be judged righteous from the end"; Distinction 40, Question 1, Article 1: "Whether 'good' and 'evil' may be essential differentiating notes of action"; and Distinction 36, Question 1, Article 5: "Whether the distinction of goods into 'good from their general class', from the end, and from the cause be fitting." The latter problem is that of scholastics who were striving for a synthesis of the various constitutive elements of morality. It must be noted, however, that none of these various Articles is really parallel to our present Article in which Saint Thomas very clearly does not want to go into the full problematic as it was discussed in the schools of his time. This he will do below, Questions 18-20.

*a. The Body of the Article*

The Body of the Article will appear hard and difficult to understand to many a modern reader of Saint Thomas. Still, such strange passages should be carefully studied; in a way, they are most characteristically Thomistic. In the human act there is a double aspect: the same act is both an

[136] "Secundum quod finis est culpabilis vel laudabilis, secundum hoc sunt opera nostra culpabilia vel laudabilia." Ibidem, t. 2, p. 713a, ll. 6-9.

action, *actio*, and a passion, *passio*. It belongs to the two categories according to the way it is considered. The human act is an actuality proceeding from the deliberate will. On one hand, insofar as the will stands under, and is dependent on, that "metaphorical" motion issuing from the end, and constituting final causality itself, the will is "passion." On the other hand, insofar as it is efficient causality, namely, the act of will intending the end, stretching itself out toward that end, it is "action." Yet in both action and passion the end appears as the act that determines a potency and therefore the end is, in both cases, or rather, under both aspects, the formal, formative, and specifying principle:

> The object of the will, however, is the "good" and the "end" ⟨to which one is "passive"⟩. Therefore, too, it is manifest that the principle of human acts, insofar as they are human, is the end. Similarly, it is the terminus of the same ⟨acts⟩ for that at which a human act terminates is that which the will intends as an end ⟨to which one is "active"⟩.[137]

This is the main part of the Body of the Article; it contains, as you see, nothing new since the division of the human act into "action" and "passion" was hinted right at the beginning of Part I-II, namely, in the Response to the first Argument in the first Article. But now the idea of thus analyzing the metaphysical structure of the act and finding it belongs to the two categories of being, namely, "action" and "passion," leads at once to the famous passage in Aristotle's *Physics*, Book 3, where motion, movement, is defined, and where, analyzing the metaphysical structure of *kinesis*, "motion," Aristotle also states that it in some way is divided into action and passion. The Aristotelian passage in the *Physics* which is the foundation of our doctrine here extends from Chapter 2 near the end over the whole of Chapter 3 (202 a 3-202b 29). In Saint Thomas's *Commentary on the Physics* one ought to read Lecture 4, especially from paragraph 9 on, and the whole of Lecture 5. This latter contains a much celebrated deduction of the ten Aristotelian "categories of being." As to motion, the point in short is this: motion supposes a mover and a movable; the same motion is both *in* the movable and *from* the mover. Thomas explains:

> It is necessary that one activity be that of both, namely, of what is

[137] "Obiectum autem voluntatis est bonum et finis. Et ideo manifestum est quod principium humanorum actuum, inquantum sunt humani, est finis. Et similiter est terminus eorundem; nam id ad quod terminatur actus humanus, est id quod voluntas intendit tanquam finem...." Ibidem in corpore; t. 2, p. 713a ll. 34-41.

> moving and of what is moved; for what is from the item moving, as an active cause, and what is in the moved item as passive and as received, is identical.[138]

In our Article Saint Thomas's example is "warming," *calefactio*, ⟨as of water boiled⟩. This is action, insofar as it proceeds from the active principle of warmth which is fire, and it is a passivity, insofar as it is the movement or alteration in the movable, for instance, in water. Whatever the physics of this may be, neither the Aristotelian nor the Thomistic analysis is here "physical"; rather it is "metaphysical." Explaining the distinction between action and passion, Saint Thomas says in his *Commentary on the Physics*:

> Nothing prevents one action from belonging to two items in such wise that it not be one and the same according to reason, although one in reality (and two in accord with reason).... For thus an action, the same in reality, belongs to two items in accord with a diverse way of thinking—to an agent in accord with the fact that it is *from* the agent, but still, to the passive item according as it is *in* this passive item.[139]

In other words, this division of one motion into action and passion is a metaphysical division answering the problem of the metaphysical structure of motion. This what Saint Thomas means by saying here in our Article that "Motion in a certain way, *quodammodo,* is distinguished through 'action' and 'passion'." As is often the case, the term *quodammodo* in the language of Saint Thomas does not have the meaning attached to our expression "in a way." If you translate "movements are, in a way, divided into action and passion," one could think that you are talking loosely and do not really mean what you say. In Saint Thomas the term most often means just what it says: *quodam-modo,* that is, "in a definite way." Movements are divided, in a definite way, into action and passion, that is, they are so divided "in accord with a metaphysical insight," according to the metaphysical, and not the physical, analysis of motion or movement. Now

[138] "Oportet unum actum esse utriusque, scilicet moventis et moti: idem enim est quod est a movente, ut a causa agente, et quod est in moto, ut in patiente et recipiente." *Super Physicam* Liber 3, Lectio 4, n. 10; Maggliolo, # 306, pp. 153b-154a.

[139] "Nihil prohibet unum actum esse duorum, ita quod non sit unus et idem secundum rationem, sed unus secundum rem (et duo secundum rationem).... Sic enim idem actus secundum rem est duorum secundum diversam rationem: agentis quidem secundum quod est ab eo, patientis autem secundum quod est in ipso." Ibidem.

the species of either action or of passion is to be taken from that which in either case is the act or actuality in opposition to what is potentiality. In the *actio*, the actuality, the entire principle of acting is that from which the motion starts, that which produces the motion. In the *passio*, the passion, on the contrary, is the terminus of motion, that in which the motion ends. "Warming" taken as action (*calefactio* means "warming-action") starts from the actual warmth of the fire and "warming" taken as passion (*calefactionis passio* or *calefieri*, "passive warming" or "to be warmed") ends in being warm, in having warmth. The definition of these two must be accordingly: warming as a an action is the motion proceeding from what has warmth; "to be warmed" is the motion towards warmth ⟨in what formerly was not warm⟩. In both cases "warmth" is the act by which a thing is defined, yet in different ways. "Warming" as action is the active principle at the beginning of the change; "warmed" as passivity is the term and end of the procedure.

This is the analogy which Saint Thomas is convinced will clear up the problem in hand. He warns the reader that in bringing in this Aristotelian metaphysics of motion he is speaking of an analogy with regard to the thing which is to be discussed and illustrated, namely, the act of the will. "And this too must be considered in its proper motions." Indeed, the action of the will is not "movement" univocally speaking since the univocal notion of movement is applicable only to the transient action in external matter. Such motion is what Aristotle analyzed; the act of the will, however, is an immanent action and therefore a "motion" improperly so-called." Yet, keeping in mind the analogy, this metaphysics of motion applies also to the act of will just as it applies to every immanent act, for instance, the act of intellect. The distinction between the "agent intellect" and the "possible intellect" rests also on the same Aristotelian metaphysics of "action" and "passion." If we now re-read the Body of our Article, I think, the light will begin to dawn upon us; through more and more reading we shall be able to grasp this logic ⟨of analogy⟩.

All of us ought to read the following passages in the works of Saint Thomas, passages which contain the same fundamental way of reasoning and which will, therefore, help to clarify the issue. First, as cited above, Lectures 4 and 5 of his *Commentary on the Physics* Book 3. Second, all the passages quoted here by the Editors as "parallel places," not "parallel" in the sense of dealing with the problem of our Article, but places in which in other circumstances elements of the argumentation are brought out. Thirdly, passages such as *On Truth* Question 22, Article 12, and *On Power* Question 6, Article 8. We ought to realize that this is a very conventional matter with editors; some sixteenth-century scholar indicated them and ever since every editor prints them again without doing very much about the matter. If only we had[140] a reliable Thomistic Index and Dictionary we could also go to work systematically and with a definite notion of "parallel places"!

*b. Responses*

*i. To the first ⟨Argument⟩*: Note the short analysis of the essential structure of a human act in which the elements of activity and passivity are put forward sharply: this very thing belongs to the notion of act, namely, that it be *from* something as regards action and that it be *with respect to* something as regards passivity.[141]

Here "to be from something" is verified by proceeding from the will as from the efficient principle; "to be with respect to something" is verified by being directed to an end and thus depending passively on the causal influence of the end or the good. That finalism in human activity implies this passivity, a passivity not like that which obtains in the relation of efficient cause-and-effect, but like that which obtains between the final cause and its proper effect.

*ii. To the second ⟨Argument⟩*: The intention, that which I want to do, is the specifying principle of my act insofar as it is human or moral acting. This intention might or might not be in conformity with what I am doing, but this is a problem which the author now takes up in the Response to the third.

*iii. To the third ⟨Argument⟩*: Recall the negative Argument:

> The same thing cannot be except in a single species;
> but, an act, numerically one, can happen to be ordered to diverse ends;
> therefore, the end does not give species to human acts.

The minor is the most important proposition: "an act, numerically one, can be ordered to diverse ends." Saint Thomas makes a distinction between

140 The fifty-volume *Concordantiae Thomisticae* edited by Roberto Busa S.J. has appeared since Eschmann's death; it more than fulfills his hopes, expressed in the days when the best available was the useful one-volume *Thomas-Lexikon*, ed. Ludwig Schütz (Paderborn: Drück und Verlag von Ferdinand Schöningh, 1895; repr. New York: Musurgia, n.d.).

141 "...et hoc idem est de ratione actus, ut scilicet sit ab aliquo, quantum ad actionem, et ut sit ad aliquid, quantum ad passionem." ST 1-2, 3, 3, Ad 1; t. 2, p. 713a, ll. 52-54.

two cases in which it happens that the same act is ordered to different ends. In the first case, an act can be integrated into a system of ends. Saint Thomas gives no example, but let us find one. I buy a ticket to go to some place; I go to that place in order to teach; I teach because I am called upon to do so and have an obligation to comply with this call. I might also want to teach in other places because I think that I have something important to say. Or, again, I might do so because I am interested in increasing my reputation or my bank account. In the concrete act which I am doing right here and now, namely, buying a railroad ticket, is a part and an element of a definite system of ends.

Now Saint Thomas's answer is that an act numerically one, inasmuch as it goes forth from an agent is not ordered except to one proximate end from which it possesses its species; but it can be ordered to many remote ends, one of which is the end of the other.[142]

The act of buying a railroad ticket is specified immediately by its closest end, namely, getting on the train. All this, however, might be part of a wider and much more complicated system of ends which then gives to my act a proper aspect and character. If we understand the minor as saying, "It happens that an act, numerically one, is ordered to diverse ends, ordered one under another," then the problem presents itself as that of a whole system of specifications. There is an immediate specification and one which enters into it somehow from farther off. The problem is here closed in one respect: as for the specification of a human act by its closest and immediate end—the "proximate end," the *finis proximus*.

On the other hand, the problem is left open, namely, for the manner in which these "remote ends" might, or might not, enter into the matter. We must wait for a decision on this problem on later occasions. As we wait, however, note that Saint Thomas opens up the "state of the question" for the following Article, for the issue in that Article will be indeed about this "act one in number," that is, one act in its relation to such diverse ends, one of which is the end of the other. In other words, the Question will be whether, in this case, there is system (or order) of ends, or whether a regress to infinity should rather be assumed.

But now, the second case. An act, numerically the same, happens to be ordered to diverse ends. Saint Thomas's example speaks for itself; it is at once clear that we are now getting off the limits of our problem as it was stated in the Argument. For Saint Thomas does not consider any long-

[142] "...idem actus numero, secundum quod semel egreditur ab agente, non ordinatur nisi ad unum finem proximum, a quo habet speciem; sed potest ordinari ad plures fines remotos, quorum unus est finis alterius." Ibidem, t. 2, p. 713b, ll. 5-10.

er one (that is, numerically one) act which might be made part of different systems of acts, but he considers the possibility of one, that is, in a certain way essentially one act. For killing a man, as the example is, as done by a public authority, and killing a man, as done by common law murderer—these are not one and the same act, either numerically or specifically or essentially speaking. Yet there is some oneness or sameness in both acts. Saint Thomas, then, as he often does (in a marginal remark, as it were) goes off into a different and wider problem. We cannot expect him at this place to give a complete solution of this problem. Still, we are again carefully to note his remarks and to keep them in mind for further reference.

There is, he says, a "natural species," a *species naturae* and distinguished from it a "moral species," a *species moralis*. In the aforementioned cases of killing (by a murderer or an execution ordered by a judge) the natural species is identical: the taking away of a human life. The act is no less or more effective whether it is done by the publicly appointed hangman or by a murderer in a crime of passion. The moral species, however, is different: "because in one mode it will be an act of virtue, in the other mode it will be an act of vice," a difference which, morally speaking, makes all the difference in the world.

Saint Thomas goes even farther: how are these two species related to each other? The answer is, they are related as substance and accident: "Moral ends qualify a natural reality and, conversely, the notion, the *ratio*, of the natural end qualifies the moral."

This is to say that *first*, the moral order is something quite different from the natural order, that is, the order of natural essences, of physical essences. In other words, there is a specific sort of being, namely, moral being, which is different from the natural or physical being. Moral being cannot be reduced to physical being. Their structures are totally different. Take an act as a natural, physical reality; it is a "motion" which has its own specification and this specification is not the one for which we are looking in our moral research. Vice versa, take an act as a moral being, and an act precisely as a human act; this, properly speaking is not a physical, but a moral, being. This act will again have its own essence, its own specific principle, namely, the end of the agent, and this specification, the essence of the act, will be quite different from the physical essence.

Then *second*, though being specifically different, the natural and the moral act are nevertheless in some way joined together. Our human acts are always at the same time physical entities and moral entities. Insofar as they are physical entities, the "end of itself," *terminus per se*, is that which is done, physically speaking, for instance, the killing of a human person. Remain with this physical essence and you will have to say that everything which is due to the moral order is accidental, *per accidens*. On the other hand, insofar as our acts are moral entities, their "end of itself" is the "end of the agent," that is, the end for which the act is done. Stay with this moral essence and you will have to say that everything which is due to the physical order is accidental with regard to the moral order. In the words of Saint Thomas (as always clearer than any "explanation" can be):

> A motion does not receive its species from that which is the end "by accident," but only from that which is the end "of itself." Moral ends are accidental to a natural reality and, conversely, the natural notion of the end is accidental with respect to the moral. And so it is that nothing prevents acts which are the same according to their natural species from being diverse according to their moral species, and the converse.[143]

What this second part of the Response to the third ⟨Argument⟩ brings out is the essential difference between the physical order and the moral order and, consequently, between the essence and methods of physical and moral science. A "moral being" properly speaking is nothing physical; it has its own constitutive principles, its own specification, its own essence, which cannot be seen or grasped or understood on the basis of physics or of physical aspects and methods. Such "being" demands the "metaphysics of morals" or "ethics." Now it is proper to metaphysics that it consider being "as being"; the being here considered is the exactly the human act in respect of it being in the sense of *esse*. This metaphysical consideration of the moral *esse*, the moral being, of human acts, does not, of course, *belong* to ethics. If it were ascribed to ethics, then any possibility of distinguishing metaphysics and ethics would be eliminated. The affirmation has been advanced recently (by F. Van Steenbergen) that ethics, among other parts of philosophy) is but a part of metaphysics. This affirmation cannot be maintained within Thomism. Saint Thomas says,

> Although the subjects of the other sciences are parts of being, which is the subject of metaphysics, the other sciences are not necessarily parts of metaphysics. For each science treats of one part of being in a special way distinct from that in which metaphysics treats of

[143] "Non enim motus recipit speciem ab eo quod est terminus per accidens, sed solum ab eo quod est terminus per se. Fines autem morales accidunt rei naturali: et e converso ratio naturalis finis accidit morali. Et ideo nihil prohibet actus qui sunt iidem secundum speciem naturae, esse diversos secundum speciem moris, et e converso." Ibidem, t. 2, p. 713b, ll. 20-28.

being....[144]

The "special way" of treating being employed in ethics or, in other words, the method of ethics, is determined by the subject of ethics, namely, being constituted by practical reason. A metaphysical method would be inadequate in ethics and so too would be a physical or psychological method. This does not mean that metaphysical or, for that matter, psychological consideration should never be taken into account; it means that their formal viewpoint is not that of ethics.

There are two kinds of being in the philosophy of Saint Thomas: being that is independent of reason and being dependent upon reason. The first sort is natural, physical, and in this sense, "real" being. The second kind must be subdivided (and this subdivision is, one might say, almost an unknown, even among some of the better scholastic philosophers today).

For the "reason" on which this vast category, "beings of reason," depends might be either "speculative reason" or it might be "practical reason." If it should be speculative reason, then we still have two kinds of such beings of reason: the "being of reason of the one reasoning," *ens rationis ratiocinantis*, or the "being of rationalized reason," *ens rationis ratiocinatae*. The difference turns on whether there is a "foundation in reality," a *fundamentum in re*. In the first case we have a pure fiction, but in the second case we have all those "beings of reason" which make up logic; the "universal" of the logician is a "being of reason" in the second sense. The universal, ⟨"horse," "triangle," "blue"⟩, has a "foundation in reality"; ⟨members of a class do have something in common as well as something they share with no other class of realities⟩.

There are also beings of reason dependent upon practical reason, that is to say, beings constituted by our practical reason; it is this which is practically unknown among modern scholastics. The "moral being," *ens morale*, is properly speaking nothing but a being of reason, that is, of

[144] "Quamvis subiecta aliarum scientiarum sint partes entis, quod est subiectum metaphysicae, non tamen oportet quod aliae scientiae sint partes ipsius. Accipit enim unaquaeque scientiarum suam partem entis quam partem entis seu specialem modum considerandi alium a modo quo consideratur ens in metaphysica...." See the English translation of the Thomist "Exposition" of Boethius, *Expositio super librum Boethii De Trinitate*, ed. B. Dekker (Leiden: E.J. Brill, 1955), (with the translator's 1986 revisions) by A.A. Maurer, *Thomas Aquinas. The Division and Methods of the Sciences*, Questions V and VI of his Commentary on the *De Trinitate* of Boethius (Toronto: Pontifical Institute of Mediaeval Studies, 1953), Question V, Article 1, Reply to 6; p. 22.

practical reason. The human act, "as human," which is to say "as moral," is nothing but a "being of reason," namely, a reality constituted by practical reason. It is dependent entirely, and in its very being, which is moral being, on the intention of the end which, as Saint Thomas will make clear later in Part II, is a matter of the "ordering of reason," *ordinatio rationis*. Here we may note that many people, many philosophers, have an aversion against, and a fear of, beings of reason that is almost pathological. They jump to the conclusion that a being of reason must be a fiction only. This unwarranted conclusion stems from an innate[145] habit of ours, that of measuring and judging everything according to physical realities.

A moral reality, that is, the human act as formally and properly human, is a being constituted by practical reason. It is the "order of reason" added to, and incident upon, the physical reality of the act. The ⟨moral⟩ law, an important moral reality, is also a "being of reason," an "ordering of reason," "something of reason," as Saint Thomas will state implicitly in Part I-II, Question 90, Article 1, Body of the Article. "Society" too is a being of reason, as Saint Thomas explicitly states in the Prologue to his *Commentary on the Politics*, discussing the "perfect ⟨that is "complete" in its order⟩ society," "community," or the "city": "The city is the most potent ⟨construct⟩ constituted by human reason."[146]

Virtue, vice, sin, obligation, and so on, all these things, measured according to their being, are "beings of reason." This does not mean that they fictions or irrelevant notions which we might neglect. The Church, as a society, is a being of reason, a being of "practical reason." In this case the fact that the practical reason ⟨at stake⟩ is, in the last instance, the divine Reason does not make any difference in the status of the Church as a being of Reason. Divine law, too, is an ordering of Reason (once more, of divine Reason) as is every law. May we not shrink from telling

145 Eschmann has written "innate" but surely intended something such as "unconscious," for this widespread attitude undoubtedly is generated by the spectacular achievements of physical science; we are hardly born with it.

146 "Est enim ciuitas principalissimum eorum que humana ratione constitui possunt, nam ad ipsam omnes communitates humane referuntur. Rursumque omnia tota que per artes mecanicas constituuntur in usum hominum uenientibus, ad homines ordinantyur sicut ad finem; si igitur principalior scientia est que est de nobiliori et perfectiori, necesse est politicam inter omnes scientias practicas esse principaliorem et architectonicam omnium aliarum, utpote considerans ultimum et perfectum bonum in rebus humanis." *Sententia libri Politicorum, Sancti Thomae de Aquino opera omnia*, Leonina Commissio (Rome: Sancta Sabina, 1971), t. 48, p. A70, ll. 95-105.

the truth. If we are asked about the being of moral realities the answer must be that they are beings of reason, not, of course, "beings of reason of the one reasoning," *entia rationis ratiocinantis*, nor even "beings of rationalized reason," *entia rationis ratiocinatae*, but "beings of practical reason," *entia rationis practicae*, that is, "beings constituted by practical reason," *entia a ratione practica constituta*.

That society is "natural" is no objection for the natural status of society is not the physical and entitative "naturality" of natural things such as humans, brute animals, plants, and so on. The natural status of society is grounded in its being ordained by the natural law. One of the precepts of natural law is indeed, according to Saint Thomas "that a human being... should live in a society."[147] That is exactly what is meant when we speak of "natural" societies. Formally speaking, and taken as a "society," matrimony is a being of reason. Such propositions sound shocking to us because we think that beings of reason are only fictions of poets which do not concern us. Then we think we should at all costs assign to these things a place among the things of nature, that is to say, in the physical world—else they would vanish from before our eyes. Matrimony quite manifestly does not exist ⟨as a "thing"⟩ in the physical world, in the world of physical realities. It is no less "real" for all that, to use this ambiguous term ⟨"real"⟩. A law announced by an authentic authority binds our conscience; matrimony is a perpetual, indissoluble bond...all this indicates that moral beings, moral entities, are indeed "real" without being *physically* real.

## O. THE EXPOSITION OF ARTICLE 4

The "state of the Question" of Article 4 is, it seems, liable to be misunderstood and, perhaps, presents a real difficulty. In fact, the commentators are by no means unanimous in explaining what this Article is about after all. Some say that its subject is a determinate action and that the question is whether this determinate action is or is not to be integrated into a closed system of ends. To use Ramirez's words by which he summarizes the opinion of Vasquez, Suárez, Wiggers, and John of Saint Thomas: "Here is canvassed ⟨an issue⟩ concerning the ultimate end in respect of a determined

[147] "Tertio modo inest homini inclinatio ad bonum secundum naturam rationis, quae est sibi propria; sicut homo habet naturalem inclinationem ad hoc quod veritatem cognoscat de Deo, et ad hoc quod in societate vivat." ST 1-2, 94, 2, corpore; t. 2, p. 1226a, ll. 3-9.

action and in any determined series and line of causes and agents."[148] In other words, here we have an action; if this action depends on several ends (the case proposed in Article 3 in Argument 3) this plurality cannot be infinite, provided that we are faced with a series of causes subordinated to each other as such, *per se*.

Manifestly these commentators are obliged to do some kind of violence to the very words in which Saint Thomas introduces his problem: "It seems that there can be no ultimate end of human life" which, translated into a question, would be "whether there be any ultimate end of human life?" Now if an author speaks in this context of "human life" he means more than a single, determinate action. His intention is wider than to prove and to verify the teleological nexus of one case, wider than that where an action has several ends, one dependent upon the other. Moreover, if we read the conclusion of the Body of the Article, carefully and without bias, the improbability of the aforementioned opinion seems to be patent:

> If there were no ultimate end of human life, nothing would be sought nor would any action be terminated, nor would the intention of an agent find rest; if, however, there were not a first in those which are directed to the end, no one would begin to do anything, nor would any plan come to term, but rather would proceed to infinity.[149]

It is not advisable to neglect the very words of the text as these commentators seem to do. Yet, on the other hand, they also seem to have a good case.

Their point, as far as I can see, is the question of Article 5. For consider this. Let us suppose that this present Article 4 proves the existence of an ultimate end in human life; what then will be left for Article 5? There Saint Thomas states the question "Whether there can be several ultimate ends for a single human being?" He decides the issue in the negative. Is it not sufficiently clear from Article 4 that there can be only one ultimate end? If it is true that there is an ultimate end in human life, then it would seem that this end has already been shown to be only one. Furthermore, does not Saint Thomas himself say so in the conclusion of the

[148] See Ramirez, op. cit., p. 280.

[149] "...si non esset ultimus finis, nihil appeteretur, nec aliqua actio terminaretur, nec etiam quiescere intentio agentis; si autem non esset primum in his quae sunt ad finem, nullus inciperet aliquid operari, nec terminaretur consilium, sed in infinitum procederet." ST 1-2, 1, 4, in corpore; t. 2, p. 714a, l. 46-b, l. 1.

"On the contrary" here in Article 4? Hence it is in view of leaving room for Article 5 that the commentators want to restrict the meaning of the problem of Article 4. They do so against the clear letter of the text. To each day its own worry! We shall worry about Article 5 later on; for the moment we are faced with Article 4. On its question and the meaning of its problem there can hardly be any doubt. It is just as Saint Thomas states in the beginning: "Whether there be some ultimate end of human life?," "Whether there is a procession to infinity in ends?" The subject of the question seems to be the main point—"human life," that is, the totality of human life.

Another point is to be remembered and noted carefully. When I say "human life" without any further specification, the term is broad and comprehensive; at this point, to speak generally, this is of course the author's intention. Human life is one single life as well as the life of all humanity. In this general sense, "human life" is made up of actions proceeding from a deliberate will and ordered to an end. That a human being is an intelligent agent must be carefully noted, else we might miss entirely Saint Thomas's point. Being an intelligent agent, an intellectual or rational agent, a human being builds that life, "The role of reason is to order" what is done. To bring order into human activity is essential to the human being. At this point, whether that order be right or wrong is no matter. This is why Saint Thomas here supposes that a human life is, speaking strictly, not a mere agglomeration of happenings, but an organic whole (let us not fall into "begging the question"!), a continuous series of ends, of which one is subordinated to another, an order of ends "of itself." The point Saint Thomas stresses here is that as soon as one goes the way of essentially subordinated ends, one cannot but come to an ultimate end. That, however, human life is such a nexus of essentially subordinated ends is, in this Article, assumed as a pre-supposed truth. It needs no proof, no demonstration, because the human agent is intelligent, or rational.

This hidden presupposition of this Article seems to cause some difficulty to some commentators and readers. Ramirez refers to a modern commentator, the Jesuit Frings, who thinks that here Saint Thomas's reasoning is rather sketchy and not quite complete. There is perhaps some truth in this remark insofar as Saint Thomas does nothing to prove that human life is a series of ends subordinated of themselves, *per se*. The point is presupposed and seems to rest on the truth that has been brought out in Article 2: to act through reason is proper to a human, and, the role of reason is to order. All that remains to be stressed after this is the possibility or impossibility of a regress to infinity.

Very characteristically Saint Thomas begins the Body of the Article by saying, "I answer that it must be stated, speaking *per se*, of ends, it is impossible to proceed to infinity." He means of course in a series of ends essentially subordinated, that is, in ends in which one is the end of another. He shows himself to be a true philosopher, preoccupied with the very last and deepest difficulty which the basic assumption of the Article might meet if it is discussed among philosophers. By the way, as we shall see later, Aristotle has already clearly shown that he was preoccupied by *this* and by no other difficulty against the assumption that human life is a "rational order." Nothing prevents infinity in a series of ends which "do not have an order *per se* (an essential order), but are joined to each other by accident, *per accidens*." Such, however, is not a human life.

*a. Arguments to the Contrary*

⟨*i. The First:*⟩ The first argument is that the very nature of the "good" (and consequently of the "end") demands an infinity of ends. The argument is *a priori*, "from beforehand, from a cause," and is taken from the very essence of an "end." According to the Pseudo-Dionysius, "Good is diffusive of itself" and Saint Thomas here adds a phrase to clarify that conventional formulation. His version is, "Good, according to its essence, is diffusive of itself." The very formality, the notion, the essence of "good" is to propagate itself, to make another good proceed, to emanate, from itself. The neo-Platonic character of this principle is evident. Where could such a process be stopped? If the propagation of good from good should terminate, the last "good" could not be what is essential to a good; as not self-propagating, that last "good" would be a pseudo-good, that is, not a good at all. Since the procession of good from good is essential to the very notion of "good," Saint Thomas ended his argument with the conclusion, "Therefore, in ends there is an infinite regress."

We have here a very strange result of dialectical skill. Saint Thomas has almost convinced us that the very notion of an "end" indicates a termination in a series; yet, the very notion of "good" (which we have seen, makes a voluntary end to be an end) entails that there can be no stopping. This argument is taken from the metaphysics of the final cause and has no explicit relation to the human act. As we shall see, Saint Thomas avails himself of the occasion to give us a short lesson in Metaphysics.

We may note on the margin of this quotation that, in medieval scholasticism, the axiom was always attributed to the Pseudo-Areopagite; in fact, it is not from him. Saint Thomas introduces it, however, not by saying "as Dionysius ⟨the pseudo-Areopagite⟩ says," but rather "as is clear through Dionysius." In the language of Saint Thomas, this last formula indicates very generally that he is aware of something wrong with the "quotation" as a quotation. Elsewhere he introduces the same axiom by saying, "as can be taken from the sayings of Dionysius" (*On Truth* 21,

1, in 4), or "as is taken from the sayings of Dionysius" (*Summa theologiae* I, 5, 4, Argument 2), or also, without any reference to a determinate author, "it is said *by some* that good, insofar that it is of this sort, is diffusive of itself" (*Summa contra Gentiles* 3, 24). In the fourth Chapter of *On the Divine Names*, the author did not speak of the "transcendental" good, but of the subsistent Good which is God. What is said of the subsistent Good cannot be extended to the transcendental "good," the common "good" of created things.[150] If this is not the well-known neo-Platonic theory of a natural, necessary, and progressive emanation from the One to the Many, it comes very close to it. In support of his own reasoning, Saint Thomas draws from every available source. This Argument, in the midst of a fundamental discussion in ethics, is very specious, but also very characteristic for the architect of the *Summa theologiae*!

⟨*ii. The Second:*⟩ There are as many ends of the will, that is, ends in human life, as there are objects presented by the practical intellect or reason as to be pursued. The practical intellect moves the will in the way that the object itself does, and that is the motion characteristic of a final cause. Now these objects presented by the practical intellect can be infinite, for the practical intellect, just as the speculative intellect too, can apprehend infinite objects, one after the other, without ever stopping; the intellect or reason can multiply its acts to infinity, that is, there is no intrinsic reason why it every should stop. Saint Thomas's example, the infinity of mathematical quantity, the infinity of numbers, is eloquent.

⟨*iii. The Third:*⟩ There are as many ends in human life as there are human acts, acts of will. Those acts are infinite in number because the will can multiply its acts to infinity, for instance, by reflecting on its own acts.

⟨*iv. "But to the contrary":*⟩ The "authority" cited as the "But to the contrary" is worthy of note because it reveals the proper source of the doctrine set out here: a passage from Book Alpha of the Aristotelian *Metaphysics* of which only one short sentence is actually quoted, 1a, 2; 994b 12; but, let us read the whole passage. In Chapter 2 Aristotle treats of the impossibility of an infinite chain of causes and also of the impossibility of an

[150] "...nam perfecta bonitas quae per omnia se diffundit, non solum ad illas optimas, quae ipsi vicinae sunt, essentias dimanat, sed ad extremas usque protenditur, aliis quidem se tota praesens, aliis autem inferiori modo, atque aliis infimo, pro captu scilicet singulorum." Latin translation of Dionysius, *De divinis nominibus*, given in the Migne edition, PG 3 719A, translation of 720A.

infinite variety of causes. Neither in material, efficient, final, or formal causes is there a series which in infinite in whatever:

> Further, the *final cause* is an end, and that sort of end which is not for the sake of something else, but for whose sake everything else is; so that if there is to be a last term of this sort, the process will not be infinite; but if there is no such term, there will be no final cause, but those who maintain the infinite series eliminate the Good without knowing it (yet no one would try to do anything if he were not going to come to a limit); nor would there be reason in the world: the reasonable man, at least, always acts for a purpose, and this is a limit; for the end is a limit.[151]

This Aristotelian text confirms the impression which I ventured to mention a moment ago. Saint Thomas does not care here, in the body of his Article, about proving the fact that human life is a series of subordinated ends. As Aristotle shows, this fact is indeed contained in the fact that a human being is a reasonable agent. The commentary of Saint Thomas on this passage (in Lecture 4) must be read here; it is a "parallel place" in the full meaning of that term.[152] On the other hand, the present Article is in its turn a new commentary on the passage in Aristotle's *Metaphysics*.

The Aristotelian *Nicomachean Ethics* is, of course, more directly the source of this Article even though there is not a single reference here to

[151] "Amplius autem quod est cujus causa finis est. Tale autem quod non alicujus causa, sed alia illius. Quare, si quidem fuerit tale ipsum ultimum, non erit infinitum; si vero nihil tale, non erit cujus causa. Sed qui infinitum faciunt, latet auferentes boni naturam. Et nullus conabitur aliquid facere ad terminum non futurus venire. Neque utique erit intellectus in talibus. Nam causa alicujus semper facit qui intellectum habet hic enim terminus finis est rei." Text of Aristotle, *Metaphysica* 2, 994b 10-14, as given in the Expositio by Aquinas, p. 108a.

[152] A summary selection from this explanation by Aquinas: "...Et ostendit propositum quatuor rationibus: quarum *prima* talis est. Id, quod est cujus causa, habet rationem finis...et si quidem fuerit...ut scilicet omnia sint propter ipsum, et ipsum non sit propter alia, ipsum erit ultimum...si autem nihil inveniatur tale, non erit finis.... *Secundam* rationem...qui ponunt infinitatem in causis finalibus, removeant csusam finalem. Remota autem causa finali, removetur natura et ratio boni.... *Tertiam* rationem...Si sit infinitum in causis finalibus, nullus poterit pervenire ad ultimum terminum...sed nullus conatur ad aliquid faciendum nisi per hoc, quod se existimat venturum ad aliquid, sicut ad ultimum terminum.... *Quartam* rationem... ita tolletur intellectus practicus. Quae cum ita sint inconvenientia, oportet removere primum, id scilicet ex quo sequuntur, scilicet ex quo sequuntur, scilicet infinitum a causis finalibus." Text of Aquinas, *In metaphysicam* Lectio 4, no. 316, p. 108a-109b.

the *Ethics,* while three other Aristotelian works are quoted: the *Metaphysics,* the *Physics,* and the *Posterior Analytics.* It will be sufficient to read the short sentence of *Ethics* 1, 2:

> If, then, there is some end of the things we do, which we desire for its own sake (everything else being desired for the sake of this), and if we do not choose everything for the sake of something else (for at that rate the process would go on to infinity, so that our desire would be empty and vain), clearly this must be the good and the chief good.[153]

Here is what Saint Thomas in his *Exposition of the Nicomachean Ethics* makes of this passage:

> The Philosopher shows that there is a certain End which is Best in human affairs.... Every end is such that we desire other things on its account and we desire it for its own sake. That end is not only Good, but the Best. Now this is apparent from the fact that there is always an end for the sake of which other ends are sought and this is the more principal one...one comes to some End which is not desired for the sake of another, or not. If there is ⟨such and end⟩, then the point has been made; if there is no such end, it follows that every end would be desired for the sake of another, and thus it would be necessary to proceed to infinity. To proceed to infinity in finite things is impossible.... This is proved...⟨i⟩f there were procession to infinity in the desire for ends...a human being would never arrive at the desired ends; thus the end of desires would be useless and vain, therefore, it follows that a natural desire be inane and empty. This, however, is impossible, for a natural desire is nothing other than an inclination inhering in things owing to the ordering ⟨of them⟩ by the First Mover, which cannot be in vain.... ⟨I⟩mpossible that in ends there be a procession to infinity...there is necessarily an Ultimate End, on account of which all others are desired...a Best End of human affairs.[154]

[153] "Si utique est aliquis finis operabilium. quem propter seipsum volumus: alia vero propter illum, et non omnia propter alterum desideramus (procedet enim in infinitum, sicque esset vacuum, et inane desiderium): manifestum quoniam hic utique erit bonus, et optimus." Aristotle, *Nicomachean Ethics* 1, 2; 1094 a 18-22; ibidem, p. 7a.

[154] "...ostendit...esse aliquem finem optimum in rebus humanis.... Quicumque finis est talis, quod alia volumus propter seipsum, et non propter aliquid aliud: ille finis, non solum est bonus, sed est optimus. Et hoc apparet ex hoc quod semper

Thus the investigation of the sources of this Article make its place as well as its object more understandable than any systematic and abstract consideration could do.

*b. The Body of the Article*

Let us note first of all the distinction between the "order of ends of themselves," *per se*, and the "conjunction of ends by accident," *per accidens*. A Thomistic example of the first can be found in the *Summa contra gentiles* 3, 17:

> In all ordered ends it is necessary that the last end be the end of all preceding ends. Thus, if a potion were prepared to give to one who was sick, but given so that the sick person be purged, purged to lose weight, and lose weight in order to be healed, then health must be the end of weight loss, and purging, and of the other preceding things.[155]

The aim of the present Article, of course, is to show more than that there are such particular lines of acting. It is to show that human life, considered as human life, that is, as composed of purposeful actions, is a line made definite by an ultimate end.

Of ends conjoined by accident there is an example in Argument 3; it is a pretty artificial one. The will reflects upon its own act, and again wills the willing of that act and so, on and on. Another (and better) he

---

finis cujus gratia alii fines quaeruntur, est principalior.... Aut ergo est devenire ad aliquem finem, qui non desideratur propter alium, aut non. Si sic, habetur propositum. Si autem non est invenire aliquem talem finem, sequitur quod omnis finis desideretur propter alium finem. Et sic oportet procedere in infinitum. Sed hoc est impossibile, quod procedatur in finibus in infinitum.... probatur...Si procedatur in infinitum in desiderio finium.... Sed frustra et vane quis desiderat id quod non potest assequi...sequitur quod naturale desiderium sit inane et vacuum, Sed hoc est impossibile. Quia naturale desiderium nihil est aliud quam inclinatio inhaerens rebus ex ordinatione primi moventis, quae non potest frustrari. Ergo impossibile est quod in finibus procedatur in infinitum. Et sic necesse est esse aliquem finem ultimum, propter quem omnia alia desiderantur, et ita necesse est esse aliquem optimum finem rerum humanarum." *In decem libros Ethicorum Aristotelis ad Nicomachum expositio*, Lectio 2, 19-22, Exposition by Aquinas pp. 7a-8a.

155 "In omnibus finibus ordinatis oportet quod ultimus finis sit finis omnium praecedentium finium: sicut, si potio conficitur ut detur aegroto, datur autem ut purgetur, purgetur autem ut extenuetur, extenuatur autem ut sanetur, oportet quod sanitas sit finis et extenuationis et purgationis et aliorum praecedentium." SCG 3, 17; p. 241b.

used in Part II-II, 95, 5: a grave-digger finds a treasure; the end intended and the end resulting are far from identical.[156] Another example would be that I take a walk for health's sake, a "constitutional." The "of itself," *per se*, order of ends is contained within this end and is composed of each and everything that I choose to do for it. On my way I meet a friend; I stop and talk to him. Again, on the way I see something displayed in a window; it attracts my attention, and I stop and buy it. All sorts of things might happen on my way and where everything might, but also might not happen, we face a series of "accidental" final causes. An international figure who knows what is wanted and who follows a plan will be countered, often enough, by random reactions on the part of rivals, trying to bargain, trying to make up for a lack of plan and goals. Those disorderly reactions will be ends "conjoined by accident."

Or think of a losing hockey team without a plan of attack or defense, hitting the puck if and only if it drifts within reach. We would say, "This is not hockey!" just as, on the political plane, we would say, "This is not politics!" and on the human level, "This is not human life!"

An accidental series of ends is often a reality in human life; we cannot do without them. We meet people and things; we are faced with an indefinite number of circumstances, unpredicted, unpredictable. Still, if a life is, speaking simply, nothing other than drifting along according to where we are pushed, then it is no human life at all. Human life as such means initiative, plan, coordination, a line of action, and the integration of all phases of our activity. Saint Thomas sets a very high standard for human life; once he had defined human action as "proceeding from a deliberate will" the rest follows logically. But let us return to the technicalities. The definition of an "essential order of causes" is that one cause depends upon the other in causing. This notion he has developed especially for series of effective or efficient causes as in his *On Truth* 2, 10:

> just as the life-principle moves natural heat, by which nerves and muscles are moved, by which are moved the hands that move the stick by which a stone is moved. In these, any one of the later causes depends *of itself*, by essence, upon any one you like of the preceding ⟨causes⟩.[157]

[156] "...homine fodiente sepulchrum, inveniatur thesaurus," cited ST 2-2, 95, 5, In corpore; 3: 1920b, ll. 33, 34; Aquinas here modified slightly Aristotle's illustration of "some one in digging a hole for a plant has found treasure" (*Metaphysics* 5, 30; 1025a 15, 16).

[157] "...sicut anima movet calorem naturalem quo moventur nervi et musculi qui-

Applying this to the chain of final causes, Saint Thomas says in the same work, 21,1, To the 1:

> Just as in other sorts of causes the bearing of the second cause depends upon the bearing of the first cause, the bearing of the first, however, does not depend on any other, so it is with final causes since secondary ends participate in the relations of the final cause from their order toward an ultimate end; that ultimate end itself, however, has this relationship "of itself."[158]

As for the multitude of accidental causes, the incidental multitude of causes,

> ...a multitude of causes "by accident" is present whenever all those contained in the multitude are, as it were, posited in place of one and are related without differentiation whether they be one or many or fewer or more numerous, just as if a builder makes a house, in the making of which he wears out many saws successively, the multitude of saws is not required for making the house, unless it be "by accident" from this, that one saw cannot last forever. Nor does how many are set out make a difference to the house, since not one owes dependence to another, as was the case when a multitude was required essentially, *per se*.[159]

A very eloquent text is also the following, taken from his commentary on the *Liber de causis*, Lecture 1:

> There is an order "by accident" whenever the meaning of "cause"

---

bus moventur manus quae movet baculum quo movetur lapis: in his enim quodlibet posteriorum per se dependet a quolibet praecedentium." *De veritate*, Quaestio 2, Articulus 10; t. 22, p. 75, ll. 54-58.

[158] "Sicut enim in aliis generibus causarum habitudo secundae causae dependet ex habitudine causae primae, primae vero causae habitudo non dependet ex aliquo alio, ita etiam est in causis finalibus quod secundi fines participant habitudinem causae finalis ex ordine ad ultimum finem, ipse autem ultimus finis habet hanc habitudinem per se ipsum." Ibidem, Quaestio 21, Articulus 1, Ad 1; t. 22, p. 594, ll. 220-228.

[159] "Sed per accidens multitudo invenitur quando omnia quae multitudine continentur quasi loco unius ponuntur ⟨et⟩ indifferenter se habent sive sint unum sive multa sive vel pauciora vel plura, sicut si aedificator facit domum in cuius factione plures essent serras consumit successive, multitudo serrarum non requiritur ad factionem domus nisi per accidens ex hoc quod una non potest semper durare, nec differt aliquid ad domum quotcumque ponantur, unde nec una earum debet dependentiam ad aliam, sicut erat quando multitudo requirebatur per se." Ibidem, ll. 58-70.

> does not proceed to anything but to the proximate effect; that something, however, should be effected from that effect is "outside the intent" of the one who effected it first, just as when some one lights a candle, it is outside the intention of that one that the candle lighted should light another, and that yet another. What is outside intent, however, we say is "by accident."[160]

In one word, then, there is an "essential order of ends" where a line of action in its entirety, in the multitude of its parts, is dependent upon the intention of the agent. There is "series of ends by accident" where a multitude of actions and ends is outside the intention of the agent.

John of Saint Thomas, if I remember correctly, proposed the following definitions of an essential order of ends: such an order obtains when the ends are coordinated by their very nature and, on the other hand, if the coordination of ends depends on the arbitrary choice of the agent, then this would be an accidental order. Economic power is ordered essentially, *per se*, to the needs of people; this constitutes an essential order of ends. Should economic power be ordered to satisfy the lust for power or some other immoral or unnatural end, then this would be an accidental nexus.

I do not think this is the Thomistic meaning of these terms, but at this point in the investigation it does not matter how, morally speaking, human life is organized or unified, whether according to reason and nature, or not. What is important here is to show that human life as such is "a line of action," a very vast line of action, but a definite one, not an endless and consequently meaningless multitude of events.

*c. To the First ⟨Argument⟩*

"It belongs to the very notion of the 'good' that from it something flows."[161] We know what this means and it is not that the good is an efficient cause, but that it is a final cause. It attracts an agent which, or who, exercises efficient causality by intention, out of love ⟨for that good⟩. "Not, however, that ⟨the good⟩ itself proceeds from yet another."[162] In

160 "...ordo per accidens...intentio causae non procedit nisi ad proximum effectum; quod autem ab illo effectu efficiatur iterum aliud, est praeter intentionem primi efficientis; sicut, cum aliquis accendit candelam, praeter intentionem eius est quod iterum accensa candela accendat aliam et illa aliam. Quod autem praeter intentionem est, dicimus esse per accidens." *Super Librum de causis*, Propositio 1, Lectio 1; #41, p. 7b.

161 "Dicendum quod de ratione boni est quod aliquid ab ipso effluat." Loc. cit., t. 2, p. 714b, ll. 9-11.

162 "...non tamen quod ipsum ab alio procedat." Ibidem, ll. 11-12.

other words, the neo-Platonic principle as expressed by Dionysius the pseudo-Areopagite, does not imply an infinite chain of goods or ends in the *upward* direction. This is clear enough from the Dionysian text itself since the author starts precisely from The One, from the Subsistent Good; it might, strictly speaking, imply the principle that there is an infinite *downward* movement: "So, since the good has the essence of end, and the First Good is the Ultimate End, this reasoning does not prove that there might not be an ultimate End, but that, from the First End posited, there might be a procession below to infinity with regard to those items which are oriented toward the End."[163] In this Saint Thomas here sees the proper point of the objection as it was proposed and he deals with that point exactly. The perfection of the First Subsistent Good (which, of course, is God) is infinite; our present world does not exhaust that infinite Perfection, nor would an infinite number of created worlds do so. If this is so, would we then not have an order of ends, "of itself," *per se*, infinite? Saint Thomas is manifestly so struck by the idea of the infinity of the Subsistent Good that, not considering anything other than this Infinitude, "...if solely the Power of the First Good, which is infinite, be considered"[164] he would concede that the admission of an order of ends, of itself infinite (which would also imply an infinite number of causes, acting of themselves) is unavoidable.

This is a certain limited admission of a neo-Platonic idea; it is, however, only hypothetical since, in truth, we cannot consider only the infinite Power of the First Good and nothing else. This notion, "Infinite Power," is indeed nothing but the product of our abstraction: "the First Good has diffusion in accord with Intellect";[165] it is always bound up with the agency of an efficient cause. The agent acts from an intention of the good and acts according to the essential conditions of that agent's being. Here we have an intellectual agent, the First Intellectual Agent. Since it is essential to an intellectual agent to cause effects in accord with a definite order and plan, "...the diffusion of goods from the First Good does not proceed to infinity, but as is said, 'God disposes all things in number, weight, and measure'" (Wisdom 11:21).

In other words, and to put the thing as clearly as possible, if we con-

[163] "Et ideo, cum bonum habeat rationem finis, et primum bonum sit ultimus finis, ratio ista non probat quod non sit ultimus finis; sed quod a fine primo supposito procedatur in infinitum inferius versus ea quae sunt ad finem." Ibidem, ll. 12-17.

[164] "...si consideretur sola virtus primi boni, quae est infinita...." Ibidem, ll. 18-19.

[165] "...primum bonum habet diffusionem secundum intellectum...." Ibidem, ll. 20-21.

sider the diffusive power of the First Good absolutely speaking, that is, if we abstract from what It really is (a potency coupled with, and informed by, wisdom and will) then we must concede that this potency, being inexhaustible, will be without limit in its "outflowing of goods." Yet even that outflowing of goods will not be an *actually* infinite multitude, as Saint Thomas holds is impossible.[166] Nor can an infinite multitude be the object of even the "absolute divine power" because "what cannot possibly exist, cannot possibly come into being, and what cannot possibly come into being, cannot possibly be made."

On the other hand, if we take the diffusive power of the First Good as the "ordered power of God," that is, such as it really is, and not as it is according to our mental abstraction, then we encounter the plan, measure, form, and order. The "absolute divine potency" plays a great role in later Scotistic and Ockhamist thought. As you see here, this absolute potency is a dangerous theory. It might lead, and it has led, to the destruction of every order and every rationality. The absolute divine potency is in theology and philosophy just what absolute power is in politics!

*d. To the Second ⟨Argument⟩*

The material objects of both our speculative and practical intellect can be infinite, that is, they can be an indefinite multitude—not an actual infinite multitude. There is no reason why the eye, after having seen one object, should not see another, and again another, and so forth. In every material multitude there is no principle, no form, which limits by itself, so long as the multitude is only material. If we take the formal object of intellect (and of the will) then we have at once unity, order, limits, and form. Let us take the practical intellect since in ethics we are concerned mainly with the practical intellect. To speak formally, all the objects of the practical intellect are reducible to three: the honest, the delightful, and the useful; or, should we take another principle of division, they are reducible to two: the goods of the soul, the goods of the body, that is to say, interior goods and exterior goods. Formally speaking all acts of the practical intellect are reducible to three: counsel, judgment, command (as we shall learn in Saint Thomas's treatise on prudence). In short, every formal consideration introduces at once order and limits into everything. We meet again, as we always meet it in Saint Thomas, the principle that the work of reason is to set in order, *rationis est ordinare.* Here he prefers to give an example of speculative reason, based on mathematics which does know

[166] For this Thomistic view, see ST 1, 7, 4 and SCG 3, 2.

"infinite numbers."[167] It is helpful to compare this with his remark in the *Summary against the Gentiles* 3, 2 on our practical rational activities:

> ...just as if a human being senses in order to imagine, imagines in order to understand, understands in order to will; or, according to the order of objects, as when I consider the body so that I might consider the soul, which I consider in order that I might consider a "separate substance" ⟨that is, an angel⟩, which I consider in order that I might consider God.[168]

*e. To the Third ⟨Argument⟩*

The Response to the Third Argument offers no difficulty after all that has been said. If the will reflects upon itself, if after willing something, I will *this* willing of mine, and again I will the willing of *that* willing, and so forth, all these acts are an "accidental" series; one element simply comes after the other, with no causal connection between them; they are juxtaposed "materially" only. We are again in the realm (if "realm" it can be called) of matter; there is no stopping unless matter be joined to form. With regard to an indefinite series of acts of the intellect reflecting upon itself Saint Thomas had said in Part I,

> In us intelligible relations are multiplied to infinity since by one act a human being understands a stone and by another act, one understands oneself to understand a stone, and by yet another understands understanding this. and so to infinity the acts of understanding are multiplied, and, in consequence, intellectual relations ⟨are multiplied to infinity⟩.[169]

[167] In his answer to the claim in Argument 2, "...mathematicae quantitates in infinitum augentur. Species etiam numerorum propter hoc possunt esse infinitae, quia, dato quolibet numero, alium maiorem excogitare potes..." (Ibidem, t. 2, p. 713b, l. 53-p. 714a, l. 2.), Saint Thomas here conceded that claim, "in huiusmodi nihil prohibet rationem procedere in infinitum" (p. 714b ll. 43, 44), but did so in the context of his appeal to Aristotle's *Posterior Analytics* 3, 2; 72b 7, on the speculative intellect in "demonstration," where a regress to infinity is impossible.

[168] "...sicut si homo sentit ut imaginetur, imaginatur autem ut intelligat, intelligit autem ut velit: vel secundum ordinem obiectorum, sicut considero corpus ut considerem animam, quam considero ut considerem substantiam separatam, quam considero ut considerem Deum." SCG 3, 2; p. 227b foot—228a head.

[169] "Dicendum quod in nobis relationes intelligibiles in infinitum multiplicantur, quia alio actu intelligit homo lapidem, et alio actu intelligit se intelligere lapidem, et alio etiam intelligit hoc intelligere; et sic in infinitum multiplicantur actus intelligendi,

## P. The Exposition of Article 5

As I warned in an earlier lecture, the "state of the question" of this Article is not easy to grasp. ⟨N.B. Eschmann, at the very beginning of his discussion on Article 4, noted that it might seem that, after the solution of Article 4, nothing could be left for Article 5.⟩ Looking merely at the words in which the problem is introduced, it would seem to be easy: "Whether it be possible that the will of one human being could be borne at once toward many ends as to ultimate ends?" In itself, this question is perfectly intelligible. Yet, as I hinted, in its context and especially with regard to Article 4, Article 5 presents a real difficulty: it seems to be superfluous. Has it not been concluded in the foregoing Article that there is *one* ultimate end in human life? Did not the "But to the contrary" state explicitly, "It is necessary, therefore, to posit *one* ultimate end"? Why then this elaborate re-statement of a problem which seems to be an "adjudged case"?

The commentators (it seems to me) show their embarrassment with sufficient candor and clarity. I have pointed to the way in which the most recent and the most comprehensive commentary, that of Ramirez, thoroughly familiar with the "classical" commentators and breathing exactly their spirit, deals with this problem. It is clear from the beginning to Ramirez that, in order to explain the structure of a Thomistic Question and to justify the presence of its single parts or Articles, only and exclusively one method is competent: that of merely abstract and logical consideration. In this way, as I said, Ramirez comes to the following hypothesis.

Articles 1-4 deal with the problem of the existence of an ultimate end in human life. What follows naturally and logically any question as to "Whether something is the case?," *An est*?, is the question "What is it?," *Quid est*? Did not Saint Thomas himself state (on another occasion of course), in Part I, 2, 2, To the Second Argument, "The question 'What is it?' follows the question, 'Whether something is?'" Hence, according to Ramirez, the constructive principle of our Question, which explains the two groups of Articles, 1-4 and 5-8, must be that sequence of two questions: first *An est?* and then *Quid est?*, first existence of an ultimate end, then the essence of an ultimate end. Now this looks very much like an aprioristic assumption: this might be true, but it must be proved.

Against this we might at once observe that the question "What might the ultimate end be?" has a definite meaning in the vocabulary of Saint Thomas. It means to ask wherein our ultimate end, or beatitude, lies and this question is treated, not in Articles 5-8, but from Questions 3-5 as the

---

et per consequens relationes intellectae...." ST 1, 28, 4, Ad 2; t. 1, p. 191a ll. 13-20.

introduction to Question 3 states explicitly: "Then there must be a demonstration of what beatitude might be." Ramirez, however, does not give up his fight for a merely abstract and logical understanding of the structure of Question 1. In his abbreviated and paraphrased view

> ...the very essence or nature of the end which is absolutely last consists in its unity, while all other ends, which are not absolutely the last, can be several.... ⟨U⟩nity is, as it were, the first quiditative predicate which formally distinguishes the last end from all other ends.... ⟨S⟩ince...non-ultimate ends are not fully sufficient with regard to the total potency of the agent, the absolutely last end is, in this respect, fully sufficient and adequate and, therefore, is, and must be, one... ⟨F⟩rom Article 4 to Article 5 we observe a turn in the procedure of this question which does full justice to the speculative genius of Saint Thomas. He now starts to investigate the specific difference of the absolutely ultimate end by which it is constituted in itself and distinguished from all other ends. This he reduces to its unity, first in Articles 5 and 6 on its unity in a single human being, in Article 7 on its unity in all humans, and finally, in Article 8, its unity in all the creatures of the whole universe.[170]

Personally I do not view these Articles in the same light. I should like to insist that the question of the unity (to be more precise, the "formal notion," the *ratio*, of the ultimate end) is radically and virtually solved in Article 4; there need not be any sequel to Article 4 on this issue from any logical viewpoint. The sequence of these two groups of Articles cannot be grasped under such a clumsy principle as that which Ramirez has advanced. Logically speaking, the later group of Articles can only be taken as a further illustration of the point made in Article 4. I fail to see why Saint Thomas should not stay with the result he obtained and then go on to *illustrate* it from different angles, so much the more since there is a sufficient *historical* reason for this further illustration.

As pointed out on a former occasion, the first 4 Articles, historically speaking, deal with a problem that has grown out of, and been inspired by, the Aristotelian ethics. The problem of these Articles is nothing but a re-statement of the ethical problem as it was stated on the first page of the *Nicomachean Ethics*. It is a treatment of that problem that is full of new ideas, new perspectives, new views, but a treatment of Aristotle's problem all the same!

[170] Ramirez *De beatitudine* 1, 424-425 nos. 728-732; *Omnia opera* (Madrid: CSIC, 1972).

Here Saint Thomas adds another group of Articles inspired by a problem historically different since in its origin it is Augustinian. That the name of Saint Augustine appears in the first lines of Article 5 is significant; moreover, this artful weaving together of an Aristotelian and an Augustinian problem, which characterizes the whole Question 1 of the Part I-II, is of great significance.

It has been mentioned, too, that the Augustinian question beneath Articles 5 and following was posed in the schools of Saint Thomas's time as "Whether all right volitions have one end?" In Saint Augustine himself, this meant all the volitions in one individual's life; this is almost the same question that is raised here in Article 5. I say "almost" because to Saint Thomas the issue was not concerned with all our "right" volitions, but with *all* our volitions, both right and not right. There is a quasi-parallel place in the *Scriptum on the Sentences*,

> Thus, therefore, it must be stated that, just as the last End of all things is One, namely, God, so too the ultimate End of all volitions is One, namely, God.[171]

At the very least, this place is the root from which the present and the following Articles have grown, the "root" because in the *Summa theologiae* we do not as yet know that God is the ultimate End; that will be treated in Question 2. However, that the ultimate end of wills and of things is one, understanding here, for the moment at least, the very notion "ultimate end," this is exactly the state of the question for Articles 5 to 8. Saint Thomas's procedure here in Part I-II is more refined, formalized, and polished in another respect as well. "All volitions, all decisions" might indeed be understood both of all those of one subject, that is, of one human being, as well as of all those of *all* human beings. In the tradition of the medieval schools on this Augustinian problem, this distinction was either somewhat obscured or left aside. Here Saint Thomas brings out the distinction and it serves him in his move from Articles 5 and 6 to Article 7. The overall scheme of these Articles is therefore:

- one end of one human being: Articles 5 and 6
- one end of all humans: Article 7
- one end of all things: Article 8.

The logical connection of this group, Articles 5-8, with the former group, Articles 1-4, in my opinion is simply this: Group I presents fundamental

171 "Sic ergo dicendum est quod sicut rerum omnium unus est finis ultimus, scilicet Deus, ita et voluntatum omnium unus est ultimus finis, scilicet Deus...." *Super Sent.* 2, Dist. 38, Q. 1, A. 1, Solutio; t. 2, p. 968.

considerations on the topic as set by the Introduction, namely, "...it is necessary first to consider the ultimate end in general, *in communi*"[172] whereas Group II presents further illustrations. Historically taken, Group I deals with the Aristotelian problem as stated in Aristotle's *Nicomachean Ethics*; Group II Articles were inspired by the Augustinian tradition from the *De trinitate*, discussed in medieval schools under the heading "Whether there be a single end of 'right' wills?" Here, however, Group II deals with the problem under the formal abstraction "'all' wills," not "'right' wills."

*a. Arguments to the Contrary*

The initial words of the Article, I think, should be paraphrased thus. In the former Articles it has been shown that there is one ultimate end in, and of, human life. Yet, do not certain facts point to the possibility of a plurality of ultimate ends? First, as concerns the individual human life, did not Saint Augustine say that some philosophers stated that the ultimate end of human life consists in four things: pleasure, rest, the primary things of nature, and power?[173]

The argument is clear and simple except for the phrase "the primary things of nature." "First things of nature" is a technical expression of the philosophical school called the "Academy," the name recalling Plato's school of which the successor, the "New Academy," was itself distinguished into at least three "Academies." An outstanding member in the first century before the Common Era was Antiochus of Ascalon and it was a disciple of his, Marcus Terentius Varro whose now no longer extant *De philosophia* Augustine cites. Cicero, however, provides an explanation of the term in his *De finibus*:

> ...others start from what they term the "primary" ⟨values⟩ of nature, among which they number the soundness and conservation of all parts, health, whole senses, freedom from pain, powers, beauty, and other things of the same sort, of which ⟨there are⟩ similar primary ⟨values⟩ of the mind....[174]

[172] "...oportet primum considerare de ultimo fine in communi...." ST 1-2, 1; 2: 710b ll. 2, 3.

[173] Augustine, *De civitate dei*, Liber 19, Caput 1; t. 48, p. 658, ll. 42-47.

[174] "...ab iis alii quae prima secundum naturam nominant profisciscuntur, in quibus numerant incolumitatem conservationemque omnium partium, valetudinem, sensus integros, doloris vacuitatem, vires, pulchritudinem, cetera generis eiusdem, quorum similia sunt prima in animis...." Marcus Tullius Cicero, *De finibus* Liber 5, vii, 18; Loeb Classical Library, p. 410, ll. 2-6.

To this catalogue both Stobaeus[175] and Saint Augustine add that "the first things of nature of the soul" were also assigned by those philosophers: shrewdness, cleverness, industriousness, steadfastness, mental power, and the like. In short, our whole corporeal and mental equipment and its good functioning are the "first things of nature."

The quotation here by Saint Thomas of a text in which Saint Augustine relates the Varronian enumeration of 288 philosophical sects is purely verbal and dialectical; as Saint Thomas correctly states in his answer to that first argument, "they used to take all that multitude under the notion of a single complete Good, constituted of them; from these they used to locate an ultimate end in them."[176] Such merely verbal and dialectical exchanges occur not infrequently in Saint Thomas—which imposes on us a readiness to take account of the demands his method of writing and constructing articles had imposed upon him! In Ramirez's commentary, however, from this playful argument the following grave difficulty has arisen:

> What has been given is, in fact, impossible; for certain people, in fact, do take all at once a number of goods as ultimate ends, for instance, riches, pleasures, and strength, as is said of Epicurus; therefore, there can be many ultimate ends at once for one human being.[177]

The objection, Ramirez says, is Saint Thomas's own, and this is his usual procedure: start with the major difficulty.[178] This is a specimen of how a speculative thinker works on a text: he forgets completely what the text means! There is no question of some people having actually done this for the question bears merely on some odd philosophical theories.

In the rest of the Arguments nothing seems especially worthy of note. Let us only point to the affirmation in the third Argument about the power ascribed to a free will. The *potentia voluntatis*, "the power of the will," is to become later an important principle both in theology and in philosophy. Saint Thomas's rebuke of the assumption made here ⟨the

[175] Ioannes Stobaeus, probably lived in the latter half of the fifth century and most probably not a Christian; his *Eclogae phusikai kai êthikai*, to which reference is made here, was summarized by Photius in that author's *Bibliotheca*.

[176] "Dicendum quod omnia illa plura accipiebantur in ratione unius boni perfecti ex his constituti, ab his qui in eis ultimum finem ponebant." ST 1-2, 1, 5, Ad 1; t. 2, p. 715b, ll. 44-47.

[177] Ramirez, *de beatitudine* 1, 451, # 787.

[178] Ibidem, 1, 450, #786.

possibility of a multiple "ultimate end"⟩ in the third Argument, is always firm and unequivocal.

*b. The Body of the Article*

The answer to the proposed Question is in the negative and the thesis clearly and categorically stated at the beginning:

> I respond: It must be stated that it is impossible that the will of a single human being relate simultaneously to many goods as to ultimate ends.[179]

The terms must be pondered. The question was asked and, therefore, will be answered from the point of view of one person's will, *voluntas unius hominis*. This point of view we should call a "psychological" one. The term may be admitted and is in some way true although we cannot and ought not to expect Saint Thomas to present a psychological demonstration in the modern sense. On the other hand, what we must not expect either is a demonstration from "the notion of the cause of the ultimate end," *ratio causae finis ultimi*, in other words, we ought not to expect a metaphysical demonstration in the sense in which Saint Thomas would build up such a demonstration. Ramirez begins his exegesis with this sort of metaphysical argument (which in itself is unobjectionable and has been hinted at by Saint Thomas elsewhere), but is not to be found in this Article; it does not fit the "state of the question" which Saint Thomas has chosen:

> For this is impossible: that there be many causes of the same ⟨effect, causes⟩ of the same sort as to genus, of themselves the same in order, although there might be many ⟨such⟩ causes ⟨either⟩ in this way, that one be proximate, another remote, or such that neither be a sufficient cause, but both conjointly are ⟨sufficient⟩, as is clear when several drag along a boat.[180]

Or, as Saint Thomas expresses the same principle elsewhere, "...it is impossible that of one and the same reality there be two complete and immedi-

[179] "Respondeo. Dicendum quod impossibile est quod voluntas unius hominis simul se habeat ad diversa, sicut ad ultimos fines." ST 1-2, 1, 5, in corpore; t. 1, p. 715a, ll. 48-51.

[180] "Hoc enim est impossibile quod ejusdem secundum idem genus, sint multae causae per se eodem ordine; licet possint esse plures causae hoc modo, quod una sit proxima, alia remota: vel ita, quod neutrum sit causa sufficiens, sed utrumque conjunctim; sicut patet in multis, qui trahunt navem...." Saint Thomas, Exp. in Metaphy. 5, 2; Lectio 2, n. 773, 1013b 5-9; p. 256b.

ate causes."[181] One would have only to subsume under this general metaphysical principle the case of the final cause in order to have a faultless metaphysical argument in favor of the unicity of an ultimate end. In itself this would be a conclusive argument, yet Saint Thomas did not use it here. The reason for this seems patent: the metaphysical aspect of the question is over and done with in Article 4; indeed, it is contained implicitly in the Body of Article 4. Saint Thomas's arguments in this Body of the Article are easy to grasp. They are based upon three definitions of the ultimate end: first (I transpose the words of Saint Thomas), "The ultimate end is that good which the seeker seeks as the good, perfect and completive of the self"; second, "The ultimate end is the natural starting point in the process of a natural appetite"; and third, "the ultimate end is that from which all objects appetible by the will inasmuch as they are of this sort, receive the formal structure of ⟨their⟩ generic kind."

In other words the first reasoning is based upon this nature of the ultimate end: it is the perfect good with regard to the one who desires it. The second assumes as its basic statement that the ultimate end is the primary natural good, the term "natural" here taken in a sense which is clear from the text of Saint Thomas. Finally, the third argument is that the ultimate end is the primary and supreme principle of human acts. Each of these definitions constitutes the major proposition in an argument the minors of which are clear from the words of Saint Thomas.

> By the words "end of the good" we mean, not that by which good is destroyed, so that it no longer exists, but that by which it is finished so that it becomes complete.[182]

Whatever the text Saint Thomas had read, it is clear that this was his understanding of Saint Augustine's words.

> ...the ultimate end so fills the total appetite of a human that nothing can remain outside that which is the object of appetite.[183]

[181] "...impossibile est quod duae causae completae sint immediate unius et eiusdem rei." ST 1, 52, 3, in corpore; ST 1, 52, 3, in corpore; t. 1, p. 327b, ll. 37-39.

[182] "Finem hominum nunc dicimus, non quod consumitur ut non sit, sed quod perficitur ut plene sit" (*De civitate dei* 19, 1) is the PL 41 621 version found in the Ottawa edition, ST 1-2, 1, 5, in corpore; t. 2, p. 715b ll. 2-4; as cited by Eschmann, however, the text is "Finem boni ergo nunc dicimus, non quo consumatur ut non sit, sed quo perficiatur ut plenum sit."

[183] "...ultimus finis ita impleat totum hominis appetitum, quod nihil extra ipsum appetendum relinquatur." Ibidem, ll. 5-7.

This is still another definition of the ultimate end, slightly different from the first.

Which cannot be if anything extraneous were required for its perfection.[184] The word "extraneous" is very significant here. The last end makes a human life a thoroughly "inside affair" in this sense: nothing outside, nothing not falling within the orbit described, and not contained by the end, is required for the perfection and fulness of this life.

The second argument is that, just as in the process of reasoning the principle is that which is known naturally, so in the process of the rational appetite, which is the will, it is necessary that the principle be that which is desired naturally.[185]

We are speaking here, indeed, not of that in which the ultimate end consists; that object, or objective good, is never desired by a natural desire. God in whom our final good consists according to the true moral doctrine, as will be shown in Question 2, is not the object of a natural desire, but of our choosing, of our decision to make Him our ultimate End. We are speaking here of the *ratio*, the "essence," the "formal structure" of the ultimate end, that is, what makes an ultimate end to be an ultimate end, no matter what we choose in the concrete to be our ultimate end. This can also be called "beatitude." It is not without interest, however, to note that in this whole Question Saint Thomas never mentions the word "beatitude" until the very last line of the very last Article of the Question, Article 8.

"Desired naturally" is here opposed, not to "supernaturally," but to "rationally." A natural desire is necessary, a rational desire is voluntary. A natural desire is not a matter of deliberation, nor of choice; it is spontaneous. A rational desire is the contrary of all this. The fundamental conviction of Saint Thomas, as of all antiquity, is that we desire beatitude, that is, in the words of our Article it is "the" good: perfect, completive, naturally, inevitably, spontaneously, apart from all effort, from all deliberation. What we thus naturally desire "must be something one, for nature tends only to what is one."[186] In our case, of course, this one thing is not a particular and determined good; it is just the "notion of the ultimate end," the "good in general," as we have learned above.

184 "Quod esse non potest, si aliquid extraneum ad ipsius perfectionem requiratur." Ibidem ll. 7-9.

185 "Secunda ratio est quia, sicut in processu rationis principium est id quod naturaliter cognoscitur, ita in processu rationalis appetitus, qui est voluntas, oportet esse principium id quod naturaliter desideratur." Ibidem, ll. 13-18.

186 "Hoc autem oportet esse unum: quia natura non tendit nisi ad unum." Ibidem, ll. 18, 19.

The "third argument" is given where Saint Thomas writes,

> ...since voluntary actions are given their *species*, their special class, from their ends...it must be that from the ultimate end which is common they be given their *genus*, their general class.[187]

Here what has been said about the double "community" or "universality" must be recalled, the one, community in predication, the other the community of a common cause. The ultimate end is a "common" end in the second of these meanings. It is a common, universal *cause*, not a common universal predicate. In the order of final causes the ultimate end is the first. The ultimate end is the common good to which all particular goods are referred, as Saint Thomas will say later in Question 90, Article 2, To the second Argument:

> Those particulars can be referred to the common good, not indeed by a community of genus or species, but by a community of final cause according to which the common good is said to be the common end.[188]

Of course we are speaking here of the common good in one individual life, but the notion of "common good" is an analogical notion which has many applications and many different meanings. It is therefore clear that, when Saint Thomas introduces the notion of "genus," he is not speaking of "genus" as used in logic. He makes this especially clear by adding "just as things of nature are placed in a genus according to their common formal notion, *rationem*."[189] Here we have the opposition between the moral genus and the natural genus. A moral genus comprises actions and their respective goods or ends, all subordinated to, and unified in, their ultimate end which constitutes the moral order. A natural genus, the natural order in which the foremost question is that of a supreme and unifying predicate, a predicate which expresses the most common "formal notion," *ratio formalis*, such as is shown in the "Porphyrian tree." All animate beings are formally comprised there under the general notion of "animated" ⟨that is,

[187] "...cum actiones voluntariae ex fine speciem sortiantur, ...oportet quod a fine ultimo qui est communis, sortiantur rationem generis...." Ibidem ll. 24-28.

[188] "...illa particularia referri possunt ad bonum commune, non quidem communitate generis vel speciei, sed communitate causae finalis, secundum quod bonum commune dicitur finis communis." ST 1-2, 90, 2, Ad 2; t. 2, p. 1207b ll. 18-22.

[189] "...sicut et naturalia ponuntur in genere secundum formalem rationem communem." ST 1-2, 5, in corpore; ST 1-2, 1, 5, in corpore; t. 2, p. 715b, ll. 28-30.

"besouled").[190] Yet, as we have seen in Article 3, the end is also the formal principle of human acts.

Hence, just as the end specifies the human act, so the ultimate end gives to all human acts their general specification and therefore it must be that the ultimate end is *one*. This reasoning in some way overlaps the intention of this Article, namely, to remain with the volitions and actions of a single person. The argument must be turned around or, let us say, restricted in some way to the matter in hand. This is the purpose of what now follows:

> Just as the ultimate end of the human being, taken without qualification, *simpliciter*, relates to the whole human race, so the ultimate end of "this" human relates to "this" human being. Hence it must be that, just as the ultimate end of all human beings is naturally one, so the will of this human being is established in one ultimate end.[191]

That the Question of Article 7, still to come, is already answered here does not matter; Saint Thomas writes Articles in a *Summa* and not a monograph.

This Body of the Article affirms categorically, but also (if I may say so) serenely and without any ado, without in any way giving to understand that there are special and extraordinary difficulties in the matter, the thesis that human activity is a teleological unity, formed by one ultimate end. This is and remains Saint Thomas's deepest conviction, one of the most fundamental assertions of his ethical thought. There cannot be a another, concurrent, "ultimate end," that is, an end not integrated into the dynamic context which is formed by the former ultimate end. There cannot be two "lasts," two "ultimates"! One might change the meaning of

[190] The "Porphyrian tree" is a diagram showing Porphyry's conception of the way in which individual beings in the world are the concluding realities to which a descending order of universals, from "substance" down, becomes more and more specific as the branches of a "tree" of universals add successive determinations: substance is thus either corporeal or incorporeal, corporeal is either animate or inanimate, and so on, until finally under "human" the logician reaches individual human beings, in the Latin version of Porphyry, Cicero, Cato, etc., represented as the "roots" of the logical "tree." See Boethius on the *Isagoge* of Porphyry, "translated by himself," CSEL 46, p. 208, l. 12-p. 209, l. 7; available also in PL 64 103 A,B.

[191] "Sicut autem se habet ultimus finis hominis simpliciter ad totum humanum genus, ita se habet ultimus finis huius hominis ad hunc hominem. Unde oportet quod, sicut omnium hominum est naturaliter unus finis ultimus, ita huius hominis voluntas in uno ultimo fine statuatur." Ibidem ll. 37-43.

one's life; in the words of Saint Thomas one might fix one's ultimate end in different goods *successively*, but one cannot have two or more "last ends" simultaneously. Saint Thomas says this and says it very calmly, without giving us to understand that he is saying a tremendous thing.

Later commentators have seldom had the courage and the peace of mind ⟨necessary⟩ to understand Saint Thomas here and to get to the bottom of this doctrine. There is perhaps no stronger witness to the radically different outlook on human life in later periods of European civilization than ⟨is⟩ the history of commentary on this Article within a school professedly guided by the authority of Master Thomas. In him, life seems to be a rather simple affair, readily comprised under one principle, the ultimate end, as he says in his "But to the contrary":

> That in which one rests as in an ultimate end, dominates the affective ⟨life⟩ of a human being because from it one accepts the rules of one's whole life.[192]

This is a fine and memorable definition of "ultimate end." To the later commentators, however, life is extremely complex and with the growing realization of this complexity, there grows also their incapacity to understand this Article and its doctrine. Their efforts tend to surround this doctrine with so many reservations, to add to the Thomistic simplicity so many distinctions and subdistinctions that in reality Saint Thomas is made to say just the contrary of what he does say and of which every unbiased mind understands him to say.

Open Suárez, for example; Suárez presents the doctrine radically inspired by this Article through several conclusions, one of which is this very Suárezian conclusion:

> The same will can intend diverse ends, each of which may be at least negatively ultimate, and in the same fashion, on their account, choose diverse means.[193]

I shall return to this conclusion in a moment and then explain this notion of "ultimate end negatively taken"; it is a very specious and sophisticated notion. Here let us simply take account of the fact that, however Suárez may wrap up his sayings, his conclusion is just the contrary of what Saint

[192] "Illud in quo quiescit aliquis sicut in ultimo fine, hominis affectui dominatur, quia ex eo totius vitae suae regulas accipit." Ibidem, p. 715a, ll. 37-40.

[193] "Eadem voluntas intendere potest diversos fines, quorum uterque sit ultimus saltem negative, atque eodem modo propter eos eligere diversa media." Suárez, in his *Tractatus de ultimo fine*; see his *Opera omnia* t. 4, p. 28b.

Thomas says.

There are two sets of problems which the commentators raise on the occasion of this Article. I perhaps ought to say that there is one which they state explicitly and another which they may not realize, but one has the impression that they are feeling it all along.

The one problem always explicitly stated at this point and discussed on page after page is this: when one commits a venial sin one's intention in this precise act is not God, but one of the goods of this earth. One chooses this against God, against one's "ultimate End." Yet the venial sinner is said to remain radically with a tendency to the ultimate end which is God; if not, the sin would be mortal. How can the theological doctrine of "venial" sin be combined with the affirmation by Saint Thomas of a necessary unicity of the ultimate end?. If we maintain the doctrine of Saint Thomas here, are we not obliged to affirm that the venial sinner, in the very act of sin, intends God as ultimate end?

It must suffice for the present to have indicated the difficulty which cannot be treated properly without a lengthy discussion of what venial sin is; there is no use in solving this difficulty here in a technical way. We must always understand the conclusions of Saint Thomas in accordance with the subject matter. They are neither mathematical nor metaphysical conclusions; they are not endowed with that absolute and invariable verifiability which characterizes the conclusions of exact sciences, of physics and mathematics. In one word, they are "moral" conclusions, conclusions of moral science about the nature of which everyone ought to read the classical warnings of Aristotle:

> Our discussion will be adequate if it has as much clarity as the subject-matter permits, for precision is not to be sought for in the same way in all discussions any more than in all the products of the crafts. ... ⟨F⟩ine and just actions, which political science investigates, admit of much variety and fluctuation of opinion.... ⟨T⟩hey may be thought to exist only by convention and not by nature.... ⟨W⟩e must be content, then, in speaking of such subjects and with such premises to indicate the truth roughly and in outline.... ⟨I⟩t is the mark of an educated man to look for precision...just so far as the nature of the subject admits; it is equally foolish to accept probable reasoning from a mathematician and to demand from a rhetorician scientific proofs.[194]

[194] Although this appeal to Aristotle's view was made, not by Saint Thomas but by Eschmann, it will not be useless to provide the way these remarks were avail-

It is characteristic of moral conclusions that they apply to a moving matter. Human life, taken as a unified movement (as it must be taken according to Saint Thomas), insofar as it is human is not immune to some erratic switching. It is true that when swallows arrive, it is summer; but it is also true that "one swallow does not make a summer" ⟨Aristotle, *Nicomachean Ethics* 1, 7; 1098a 19, but The Philosopher, who was also an observer of nature, said "spring," *éar*, not "summer"!⟩. There is no contradiction between the two statements.

The other difficulty which the commentators feel here is perhaps more serious. It crops up in the text from Suárez which I read a while ago. What Suárez means by an end "negatively ultimate" in his own words is this:

> The nature of an ultimate end, taken without qualification, is especially this: that a human being refer to it as what is owing and thanks to its merits both the self and all that one possesses, absolutely and without reservation. Hence, in order that the intention of the ultimate end be complete in every sense, it is necessary that nothing which is not referable to such an end be admitted in a human being; in order, however, that it be maintained in an absolute and unqualified sense it is sufficient that one admit nothing which is absolutely contrary to such an end and totally inconsistent with attaining it.[195]

In other words, it is true that speaking of the ultimate end positively and absolutely, in accordance with the strictest significance of the word, it is

---

able to Saint Thomas as found in the edition cited of his Exp. in Ethicam 3, 2; p. 11a, on the text of Aristotle *Nicomachean Ethics* 1, 2; 1094b 12-28: "Dicetur autem utique sufficienter, si secundum subjectam materiam manifestetur. Certum enim non similiter in omnibus sermonibus quaerendum est.... Bona autem et justa, de quibus civilis intendit, tantam habent differentiam et errorem, ut videantur lege sola esse, natura vero non.... Amabile igitur de talibus et ex talibus dicentes grosse et figuraliter veritatem ostendere.... Disciplinati enim est, in tantum certitudinem quaerere secundum unumquodque genus, in quantum rei natura recipit: proximum enim videtur et mathematicum persuadentem acceptare, et rhetoricum demonstrationes expetere."

[195] "Quodcirca de ratione finis ultimi simpliciter, imprimis est, ut ex debito et meritis ejus, homo referat in ipsum se, et omnia sua absolute et simpliciter: unde, ut intentio ultimi finis undequaque perfecta sit, necesse est ut nihil in homine admittat, quod non sit referible in talem finem; ut autem absolute et simpliciter conservetur, quamvis non cum tota perfectione sua, satis est ut nihil admittat, quod sit absolute contrarium tali fini, et omnino repugnet consecutioni ejus." Suárez *Tractatus de ultimo fine* Disputatio 1, Sectio 6, N. 3; *Opera* t. 4, p. 13a-b.

that end to which everything else is ordered. However, we need not speak always in this absolute and positive sense of ultimate end. We might indeed call "ultimate end" another end which is not *ordered* to the former one, but could be so ordered in such a way that contains nothing which is absolutely contrary to the former end. Under such circumstances, as Suárez has told us before, we might admit the possibility of two "ultimates."

There is in the treatment of this matter by Suárez not a single allusion to the problem of the relationship between Church and State; yet I am sure that this problem is somehow at the back of his mind, even though he might not have been actually aware of it, when he develops these distinctions. What makes me think of the connection between these two sets of doctrines, is the fact that ever since the beginning of the fourteenth century people have tried to solve the main political problem in Christendom, namely, the relationship between ecclesiastical and secular power with the assumption, more or less clearly set forth, of what Dante says explicitly are the "Two ultimates." Dante is perhaps, among all medieval thinkers, the one who has affirmed this thesis in the most explicit and forceful manner. He says, in the last Chapter of his *De monarchia* 3, 16,

> If, therefore, the human being is a kind of mean between the corruptibles and the incorruptibles, since every mean carries an air of the nature of each extreme, it is necessary that the human carry the air of each of these two natures. Besides, since every nature is ordered to some ultimate end, it follows that a double end of the human must exist, with the result that, just as the human alone among all beings participates incorruptibility and corruptibility, so too is the human ordered to two ultimates, one of which is the end inasmuch as corruptible and the other inasmuch as incorruptible. The inerrant Providence, therefore,...has proposed two ends that must be sought by a human being, namely, beatitude in this life which consists in the exercise of one's own power...and the beatitude of eternal life which consists in the enjoyment of the divine vision, to which one cannot ascend by one's own power unless aided by divine light.[196]

[196] "Si ergo homo medium quoddam est corruptibilium et incorruptibilium, cum omne medium sapiat naturam extremorum, necesse est hominem sapere utramque naturam. Et cum omnis natura ad ultimum quemdam finem ordinetur, consequitur ut hominis duplex finis existat; ut, sicut inter omnia entia solus incorruptibilitatem et corruptibilitatem participat, sic solus inter omna entia in duo ultima ordinetur, quorum alterum sit finis eius prout corruptibilis est, alterum vero prout incorruptibilis.

Every one of you ought to read Gilson's very apt and extremely interesting commentary on this passage.[197] One of the key assertions of Saint Thomas in his *On Kingship* is that there is but one ultimate end of the human being.[198] Gilson very effectively destroys the legend of Dante's "Thomism" by his acutely observing,

> St. Thomas certainly does not deny that natural man has a natural goal to seek and attain in this life.... ⟨O⟩f all the theologians of the Middle Ages, none did more than he to establish this thesis. It is inseparable from his differentiation between nature and grace...accompanied by unity in the Thomistic doctrine only because here differentiation between the orders entails their gradation.... ⟨T⟩he final goal of the body of society is not to live in accordance with virtue, but through a virtuous life, to come to the enjoyment of God....[199]

Dante's scheme is dualistic: here Church, there State, each completely autonomous, each completely independent of the other. The last ethical reduction of this scheme is the thesis of the two "ultimates" as expressed in the *De monarchia*. Saint Thomas's scheme is unitarian, it is the conception of the one Christianity within which there are two powers. The last ethical reduction of this Thomistic scheme is found in our Article and its thesis, "It is impossible that...." What Dante destroys is, in truth, the unity of human life. Dante's gigantic struggle between Empire and Priesthood, *Imperium et Sacerdotium*, will be fought out in the soul of man who, as Saint Thomas held, naturally strives for the unity of his life. Dante's scheme is the modern scheme, that of the world of our "States"; Saint

---

Duos igitur fines Providentia illa inerrabilis homini proposuit intendendos: beatitudinem scilicet huius vite, que in operatione proprie virtutis consistit...et beatitudinem vite eterne, que in fruitione divini aspectus ad quam propria virtus ascendere non potest nisi lumine divino adiuta...." Dante *De monarchia* 3, 15, 5-7; *Opere minori* ed. Bruno Nardi (Milan, Naples: Riccardo Ricciardi, 1979), pp. 496-498.

197 Etienne Gilson, *Dante et la philosophie*, Chapitre 3, "La philosophie dans la *Monarchie*," especially n. 4, pp. 190 sqq.

198 *St. Thomas Aquinas. On Kingship, to the King of Cyprus*, tr. G.B. Phelan as "On the Governance of Rulers," revised with introduction and notes by I. Th. Eschmann O.P. (Toronto: Pontifical Institute of Mediaeval Studies, 1949), 1, 8, pp. 34-43. Eschmann's class notes edited here seem to pre-date his own revision (after considerable manuscript work) of the Phelan translation; see p. v (unnumbered of revised translation).

199 E. Gilson, *Dante The Philosopher*, tr. D. Moore (London: Sheed & Ward, 1948), pp. 192, 193. Eschmann did not use this translation but, perhaps, made his own from Gilson's French.

Thomas's scheme is the medieval scheme, that of Christendom where "The Pope holds the apex of the twofold power."

Suárez does not say as bluntly as Dante that there are two "ultimates"; he would say that there are two ultimates "in some way"; there is one "negative ultimate" and one "positive ultimate." What is this positive ultimate? According to Suárez it is that end to which we finally refer all actions and particular ends. Very well; but then, what is the negative ultimate? It is also an ultimate end and thus we refer to it all our actions. The coexistence of these two ultimate ends is guaranteed, according to Suárez, in this: that we assume that one ultimate and its order contains nothing contrary to the other ultimate end and its order. The first is by no means directly and positively ordered to the other for such an ordering would make of it a "non-ultimate" end. Although the first is disparate with respect to the other, it is quite different, something other, and yet not contrary to the second.

Behind these abstract discussions there looms before my mind the whole modern system of Church and State which is one of the capital points, if not the absolutely capital point, of the modern system of life. I wonder why Suárez at this point did not speak of this explicitly. Of course the Suárezian doctrine of a negative ultimate end would need further study and investigation. The few hints which I have given may be sufficient for the moment to illustrate our present Article and to give some flesh and nerves to the somewhat dry bones of its reasoning.

## Q. THE EXPOSITION OF ARTICLE 6

*a. The State of the Question*

*i. Systematic Considerations*: This Article is manifestly dedicated to a more concrete verification of the doctrine of Article 5. If, at a given moment, the whole activity and life of the human race is unified in, and by, an ultimate end which we desire *as* ultimate, then it follows that all and everything else, which we might also desire, is desired for the sake of this ultimate end. It is part of that teleological system, the first principle and formal measure of which is that ultimate end. Yet certain facts seems to contradict this conclusion, contained virtually, at least in the foregoing Article. Those facts are enumerated in the Arguments to the contrary of the present Article. Hence, on account of these precise facts, the conclusion, although in itself evident from the foregoing Article, needs some further clarifications. The present Article is nothing but such further illustration of the statement made formerly. In Article 5 we focussed on the last end and its unity; here we descend to the ordering ⟨of subordinated ends⟩ which is formed by the ultimate end and, on account of certain difficulties, investigate how this ordering is formed and integrated under the ultimate end.

This having been clarified under a logical and systematic point of view, the present Article has a clearly marked historical starting point. History here is of peculiar interest, indeed more interesting than the logical transition from Article 5 to Article 6. I doubt that Saint Thomas would have written this Article, the formal statement and proof of which have been virtually contained in the former Article, had there not been a historical reason for it. Saint Thomas always takes account of what is said and discussed in the schools of his time and here we definitely touch upon a point which is an actual discussion in the time of Aquinas. We must, therefore, investigate the "state of the question" of this Article from the historical point of view.

*ii. Historical consideration*: It is usually wise, in this sort of study, to pay attention to a parallel place in the *Scriptum super Sententiis*. In that work, more than in any other, Saint Thomas is always in close contact with what was going on around him in the other schools. Now here, as the editions point out, we have a parallel place in the *Scriptum*: Book 4, Distinction 49, Question 1, Article 3, Quaestiuncula 4, an Article (or better, a *part* of an Article) belonging to the treatise on the "Last Things" which concludes this handbook of medieval theology. Peter Lombard there reminds us in Chapter 2 of Distinction 49 that ⟨it was⟩ usually in this context ⟨that⟩ the old Augustinian problem of whether all human beings desire beatitude, is raised and discussed. The Master of the Sentences leaves the solution of the problem to the Augustinian text in which mainly it had arisen in the medieval mind, namely, *On the Trinity*, Book 13.[200] As he often does, this author patches together his text from several Augustinian fragments:

> This is surprising, since the will to obtain and to retain blessedness is one in ⟨us⟩ all, whence comes on the other hand, such a variety and diversity of wills concerning that blessedness itself? Not that anyone is unwilling to have it, but that not all know it. For if all knew this, it would not be thought by some to be in goodness of mind, by others in pleasure of the body, by others in both, by others somewhere else and by yet others somewhere else again.... How then

[200] *IV Libri Sententiarum* 4, Dist. 49, Cap. 1, n. 3: "Solet etiam quaeri de beatitudine, utrum omnes eam velint, et sciant quae sit vera beatitudo."

> do all love so warmly what not all know? Who can love what is not known? Since blessedness is loved by all, is it, nevertheless, not known by all? Perhaps all do know *what* it is, but not all know *where* it is, and the dispute arises from that?... Or is this perhaps false which we have assumed to be most true and most certain, namely, that "All humans will to live blessedly"?... Shall we, therefore, hold that to be false of which the Academic Cicero himself did not doubt (although Academics doubt everything) who when, in his dialogue *Hortensius*, he wanted an issue so certain that no one would waver on it he says, "Certainly we all wish to be happy." Far be it from us to say this is false!...[201]

After a lengthy discussion, extending over pages and pages, Augustine concludes finally in Chapter 20 and this conclusion is also given by the Lombard who, moreover, makes some extracts from the intermediate Chapters:

> Let us see what this prolix discourse has effected, what it has garnered, whereto it has reached. To will themselves blessed belongs to all human beings, but not all humans have the faith whereby the heart is cleansed and arrives at blessedness. Thus does it comes to pass that through this, which not all will, one must contend for the blessedness which there can be no one who does not will![202]

[201] "Mirum est autem cum capessendae atque retinendae beatitudinis voluntas una sit omnium, unde tanta exsistat de ipsa beatitudine rursus varietas et diversitas voluntatum, non quod aliquis eam nolit, sed quod non omnes eam norint. Si enim omnes eam nossent, non ab aliis putaretur esse in virtute animi, aliis in corporis voluptate, aliis in utraque, at aliis atque aliis, alibi atque alibi... Quomodo igitur ferventissime amant omnes quod non omnes sciunt? Quis potest amare quod nescit...? Cum ergo beatitudo amatur ab omnibus nec tamen scitur ab omnibus? An forte sciunt omnes ipsa quae sit, sed non omnes sciunt ubi sit et inde contentio est?... An forte falsum est quod pro verissimo certissimoque posuimus, 'beate vivere omnes homines velle'?... Itane falsum erit unde nec ipse, cum academicis omnia dubia sint, academicus Cicero dubitavit qui cum vellet in Hortensio dialogo ab aliqua re certa de qua nullus ambigeret sumere suae disputationis exordium, 'Beati certe,' inquit, 'omnes esse volumus.' Absit ut hoc falsum esse dicamus...." Augustine, *De trinitate* 13, 4, 7; CCL 50A, 389-391, ll. 1-7, 8-13, 24, 25, 32-36; cited by Peter Lombard, *Sent.* 4, Dist. 9, cap. 1; p. 1028, no. 436.

[202] "Iam itaque videamus quid sermo iste prolixus effecerit, quod collegerit, quo pervenerit. "Beatos esse se velle" omnium hominum est, nec tamen omnium est fides qua cor mundante ad beatitudinem pervenitur. Ita fit ut per istam quam non omnes volunt ad illam tendendum sit quam nemo potest esse qui nolit." Ibidem,

From this text the kind of problem with which scholasticism will be faced once it comes to discuss the question is immediately clear. In what way is the universal tendency to beatitude, to blessedness, a sign of "the soul, naturally Christian"?[203]

How far does reasoning reach and where does faith begin? This is one set of problems connected with the Augustinian questions; it is the problem of faith and reason, the problem of the Christian meaning of our life. Yet another problem is this: in the tendency to beatitude Saint Augustine sees a vestige of God in human nature. Now we may at once foresee that it would be a properly Augustinian trend of thinking to explain this vestige in the way of the typical Augustinian "exemplarism." Do we, through the object of our volitions, have the same immediate contact with something divine, with the divine reality, as we have (according to Augustinism) through the object of our knowledge? In fact, this is the outstanding problem arising from the text for the medieval schools. It is easy to verify this in both Albert and Bonaventure; let us cast a glance at Saint Albert's text *In IV Sententiarum* Distinctio 49, Articulus 7; Albert's question in this place is "Whether all wish to be blessed?"[204] Starting the line of arguments for this thesis Albert at once quotes Dionysius:

> Dionysius says in the Book *On the Divine Names* that all ⟨beings⟩ seek the Good and Beautiful and, on this account, do whatever they do. Therefore, by much more do all ⟨humans⟩ desire to be blessed.[205]

To desire a good, whatever it is, is enough to reach God who is the supreme Fountainhead of Goodness, the Principle of the universal "flowing forth of the Good"? This meaning of the doctrine comes out more clearly in the following Argument, the fifth in the file, in which a text from the *Confessions* is quoted:

> Perversely do they all imitate You who make themselves far from

---

pp. 417, l. 64-p. 418, l. 4. While Peter Lombard's text justifies the previous note, the present material seems not to be indentifiable in his *Sent.* 4.

203 "anima naturaliter christiana," a celebrated phrase coined by Tertullian; see his *Apologia* 17; AN 17.

204 Albert, *In IV Sententiarum* Dist. 49 B, Art. 7; 40: 677.

205 "1. Dicit Dionysius in libro de *Divinis nominibus*, quod 'omnia bonum et pulchrum concupiscunt: et propter illud agunt, quidquid agunt.' Ergo multo magis omnes homines volunt esse beati." *Beati Alberti Opera omnia* (Paris: Vivès, 1894), t. 30, p. 677a.

> You and raise themselves against You. For even by imitating You thus do they pass judgment that You are the Creator of every creature and, therefore, there is no one who recedes totally from You.... From this it is taken that every human being seeks similitude with God and, for the sake of this, does whatever that one does. Now only this sort beatifies; therefore, every human seeks beatitude.[206]

In one word: only God can beatify us. Still, every good which we desire is a similitude of God; this is enough to solve the Augustinian antinomy, namely, that all human beings want to be blessed, yet not all acknowledge that their blessedness lies in God. Whether they acknowledge it or not, they are on their way to God. Albert states this more explicitly in the Body of the Article:

> ...then anything you like that beatifies possesses an imitation of Uncreated Beatitude, and from this fact, that it is patterned after It, has the power to move an appetite; and thus, everything which exists seeks blessedness in accord with the fact that it is patterned after the First Blessedness....[207]

This is a clear statement of exemplarism in this matter, of the Platonic-Augustinian idea of "participation" to which a claim is made to help on the solution of the proposed problem. Saint Thomas's solution to the same problem, although it sticks to the Augustinian terminology (as we have read it in Saint Albert) will, however, at once appear in its originality as well as in its differences as soon as we read a few words of his Article in the *Scriptum* at the place cited:

> And because all things proceed from God, inasmuch as He is Good, (NB not "all things proceed" (that is, *flow*) "from the *divine Goodness*"—Saint Thomas is very careful in his choice of words) as Augustine and Dionysius say; therefore, all created things, in accord with

[206] "5. Adhuc autem Augustinus, ibidem ⟨in libro 2 *Confessionum*, no. 4, p. 677a⟩: 'Perverse te imitantur omnes, qui longe se a te faciunt, et extollunt se adversum te. Sed etiam sic te imitando judicant Creatorem te esse omnis creaturae, et ideo non esse qui a te omnino recedatur.' Ex hoc accipitur, quod omnis homo similitudinem Dei appetit: et illius gratia agit quidquid agit: sed sola talis species beatificat: ergo omnis homo appetit beatitudinem." Ibidem p. 677b.

[207] "...tunc quodlibet beatificantium habet imitationem ad beatitudinem increatam: et ex hoc quod est exemplatum ab ipsa, habet movere appetitum: et sic omne quod est, appetit beatitudinem, secundum quod est exemplatum primae beatitudinis...." Ibidem p. 678b.

> an impression received from the Creator, are inclined to seek the good, each in accord with its own modality.[208]

Although Saint Thomas gives due credit to the fundamental Augustinian tenet, namely, that every created good is a participation of the Uncreated Good—which, indeed, is also a truly Thomistic proposition—yet he insists on the activity of the secondary causes. Just as in the order of knowledge, what is divine in a human person is the "light" of the agent intellect, so in the order of appetitive tendency the inclination, and not the object, is divine, that is, given by, impressed by, the Creator. Before going on to the Body of the Article, I should like to expedite the question of a second "parallel text" which you will find in the editions. The Leonine gives simply "*Contra gentiles* Capitulum 101" with no indication of the Book in which this Chapter is supposed to be; the Ottawa editor supplies "Book 2." Everyone can see easily that "Book 2, Chapter 101" has absolutely nothing to do with the problem in hand. Some editors have a "horror of a vacuum"; they prefer to give a wrong reference than no reference at all! In the *Summa contra gentiles* there is no parallel place, but there is in Book 1, Chapter 101, a chapter entitled "That God is His own beatitude" which in its first part uses a similar idea as that in the *Scriptum*. This includes a passing remark of such a sort that perhaps more than one ⟨like it⟩ could be found in the works of Saint Thomas. It is interesting, however, because it shows, albeit sketchily, a stage of his thought between the *Scriptum* and the *Summa theologiae*. The remark proves, too, that this Article is in its way a continuation and a further illustration of what has been said in Article 4, an Article that is indeed the culminating point of the whole doctrine.

*b. The Body of the Article*

It is most interesting and illuminating to compare this "Body of the Article" with the parallel place, *On the Sentences*:

> ...according to The Philosopher in the *VII Ethics*, the end in the order of appetibles is related just as is a principle in the order of intelligibles. Since, however, that which is the first and the maximum in any order you like is the cause of those items which come later, therefore in speculative matters knowledge of the principle is the cause of knowing all else; and similarly, so the appetite for the end

[208] "Et quia omnia procedunt a Deo inquantum bonus est ut dicit Augustinus et Dionysius: ideo omnia creata secundum impressionem a Creatore receptam inclinantur in bonum appetendum secundum suum modum." *Super Sent.* 4, dist. 49, q. 1, a. 3, qcla. 4, sol. 1; Vivès, t. 11, p. 472b.

> is the cause of the appetite for all others which are related to the end. Hence, since blessedness is the end of a human life, whatever the will has an appetite to do, it orders to blessedness....[209]

Clearly this same argument re-appears here in the *Summary of Theology* as the second argument presented in the Body of the Article:

> Second, that the ultimate end is related in moving appetite as the "prime mover" is related in other motions. It is manifest, however, that secondary moving causes do not move *except* as they are moved by the prime mover. Hence, secondary objects of appetite do not move the appetite except in an ordering to the first object of appetite, which is the ultimate end.[210]

The difference between the *Summa* and the *Scriptum* is only that, while in the earlier work the analogy of the "process of knowing" with any set of ordered causes is assumed, in the later work it is explicit; in both the whole reasoning is based upon the principle "that which is first in any genus is the cause of that which is later." The two reasonings are, therefore, identical in substance. It is clear that with this argument we learn nothing new since it is also found in Article 4. That Saint Thomas does not note this repetition is owing to the technique of a *Summa*; each Article is (or tends to be) a structure in itself.

The text of the *Scriptum* continues:

> ...this is evident by experience. For whoever has an appetite for anything, has that appetite for it insofar as it is thought to be good.

209 "...secundum Philosophum in VII Ethicorum, in ordine appetibilium hoc modo se habet finis sicut principium in ordine intelligibilium. Quia autem illud quod est primum in quolibet genere et maximum, est causa eorum quae sunt post, ideo cognitio principii in speculativis est causa cognitionis omnium aliorum; et similiter appetitus finis est causa appetendi omnia alia quae sunt ad finem. Unde cum beatitudo sit finis humanae vitae quidquid voluntas appetit facere, ad beatitudinem ordinat...." *Super IV Sententiarum* Distinctio 49, Quaestio 1, Articulus 3, Quaestiuncula 4, Solutio 4; t. 2, p. 474b.

210 "Secundo, quia ultimus finis hoc modo se habet in movendo appetitum, sicut se habet in aliis motionibus primum movens. Manifestum est autem quod causae secundae moventes non movent [nisi] secundum quod moventur a primo movente. Unde secunda appetibilia non movent appetitum nisi in ordine ad primum appetibile, quod est ultimus finis." ST 1-2, 1, 6, in corpore; t. 2, p. 716b, ll. 1-9. NB: the Ottawa editors were allowed by the Leonine Commission to record significant Leonine variations; here the word "nisi," *except*, essential to the sense, has been Italicized in the English translation and printed with square brackets in this note.

> Now through this, that one possesses something one counts good, one judges oneself the closer to blessedness, for the addition of good upon good makes one approach all the more to the complete good which is blessedness itself. Therefore, every appetite you like is ordered to blessedness.[211]

Here it is manifest, first, that in the first argument of our present Article we have a re-statement of what was the second argument in the *Scriptum* and second: that this argument has undergone a very decisive correction. We are in the presence of one of those various and frequent cases where Saint Thomas corrected himself and gave to one of his former views and arguments a more solid basis. The first argument makes one think that "the complete, the perfect, good" consists of a great number of goods piled up, one upon another. Such a notion cannot stand any severe test. The human "perfect good" is not a mass of goods, but an indivisible, formal entity, and this is exactly the point which Saint Thomas now corrects in the *Summa theologiae*:

> This is apparent for a twofold reason. First, because for whatever a human being has an appetite, that appetite is had under the notion of good. However, if it is not the object of appetite as the perfect good (which is the ultimate end), it is necessary that this be an object of appetite as tending toward the perfect good, because the beginning of anything is ordered to its consummation, as is evident in what comes to pass by nature as well as in those things which come to pass by art. Besides, thus every beginning of perfection is ordered to perfection consummated, which is for the sake of the ultimate end.[212]

[211] "...quod etiam experimento patet. Quicumque enim appetit aliquid, appetit illud inquantum est aestimatum bonum. Per hoc autem quod aliquis habet aliquid quod aestimat bonum, reputat se ut beatitudini propinquiorem: quia additio boni super bonum facit magis appropinquare bono perfecto, quod est ipsa beatitudo. Et ideo quilibet appetitus in beatitudinem ordinatur." *Scriptum super Sententias IV* Distinctio 49, Quaestio 1, Articulus 3, Quaestiuncula 4, Solutio 4; t. 2, pp. 474b, 475a.

[212] "Primo quidem quia quidquid homo appetit, appetit sub ratione boni. Quod quidem si non appetitur ut bonum perfectum, quod est ultimus finis, necesse est ut appetatur ut tendens in bonum perfectum; quia semper inchoatio alicuius ordinatur ad consummationem ipsius; sicut patet in his quae fiunt a natura, quam in his quae fiunt ab arte. Et ita omnis inchoatio perfectionis ordinatur in perfectionem consummatam, quae est propter ultimum finem." ST 1-2, 1, 6, in corpore; t. 2, p. 716a l. 40-716b l. 1.

In the light of the *Summa*, what is wrong, or rather what is not entirely good and solid, in the argumentation of the *Scriptum* is this: the argument is a strange mixture of experience and metaphysical principle. It started out by saying that it wanted to be a reasoning from experience and it bravely kept to the line of experience. Should you have obtained a good you think yourself nearer to blessedness; this *Scriptum* version manifestly makes you think in a material way of the "perfect good" whereas the later version presents a formal conception of that ultimate good, not material, not quasi-quantitative. Where we had a pretended "experience" of coming nearer to the end, here we have a solid metaphysical principle, namely, that "the beginning of anything is ordered to its consummation."

The correction is quite noticeable and I should like you to take note of it as an example of how Saint Thomas worked on his own earlier statements. Surely such corrections can be turned into valid arguments for fixing Thomistic chronology. Of course there is no doubt about the chronology of these two writings; one is more than ten years earlier than the other. Suppose, however, that we find such and similar corrections in two works, the chronology of which is not established and can be established only by such comparisons. In the presence of such corrections (and most are much more subtle than this one), then we have a sure criterion for fixing the relative chronology of those two writings.

The present case serves also to show that, and how, Saint Thomas corrected himself; he does so pretty often and in a thousand subtle ways which not infrequently need careful study to be perceived. Now, what would you say about an author, a commentator, repeating the argument of the *Scriptum* and presenting it as Thomistic argument? I know of no one who does so in this particular case, but many examples can be found of commentators who use earlier arguments that Saint Thomas himself eliminated in his later writings. Saint Thomas never corrects himself explicitly, almost never says "So I held in my former works, but I now wish to correct this opinion." Implicit corrections, however, and often of a very subtle type in expressions, in the ways of saying things, in such corrections his writings abound.

In a way, the present case is typical because such re-organization, brought about by the discovery of a new principle upon which to base it, or by making a former principle more explicit—this kind of re-organization is pretty frequent in the writings of Saint Thomas. Re-organized then, as the former argument now is, it deserves to occupy first place in the Body of the Article, for the first place is also, in the construction of a Thomistic Article, the place of honor. This is warranted by the context for, if you look more closely into it, you will see that it is nothing other than a development of the thesis which has been central to this whole Question from the beginning. This thesis is that "the object of the will is the end and the good"; here Saint Thomas evidently develops this same principle or, perhaps, formulates it anew by saying at the beginning of this argument, "Whatever a human being desires, *appetit*, is desired under the notion of the good."

There is nothing Platonic about this Article or about the one in the *Scriptum* either. Historically speaking, this is perhaps the most noteworthy feature about the doctrine as a whole. The Platonic way of arguing here would be to stress the similitude of every good with the first and subsistent good so that whatever a human being does touches on the divine. Saint Thomas refuses to follow this line of thinking though, of course, it is true that every created good is a participation in the Uncreated Good. As the *Summa contra gentiles* 3, 19, states explicitly, "All things by their movements and actions, tend to the divine similitude as to the ultimate end."[213]

In this place such an argument would be of no avail since we are speaking always of the notion, the *ratio*, of the ultimate end and are not supposed to know in what concrete good the notion of the ultimate end finds its place and its fulfillment. The reasonings in this first Question are in a peculiar way strictly philosophical although they serve as an introduction to the theology of the ultimate end and of beatitude.

*c. The Responses*

As to the first Argument, Saint Thomas knows nothing of professional "playing" which, of course, is a contradiction in terms; playing for money is not play and is called "play" abusively! As Saint Thomas understands play it is "an action which is not ordered to any extrinsic end," it is gratuitous and, objectively speaking, has its end in itself; it has no part in a scheme or a plan, no part in an order of actions. Speaking of the playing subject, however, the picture changes; "playful actions are ordered to the good of the one playing insofar as they delight or offer rest." Therefore, thanks to the exercise of the action, not of its specification, these "playful actions" are part and parcel of the whole system of a life unified in the ultimate end.

To the second Argument, the same obtains with respect to speculation. From the point of view of its object, metaphysics refuses to be subordinated to any other end; it can never become a means. Saint Thomas

[213] "In tantum autem aliquid de bono participat, in quantum assimilatur primae bonitati, quae Deus est. Omnia igitur per motus suos et actiones tendunt in divinam similitudinem sicut in finem ultimum." SCG 3, 19; p. 243a, b.

wants us to remember what has been stated earlier in Article 1 in the Response there to Argument 2, where it was said, or at least hinted, that although this is true from the point of view of the specification of the act, that is, of its object, it is not true if one considers the "exercise" of the act, that is, its concrete and psychological reality. "Speculative knowledge," Saint Thomas says here, "which is sought as a kind of 'good of the one who speculates', is comprehended under the complete and perfect good which is the ultimate end."[214] This is also the reason that the will, the principle of every "exercised act" is in this line the supreme human power, subordinating everything to its object—which is the total good of that living being who acts and lives.

Looking at the implications of this fine answer we see that, to Saint Thomas, there is not and there never can be, a completely and absolutely "selfless act" in the sense that the acting or desiring subject would abandon the self completely and absolutely, in other words, one would annihilate oneself! With respect to the agent, every good that agent desires is at least that agent's good. It is not always a genuine good, which of itself would be subordinated to that agent and less a good than is the agent. Still, if it were not the agent's "good," it would never arouse the desire of the agent. This applies as well to the Supreme Good. There is a theological virtue: cultivating the love of God insofar as this is useful to the lover. This is hope, for in hope we love God insofar as He is our Good, our help and our aid. Certain Pietists and mystics have never understood this and there are whole theological systems to eliminate hope from the catalogue of theological virtues. In hope, however, I do not degrade God, the highest Good, to the level of a means or a tool in my selfish interest. Hope stresses only and simply the relationship which every good at least in the exercise of an act, has to one for whom it is good. "The good is what all desire"; in this definition the relationship of fittingness with respect to a desiring subject is expressed. This relationship cannot be eliminated because in eliminating it we would destroy the very nature of good.

In consequence, selfishness cannot be defined simply as the fact that in acting one refers the object loved to oneself; if that were selfishness (and so to be avoided) there could be no love at all. Selfishness is defined rather by the fact that one makes the self and the advantage of the self the *ultimate* end, makes oneself the perfect and consummate good. Saint Thomas's ethical doctrine is outstanding for having preserved a natural and

[214] "...scientia speculativa; quae appetitur ut bonum quoddam speculantis, quod comprehenditur sub bono completo et perfecto, quod est ultimus finis." ST 1-2, 1, 6, Ad 2; t. 2, p. 716b, ll. 18-21.

rightful place for an "ordered love of self." Our text gives us only a small hint which it would not be convenient to follow out too much. Note, however, the different ways in which Saint Thomas expresses himself in his Response to 1 and to 2. Of the acts of play he says "they are ordered to the good of the one who plays" while of speculative knowledge he says "it is sought as a kind of good of the one who speculates." The technical expressions for these different relationships would be that the playful acts are *on account of* the good of the one who plays whereas speculation is not *on account of* the one speculating, but is a "good for" the one speculating. That which is "on my account" is subordinated to me; hence it must be a lesser good in the scale of values than I am myself. The scholastic example is "Wine is for my sake"; all corporeal and exterior goods are for the sake of the human race. That, however, which is "good for me" might also be a superior good: God is "good for me" and all spiritual goods are "good for me." In Latin, the dative case expresses their relationship to the subject desiring them. Without that relationship the very notion of "good" would not be fulfilled; yet this relationship implies no subordination.

To the third Argument, which was that to act for an end implies that one thinks of that end; of course we are not always doing that with respect to the ultimate end of a human life. The response by Saint Thomas is a famous text and has given rise to the major scholastic dispute connected with this Article. The Thomistic solution of the difficulty lies in the distinction between "actual intention" and "virtual intention." The ultimate end ought not to be intended actually in all our actions, but a first actual intention of it and the force, the *virtus*, of that intention, remains in all subsequent intentions:

> ...the force of the first intention with respect to the ultimate end remains in every desire of anything you like, even if there is no actual thought of the ultimate end, just as it is not necessary that one who goes down a path think of the end at each step.[215]

Among the many Thomistic texts expressing the same doctrine the outstanding one is perhaps that of *On Charity*:

> Just as in efficient causes the force of the first cause remains in all the secondary causes, so too the originating, *principalis*, intention of

[215] "...virtus primae intentionis, quae est respectu ultimi finis, manet in quolibet appetitu cuiuscumque rei, etiam si de ultimo fine actu non cogitetur. Sicut non oportet quod qui vadit per viam, in quolibet passu cogitet de fine." ST I-II, 1, 6, Ad 3; t. 2, p. 716b ll. 25-30.

> the end remains in force in all secondary ends whence whoever intends some secondary end is virtually intending the originating end. Just as the medical practitioner, while actually collecting herbs to concoct a potion, perhaps thinking not at all of health, is nonetheless *virtually* intending health, on account of which he gives the potion.[216]

Anyone reading this text will have no trouble in understanding that this doctrine has always been the object of much controversy. Other possible ways of "intending" have been brought to students' attention and claimed to be, more or less, the "virtual intention" of Saint Thomas, as for instance, "habitual intention" and the "interpretative intention." The latter especially has been adopted by Suárez and all the minimizing theologians because it permits them to get out of many troubles easily, troubles which are caused by the Thomistic "virtual intention." As Saint Thomas explains it, the "virtual intention" is the *virtus*, the force, of a first cause that remains and is continued in all subsequent causes. Now, that I intend an end (or better, the ultimate end) *only* by way of "interpretation" is clearly no longer a "virtual" intention.

For this interpretation means that, whatever the facts are, whether I intend the ultimate end or not, my action might be taken by some one else as directed toward the ultimate end. Every action which is not contrary to the ultimate end might, by interpretation, be taken as such an intention, or as revealing such an intention, whatever the real facts on the action are. The doctrine of the "interpretative intention" thus takes no account of the facts. Yet manifestly, the virtual intention in Saint Thomas is a fact; it is, of course, no actual fact, but it is the fact and the reality which remains after an actual fact, an actual intention, has passed.

The interpretation of our acts, the judgment on them in spite of what they really are, is a means properly used by jurists. It is the principle upon which the so-called "proof by circumstantial evidence" is founded. This an aprioristic presumption, which might or might not be true, is a means of "knowledge" necessary for the jurist, but one revealing the limits of human knowledge about human things. Humans can only judge humans

[216] "Sicut in causis efficientibus virtus primae causae manet in omnibus causis secundis, ita etiam intentio principalis finis virtute manet in omnibus finibus secundariis, unde quicumque actu intendit aliquem finem secundarium virtute intendit finem principalem. Sicut medicus, dum colligit herbas actu intendit conficere potionem, nihil fortasse de sanitate cogitans. Virtualiter tamen intendit sanitatem propter quam potionem dat." *Quaestiones disputatae de caritate*, ed. Odetto, ed. cit. Quaestio unica, Articulus 11, Ad 2; p. 782b.

according to exterior appearances. It is very characteristic of sixteenth-century theologians to have thus "juridified" moral doctrine, a moral doctrine which is not about what appears, but about what *is*. In Suárez this juridification is one of many, almost countless, instances where he has done the same thing with the philosophical and substantial doctrine of Saint Thomas.

Now the difficulty comes up which is also at the bottom of Suárez's interpretation. Saint Thomas supposes that, in everyone's life, and even at the beginning of that life, that is, when reason is awake and one is able to posit a human act, an actual decision about the ultimate end of one's life is made. The "first thing willed" according to this doctrine, will and must be, the intention of the ultimate end.

Is this true?

Is this verifiable?

One can easily understand that to avoid this consequence the theologians have taken refuge in the "interpretative" ⟨intention⟩, for with this, no actual intention is required at that moment. It is enough, for instance, that the child begin to live a good life, do good actions, and those actions "interpretatively," that is, neither actually nor virtually, contain the intention of the true ultimate end. Yet Saint Thomas explicitly faces this consequence in I-II, 89, 6, Body of the Article, and at To Argument 3:

> What first occurs to a human possessed of discretion, is thinking of oneself to whom one orders other things as to their end, for the end is prior in intention. And therefore, this is the time in which there is an obligation by the affirmative precept from God in which the Lord says, "Convert yourselves to Me and I shall convert Myself to you" (Zachariah 1:3).[217]

Many theologians, even so-called "Thomists" of the strict observance, like Billuart, have tried hard, but in vain, to get around and to minimize this clear and absolutely logical text of Saint Thomas. On the supposition, of course, of the total Thomistic ethical system, I find no difficulty in it. Moreover, two suppositions must be made.

First, it is difficult to fix the time in a child's, or in an adolescent's

[217] "Primum enim quod occurrit homini discretionem habenti est quod de seipso cogitet, ad quem alia ordinet sicut ad finem: finis enim est prior in intentione. Et ideo hoc est tempus pro quo obligatur ex Deo praecepto affirmativo, quo Dominus dicit: 'Convertimini ad me, et ego convertar ad vos,' Zach. 1:3." ST 1-2, 89, 6, Ad 3; t. 2, p. 1205b, ll. 6-13. Although Eschmann mentioned the Body of the Article, he has cited only the Response as given here.

life, when this obligation occurs. Of course, it need not coincide with the time when jurists, according to their diverse legislative views, declare a child to be capable of the use of reason, based on no direct fact; this is an assumption based on interpretation, on circumstantial evidence. The process of awakening of reason is slow and, perhaps, if we could indicate it in every individual case, the results of this kind of statistics would be very surprising indeed.

Second, a very important supposition has to be made, one which results from I-II, 9, 4, one of the deepest considerations of the will which have ever been written in the whole of human literature. Saint Thomas there says this:

> It is necesary to posit that, in the first motion of the will, the will proceeds from the instinct of some exterior mover, as Aristotle concluded in some Chapter of the *Eudemian Ethics*.[218]

The intention of the ultimate end is the very first motion of the will. For it the "first mover of the will" is necessary, else we should have one of those "regressions into infinity" which Saint Thomas is always so careful to avoid.

This "first mover of the will" is God and it is God, but as a natural Agent, as Creator and Provider of the universe, not as supernatural. Without God we cannot explain the advance of will from the first moment of life till the end of it. That is why we pray for our children and we carefully educate them so that their first decision will be in conformity with what Saint Thomas declares to be a precept—Saint Thomas who knows a lot more precepts than the ordinary theologian of today who knows only ten commandments and thinks he can master the whole of moral life with those ten commandments—"Convert yourselves to Me and I shall be converted to you"!

## R. THE EXPOSITION OF ARTICLE 7

### *a. The State of the Question*

The state of the Question here will be exactly understood when we remember the historical occasion of this whole group of Articles. It is (as we found on the occasion of Article 5) the Lombardian question debated in the medieval schools, namely, that of *Sententiarum* liber 2, Distinctio 38,

[218] "Unde necesse est ponere quod in primum motum voluntatis voluntas prodeat ex instinctu alicuius exterioris moventis, ut Aristoteles concludit in quodam capitulo *Ethica Eudemiana*" (7, 14; 1248a 14). ST 1-2, 9, 4, in corpore; t. 2, p. 771a, ll. 8-12.

a Question inspired by Saint Augustine's problem, "Whether there be one single end of all right wills?" ⟨Here "wills" translates *voluntates*, that is, "decisions" of the will.⟩

In the *Summa theologiae* of Saint Thomas the treatment of this question as compared to his treatment of it in the *Scriptum* appears to be formalized insofar as the problem is no longer stated with respect to "all righteous wills," but with respect to "all wills." The determination "righteous," *rectae*, has been eliminated in conformity with the abstract intention of this whole Question.

Second, as I pointed out formerly, the question is divided into two. It concerns first "all wills," that is "all the volitions of a single human," and second, "all the wills of all humans." Thus the problem we now face is the last and second member of this multiform problem, "Whether there be one ultimate end of all humans?"

Inspecting nothing but the abstract formula of this problem one could imagine finding there an instance of what we should today call a "sociological" problem, namely, the problem of the deepest and last foundation of the unity of the human race as a community. For if there is a unique aspiration in humanity as such, that is, one ultimate end, why should humanity not form a community around this unique and common goal? Would this not be, according to Saint Thomas's famous definition of a community in his tract *Against those Impugning the Cult and Religion of God* 3, par. 4, "A union of many human beings in order to do some one thing in common"?[219]

Dante, (who was an eminent social and political thinker, much more aware of social and political problems than Saint Thomas ever was and, mind you, among all thirteenth-century theologians, Aquinas is evidently the keenest mind with respect to social implications of his own doctrine!) Dante, I say, has set out in his *De monarchia* to state and to answer this social and political problem. His answer is that the common and earthly goal of all humanity is to exhaust the possibilities of the agent intellect, to reduce to act all that is potentially included in the human intellect. This reduction is not possible for any single human being and therefore needs the cooperation of all. This cooperation, for Dante is the basis of the required political unity of all humanity. I am afraid that Saint Thomas will disappoint us if we expect him to treat, or even to hint at, such a problem. There is no explicit social philosophy in this Article, and in its Body, there

[219] "Est enim societas, ut dictum est, adunatio hominum ad aliquid unum perficiendum." *Contra impugnantes Dei cultum et religionem* capitulum 3, par. 4, in *Sancti Thomae de Aquino Opera omnia*, Leonine edition, t. 41, p. A 65, ll. 235-237.

are even a few hints that nothing is farther from the mind of Saint Thomas than the Dantesque problem.

*b. Arguments to the contrary*[220]

These arguments are easy to grasp. Three diversities are envisaged among human beings, the first of which (and to a theologian this is naturally the most important) is that between those who are good and those who are sinners.

The second is among human beings with different *studia vivendi*, the precise meaning of which phrase we shall investigate in a moment.

The third is that among individuals as such, for it seems that, if there is a unity among us all as to the ultimate end, this unity must have something to do with the basic and essential unity of the human race, namely, the unity of our species. The species, however, does not exist; what exists is the individual only; in existence, humans are diversified; hence, we seem to be diversified in our ultimate goal as well.

What does *studia vivendi* mean? An English translation has rendered this "pursuits in life." This translation is acceptable if it means the *human* pursuit, that is, what a human being pursues *as* a human being, not what is pursued "as a teacher," "as a student," "as a physician," or whatever one's limited and specified occupation may be. I should prefer "pursuits *of* life" instead of "pursuits *in* life.

Ramirez identifies *studia vitae* with "sorts of life," *genera vitae* and thinks them (at least insofar as good human beings are concerned) the "contemplative" life, the "active" life, and the so-called "mixed" life. This does not appeal to me because, as the Response to 2 implies, the "pursuits of life" cut deeper into one's life and diversify us more thoroughly than do these forms of life. Saint Thomas says explicitly (and this is almost a definition of what he means by "pursuits of life"),

> Diverse pursuits of life occur in humans on account of the diverse things in which the formal notion, the *ratio*, of the highest good is sought.[221]

[220] Professor Jordan has noted that, although Eschmann here scored out almost two full pages of single-spaced typing, much of it dealing with "parallel passages," lines dealing with the "Arguments" seem to have been excluded by error and thus ought to be retained in this edition. As so often is the case, Jordan's view here seems to be well founded and has been followed.

[221] "Dicendum quod diversa studia vivendi contingunt in hominibus propter diversas res in quibus quaeritur rationem summi boni." ST 1-2, 1, 7, Ad 2; t. 2, p. 717a ll. 44-47.

Examples of those things are given in the Body of the Article:

> Some have an appetite for riches...some for pleasure...some for something else....[222]

These are the "pursuits of life" and we might call them so, either in the universal sense which I pointed at awhile ago, or "modes of life." Epicureans, Stoics, Materialists, Spiritualists—all these are profoundly diversified by their different "pursuits of life." In addition, "pursuits of life" seems to be a Ciceronian notion and ought to be investigated in Cicero and in ancient Latin literature.

*c. The Body of the Article*

The Body of the Article contains two themes. First, the division of the ultimate end considered according to the formal notion of ultimate end, that is, "formally speaking." Second, the ultimate end according to that in which the formal notion of the ultimate end is found, that is, "materially speaking." The Body of the Article contains this basic division and the ensuing decision as to the point in question.

Second, it enlarges this basic decision and gives us to understand that the ultimate end, materially speaking, is to be found in truth. From the point of view of logic and monographic method, this second part overlaps the original intentions and limits of this whole Question. As we know by now, however, a *Summa* is quite different from a modern treatise in monographic form. The division of the ultimate end "formally speaking" and the ultimate end "materially speaking" is already known to us. It is a division that plays an important role in Saint Thomas's moral philosophy as well as elsewhere. It gave the constructive principle for the first Questions of the I-II; for Question 1 is precisely about the formal notion of the ultimate end, and the rest of the first five Questions in this Part, 2-5, are about "that in which the ultimate end is found." The distinction is familiar to every reader of Saint Thomas: the distinction between the "formal object" and the "material object" (or, as it also expressed, for this means the same, between the "formal object by which," *quo* and the "formal object which," *quod*). Here is a text from the *On Charity* which may be illuminating with respect to this distinction:

> ...in an object something is considered as "formal" and something as "material." What is formal in an object is that according to which the

222 "....quidam appetunt divitias tanquam consummatum bonum, quidam vero voluptatem, quidam vero quodcumque aliud." Ibidem, in corpore; p. 717a, ll. 26-29.

> object is referred to a power or a habit; the material, however, is that in which this is founded, Thus, if we speak about the object of the power of sight, its formal object is color or something of that sort; for insofar as anything is colored, to that point it is visible. The material in the object is the body to which color comes.[223]

Saint Thomas wants here to lift the veil a little for the Body of the Article would indeed be a bit meagre and uninformative had he stopped here. The following passage is most interesting since Saint Thomas gives an example of the foregoing part of the Body:

> Just as anything sweet is delectable to everyone, but for some people this is the sweetness of wine, for some the sweetness of honey or something of that sort. That sweetness, however, necessarily must be, without reservation, the "better" delectable in which one who has the best taste is most delighted. And in like manner that good must be the most complete which the one who possesses a well-disposed affection seeks as the ultimate end.[224]

Saint Thomas does not leave things at the level of the well-known principle: "On tastes there must be no disputing." He would not admit such a principle: There is good taste and bad taste; there are judges of what is good taste and what is bad taste. The judge of good taste is the one who has the best disposed organ for tasting; what delights this judge is "most delightful, without reservation, *simpliciter*." Likewise, if we ask, "What is the most complete good?" then the one to ask is the one who is wise, the *sapiens*. The Latin terms, *sapere*, "to be wise," *sapiens*, "one who is wise," *sapientia*, "wisdom," all come etymologically from a root that means "to taste." The judgment of the one who is wise will be right because that is

[223] "Sed in obiecto consideratur aliquid ut formale et aliquid ut materiale. Formale autem in obiecto est id secundum quod obiectum refertur ad potentiam vel habitum; materiale autem id in quod hoc fundatur: ut si loquamur de obiecto potentiae visivae, obiectum eius formale est color, vel aliquid huiusmodi, in quantum enim aliquid coloratum est, in tantum visibile est; sed materiale in obiecto est corpus cui accidit color." *Quaestiones disputatae de virtutibus*, De caritate, ed. P.A. Odetto O.P. (Turin: Marietti, 1940 sqq.), p. 763b.

[224] "Sicut et omni gustui delectabile est dulce, sed quibusdam maxime delectabilis est dulcedo vini, quibusdam dulcedo mellis, aut alicuius talium. Illud tamen dulce oportet simpliciter esse melius delectabilis, in quo maxime delectatur qui habet optimum gustum. Et similiter illud bonum oportet esse completissimum, quod tanquam ultimum finem appetit habens affectum bene dispositum." ST 1-2, 1, 7, in corpore; t. 2, p. 717a, ll. 29-38.

the one who possesses a well-disposed affection. Because the ultimate judgment about "the good" comes, not from the intellect (although it is the intellect that judges), but from the good will: "that which is in truth an object of wish is an object of wish to a good man, while any chance thing may be so to the bad man" says Aristotle (see the text cited below at note 226). In order to judge about the right and best ultimate end, one must be marked by virtue in the full sense of the term, "possess a well-disposed affection."

This little remark of Saint Thomas is full of suppositions and connotations that come out slowly in later Questions and Articles of the *Summa theologiae*. The proper place to discuss the whole problem is I-II, 58, 4 and 5. Moral virtue depends upon prudence, that is, on an intellectual virtue. Still, this intellectual virtue depends in its turn on moral virtue, that is, on the perfection of some habit, as Saint Thomas says in the place cited, Article 5, "...through certain habits in accord with which it becomes in some way connatural to a human being to judge rightly concerning the end."[225] In order to be good and to act well (in the sense of moral virtue) one must be prudent, in the sense of possessing the intellectual virtue of prudence. In order to be prudent, however, one must be good! A further explanation of this organism of intellectual and moral virtues pertains to later Articles, especially to those just quoted, but also those in II-II, 47, "On Prudence."

Saint Thomas is an aristocrat here. He would not go along with the greatest number, with the fifty-one per cent, to let them decide what is good, good taste, and good behavior. The fifty-one per cent surely reflect the greatest prejudices, the inconsistent, the irresponsible, the trite, and the maudlin! In Aristotle's *Ethics* the judgment of the *spoudaios*, of the "earnest, serious, weighty" human person, is of decisive value. In fact, there is no doubt but that Saint Thomas here has in mind a text from the *Nicomachean Ethics*:

> ...while those who say the apparent good is the object of wish must admit that there is no natural object of wish, but only what seems good to each. Now different things appear good to different people, and, if it so happens, even contrary things. If these consequences are unpleasing, are we to say that absolutely and in truth the good is the object of wish, but for each person the apparent good; that which is in truth an object of wish is an object of wish to the good person, while any chance thing may be so to the bad person, as in the case

[225] "...per aliquos habitus secundum quos fiat quodammodo homini connaturale recte judicare de fine." ST 1-2, 58, 5 in corpore; t. 2, p. 1016b, ll. 2-4.

> of bodies also the things that are in truth wholesome are wholesome for bodies which are in good condition, while for those that are diseased other things are wholesome—or bitter or sweet or hot or heavy, and so on; since the good person judges each class of things rightly, and in each the truth appears to him?[226]

For the good person judges everything correctly, what things truly are, they seem to him to be, and this in every department. That is why Aristotle, referring to this place in his Book 9, Chapter 4, says, "For it seems, as has been said in some way, that virtue is the measure of everything and ⟨so is⟩ the one who studies ⟨virtue⟩."[227] Saint Thomas explains in his *Exposition*:

> ...a person of virtue judges rightly of the singulars which pertain to human operations and in singular actions, the truth is apparent to this one. With respect to every ⟨moral⟩ habit, that one's are what are good and delightful. And the studious one differs perhaps mainly in this: seeing the truth in single cases, as if that one person were the rule and measure of those things.[228]

This aristocratic principle makes of Aristotelian and Thomist ethics, not merely an abstract, but a very concrete, science. It allows tradition and the concrete examples of virtuous people to enter very largely into moral teaching, as do the saints for Saint Thomas.

Nothing is particularly noteworthy about the Responses.

[226] "Rursus autem apparens bonum voluntabile dicentibus non esse natura per se bonum, voluntabile, sed unicuique quod videtur. Alii autem aliud videtur. Et sic contingit contraria.

Si autem utique haec non placent, ergo dicendum simpliciter quidem et secundum veritatem voluntabile esse per se bonum, unicuique autem, quod videtur. Studioso quidem igitur, quod secundum veritatem esse; pravo autem, quod contingit. Quemadmodum et in corporibus bene dospositis sana sunt secundum veritatem talia existentia, infirmis autem altera. Similiter autemet amara et dulcia et calida et gravia et aliorum talia singula. Studiosus enim singula judicat recte, et in singulis verum ei apparet." *Ethicorum ad Nicomachum Expositio*, Liber 3, Lectio 10; (1113a 20-31) p. 166a, 22-31.

[227] "Videtur enim, quemadmodum dictum est, mensura uniuscujusque, virtus et studiosus esse." Ibidem, 9, 4; 1166a 13; p. 578a, ll. ca 13,14.

[228] "Studiosus enim singula judicat recte, et in singulis verum ei apparet. Secundum unumquemque enim habitum propria sunt et bona et delectabilia. Et differt plurimum forsitan studiosus hoc, verum in singulis videre, quemadmodum regula et mensura existens ipsorum." Ibidem, Liber 3, Lectio 10; 1113a 30-34; p. 166b.

## 5. THE EXPOSITION OF ARTICLE 8

*a. The State of the Question*

It is evident at once that the object of this Article overlaps the proper object of the whole Question 1. The evidence of this fact lies in that Saint Thomas is unable to prove his thesis here save by anticipating a thesis which (although the reader knows it even before the *Summa theologiae* has been opened) has been carefully and on purpose kept out of the picture so far. This assertion is that God is the ultimate end of the human race and, indeed, of everything.

The demonstration of this will occupy the whole of Question 2, but in Question 1, we are supposed not to know this! We are not yet concerned with *what* is the true end of humanity, *wherein* it lies, but rather with the "formal notion" of the ultimate end, the *ratio ultimi finis*, as such, of something (which "something," to repeat), is as yet unknown to us. The state of the Question of this Article is thus not understandable from the standpoint of mere logic and of the monographic method of dealing with a problem. It is plainly and very characteristically indeed, more than anyone of the seven Articles we have seen so far, a piece of a medieval *Summa*, of a Thomistic *Summa*.

It owes its origin to two inspirations and preoccupations. First, from Article 5 on we have been moving in the orbit of that Augustinian-Lombardian problem which is known to you by now. Saint Thomas here simply follows out the line of this problem as it used to be stated and discussed in the medieval school. He wants to deal with it in a complete fashion, leaving nothing unsaid that rightly pertains to it. Therefore, the *Sentences* Book 2, Distinction 38, is the source of the present Article. (Here, as you see, the Editors finally decide to indicate this place in their noting of the parallel places, an indication which, as I have said repeatedly, comes too late and is therefore a bit out of place!)

The second inspiration of this Article is the characteristically medieval tendency to synthesize and to round out a doctrine which an author has begun to discuss. After having considered the unity of the last end in one human being, and then in all humans, it comes very naturally to the medieval mind to round out that question. Thus, Article 8 is a very noteworthy expression of medieval *Weltanschauung*, the medieval "world view." It is also a very typical piece of Saint Thomas's method of proceeding in this *Summa* and elsewhere—synthesis and unification; broad views are put forward, even if the logical sequence of the teaching is thereby somehow interrupted. Today we should put the contents of this Article in a note! The medieval writer knows nothing of the technique of notes; he has to construct a complete, full-fledged Article with "Arguments to the contrary," a "But to the contrary" ⟨with respect to those Arguments⟩, and a "Body," and all the paraphernalia. Saint Thomas here, however, dispenses with an explicit answer to the ⟨preliminary⟩ Arguments to the contrary.

*b. Sources of the Doctrine*

The indication of the sources lies in Argument 2, in the reference to Dionysius: "God turns all things to Himself as to the ultimate end."[229] It is this great topic which is carefully pursued in the *Summa contra gentiles* Book 3, Chapters 17-20, four Chapters which ought to be given as "parallel texts." Chapter 17 concludes with the two Scriptural texts which contain a doctrine equivalent to Dionysius's: "Hence it is that it is said in Proverbs 16:⟨4⟩ 'God has wrought the cosmos for His own sake'" and Apocalypse, the last Chapter ⟨22:13⟩ "I am Alpha and Omega, the First and the Last." Chapter 18 goes into a particular point of no immediate interest for us here; Chapter 19 develops ⟨it is the title of the Chapter⟩ "That all things tend to be assimilated to God," and concludes that "All things, therefore, through their motions and actions tend to the divine similitude as to the ultimate end."[230] Chapter 20 adds, "Therefore things tend to this, that they be assimilated to God, properly ⟨speaking⟩ *proprie*, inasmuch as He is good."

In its historical roots, this doctrine is Platonic and neo-Platonic; every time we meet with the idea of "participation" and of "similitude" we are in an originally Platonic context. To get closer to the sources of this doctrine you may compare the two texts of the *Enneads* (1, 7, 1 and 6, 9, 7) which have been collected by Schuster.[231] Not only has Plotinus seen and taught that all things tend to a similitude with the One and the Subsistent Good, but also that, as he says, there are two "methods" of reaching this goal, two methods of participation in the Good. The first is to become similar to It; the second is to direct one's activity towards It.

This is said by Plotinus and it is a topic often re-worked by the various neo-Platonic writers after Plotinus with whom the Latins and the Moslems came into contact, and whose teachings were transmitted to the West. When Saint Thomas wrote his *Summa contra gentiles*, the "gentiles" or "pa-

[229] See Saint Thomas, *In lib. Dionysii De divinis nominibus*, Lectio II, (12a), no. 4.112 sqq., p. 95, where the Greek text of Dionysius, PG 3 697 sqq, is given with its Latin translation.

[230] "Omnia igitur per motus suos et actiones tendunt in divinam similitudinem sicut in finem ultimum." SCG 3, 19; p. 243a.

[231] J.B. Schuster S.J., *De eudaimonia sive de beatitudine: Textus ex philosophis antiquis*, Textus et documenta (Rome: Gregorian University, 1933), pp. 33 sqq.

gans" ⟨against whom he wrote were⟩ the Moslems and when he touched (in 3, 17 sqq.) on a doctrine with which those philosophers were well-acquainted, he gave, of course, a Christian version of it.[232] The main witness of this important doctrine of Platonic and neo-Platonic origins was Dionysius who is, for the Christian Middle Ages, the all-important transmitter of this ancient tradition.

The point which I want to stress here is that Aristotle, who appears in such a prominent place at the beginning of the Body of this Article, has in reality little or nothing to do with the doctrine which is taught here. We might even say that this Aristotelian quotation rests upon a mistranslation and a misunderstanding of Aristotle. But more about this when we arrive at the Body of the Article.

Since nothing in the preliminary Arguments to the contrary needs explanation, it may be remarked that the text of Saint Augustine in the "But to the contrary" is a common Greek conviction, namely, that happiness, *eudaimonía*, is something which can come only to rational or intellectual creatures (compare *Ethics* 1, 1; 1098a 2). Beatitude essentially needs consciousness. That is why beatitude and ultimate end do not coincide perfectly and absolutely. For all creatures have an ultimate end, but beatitude is not the ultimate end of all creatures. In humans, however, the two notions coincide. I remarked in one of the former lectures that Saint Thomas during this whole Question, up to the very last Article, avoids the term "beatitude." The reason is probably that he wanted to discuss this subject under the heading of "ultimate end" which, as appears here, is not *absolutely* the same as "beatitude." Yet, relatively speaking, that is, with respect to the human ultimate end there is no difference between the two notions.

*c. The Body of the Article*

The first thing to be noted here is the quotation from Aristotle. The text of the Leonine[233] ⟨edition of the *Summa theologiae*⟩ has "ut Philoso-

[232] This identification of the "gentiles" as Moslems has not met with universal acceptance; see, v.g., discussion in J.-P. Torrell O.P., *Saint Thomas Aquinas* t. 1, *The Person and His Work*, pp. 105-107. It was defended by Eschmann in his 1955 "A Catalogue of St. Thomas's Works" for E. Gilson's *The Christian Philosophy of St. Thomas Aquinas*, pp. 385, 386: "The tradition linking the work with the Dominican missionary cause much cherished by every Dominican in the thirteenth century is still sound" (p. 385); see above, note 12.

[233] Here the term "Leonine" refers to the edition of the *Opera omnia* of Saint Thomas, begun in the last century under the authority of Pope Leo XIII; since the ST,

phus dicit in II Phys. et in V Metaph.," that is, "as The Philosopher says in the Second Book of the *Physics* and in the Fifth Book of the *Metaphysics.*" The text alleged to be from the *Metaphysics* is unidentifiable and the Ottawa editors follow the Leonine in identifying that citation as from the *De anima* 2, 4 (415b 2, and b 20). There is manifestly great confusion here.

The first possibility is that Saint Thomas has given no reference at this place; in some manuscript texts, at least in some places, such references are later additions made by the copyists.

A second is that the distinction which Saint Thomas presented here as "Aristotelian" is not Aristotelian at all. To make a long story short, let me refer to the note of R.D. Hicks in his commentary on the *De anima* at the location suggested above (Bekker 415b 2): Hicks suggests that the phrase is "in the nature of a footnote," that a similar phrase in the *Metaphysics* (1072b 2) actually interrupts the argument and that the doctrine is similar to one taught in "scholasticism."[234] Scholasticism has elaborated a similar, or rather, the same distinction which it presents as the "end of which," *finis cuius,* and the "end to which," *finis cui,* apparently the distinction Aristotle has in mind in his *Metaphysics, Physics,* and *De anima.*

The distinction made by Saint Thomas, that between "the end of which," *finis cuius,* and "the end by which," *finis quo,* is quite different from all this, but I am unable to explain how the mistake of Saint Thomas has come about, I mean a "mistake" with respect to our modern knowledge of the correct reading of Aristotle's text.[235]

The more interesting question in this regard is, was it possible for Aristotle to have thought of this distinction between the "end of which" and the "end by which"? As Michael Wittman notes in his *Die Ethik des hl.*

---

the most important of Saint Thomas's works was published more than a century ago and so could not meet the exacting standards of text-edition developed since, the "Leonine Commission" charged in our time with this project has begun to re-edit the earliest volumes, some of which are now available. The "Piana" edition to which Eschmann refers has been mentioned in the Introduction as available in a new "Ottawa" edition on which Eschmann worked when he was first in Canada and is the text cited here.

[234] "This is of the nature of a footnote" (with respect to 415b 2), R.D. Hicks, *Aristotle. De Anima* (Cambridge: University Press, 1907), p. 340.

[235] Eschmann here noted that "we do not as yet have a critical text of the medieval Aristotle." This was true in his day, but true no longer, thanks to the *Aristoteles latinus* project. Begun with two preliminary volumes on sources, "Pars prior" (Rome: Libreria dello Stato, 1939), and "Pars posterior" (Cambridge: University Press, 1955), it has produced a large number of the medieval Aristotelian Latin translations, many edited by L. Minio-Paluello at Oxford; the series continues.

*Thomas von Aquin*, there is a fundamental difference between two types of ethical doctrine. One is the Aristotelian type of a teleological and immanent ethics: the last end of life is not life itself, but a good and goods outside a human being's life by which this life is enriched. In this sort of ethics the possession of these goods is of great importance; the possession and fruition of good is exactly what is meant by the "end by which." The Aristotelian ethics did not develop or even mention this idea. It is nevertheless a Greek notion, especially developed by the Stoics, the neo-Platonists, and by the later Aristotelians.[236]

Saint Thomas's definition of human life by means of the principle of final causality comes out of this larger tradition, draws this tradition in with the Aristotelian materials of the earlier Articles. Indeed, it reaches farther than that. In this first Question Saint Thomas has achieved the first task of a science, the definition of its object: human action, human life. That object has been understood comprehensively and in many ways in relation to the end, but we are reminded in this last Article of the universal participation of all creatures in the likeness of God. The intellectual creatures that know and love God—we human creatures—are destined to much more than just a "likeness." As Thomas will say later, our end is an assimilation to God "by means of union and the giving of form," *per unionem et informationem*.[237]

## T. Conclusion[238]

With the foregoing we terminate our studies insofar as they concern the textual matter which was their basis. We have not covered a large slice of text. This, as you will agree, was owing to the extreme difficulty of our text. I have always found, and still find, that breaking into the I-II is an awfully hard task. I frankly confess that I am by no means sure that I understand every bit of text which we have tried to cover. I have never found any author of real help in this study. Modern popular authors are,

[236] Michael Wittman, *Die Ethik des hl. Thomas von Aquin...* (Munich: Max Huber, 1933), pp. 25 sqq.

[237] "beatitudo magis consistit in operatione speculativi intellectus quam practici.... Ad 1: assimilatio intellectus speculativi ad Deum est secundum unionem vel informationem; quae est multo maior assimilatio." ST 1-2, 3, 5, in corpore and Ad 1; t. 2, p. 731a, ll. 34-36, 731b, ll. 29-32.

[238] This concluding material is from two unnumbered pages marked by Eschmann, *Einlage Schluss T⟨oronto⟩ 52/53*.

of course, out of question here, but even the great commentators are deficient in this respect. The trouble with them, if I am not mistaken, is that they did their commenting on Part I. One would say that, after that, there simply was no time left for a thorough-going and complete work on the I-II. Take Cajetan. It is—once again, if I am not mistaken!—noticeable in Cajetan with regard to Part I-II, 9 and 10, that he went to those Questions with his mind made up on the basis of Part I, 82 and 84. What he had learned and meditated there was a sort of gospel to him and to which he simply bent the doctrine of Part I-II.

The fact of the sequence of Saint Thomas's books is an interesting and important factor in Thomistic studies. In the early Thomist school at the beginning of the fourteenth century they knew Thomas's *Scriptum super Sententiis* inside and out, but they knew much less about the *Summa theologiae.* Later on it was the same with regard to Part I and Part I-II. The fact is that commentaries on Part I are much more numerous and of a much more thorough-going character than are those on other Parts of the work. In this context it must also be considered that of course the I-II was written after and on the basis of the Part I.[239] In the I-II Saint Thomas did not start something afresh. With the specialization to which we are accustomed now, we are likely to overlook this fact. A through-going knowledge of the whole Part I is especially needed for that breaking into Part I-II. The really big problems of those first pages are stated and solved in the Part I with the result that Thomas here is doing nothing but recapitulating and adapting these teachings more definitely to the matter in hand. Take the issue of "action," its origin in being, of will, of intellect. These are considered three times in the Part I: first, in relation to God, second in relation to angels, third in relation to human creatures. These are taken up a fourth time in I-II under the aspect of the "return of the rational creature to God." A major mistake in reading Saint Thomas is certainly that we are inclined to take his works as an encyclopedia which we consult by bits and pieces according to our specialized interests. Obviously Saint Thomas cannot be read that way.

Now I should like to end with a recapitulation and, most of all, a synthesis of the points which we have been studying. I have a feeling that since our studies were based on the text, their coherence and their se-

[239] Here it will be useful to note the later refinements made by Boyle: "By prefacing the Secunda or "moral" part with a Prima pars on God, Trinity, and Creation, and then rounding it off with a Tertia pars on the Son of God, Incarnation and the Sacraments, Thomas put practical theology, the study of Christian man, his virtues and vices, in a full theological context...." Op. cit. p. 16.

quence might easily escape us.

The first three Articles of Part I-II, with their Prologue, may be considered as a treatise on the *subject* of a "moral Part" within the total *Summa theologiae*. The first issue to be determined in any science is its subject for, without a clearly defined subject, a science could neither know nor express what it is about, nor identify the special aspect under which its subject is considered.

First, the subject has a logical meaning. It is the "subject" of all predications to be made in the development of the science; the subject is the support of what can be called the "passivities of the subject," the *passiones subiecti*.

Still, the meaning of "subject" is not merely its logical import. It designates the very principle of that "order of what is knowable," the order of all that falls within the orbit of a science, of all items which, indeed, constitute that science.

Hence, that subject is the supreme criterion, the rule, by which all predications are weighed and measured as to their scientific value or importance in the science. This is the reason that Saint Thomas, in stressing that God is the ultimate subject of theology (Part I, 1, 7), adds that "under the formality of God, all things are considered in theology." Any proposition is "theological" when, and to the extent that, a thing is considered "under the formality of God." As subject of theology, God is the Principle of an order of knowable things. Any and every proposition in the *Summa theologiae* will deliver to us its full and complete meaning only when we remember that it is said by Saint Thomas "under the formality of God," that its full and complete meaning is theological, no matter what the surface might appear to be at a first and superficial glance. Our encyclopedic way of using the work has done much to obliterate this fact. All who have thought that, with scissors and paste, they could put together a philosophy from texts of the work have failed, and must fail. This cannot be otherwise because of the formal declaration of the author at the beginning of his work: "All things in this science are considered under the formal aspect of God." Things thus fall under this formal object "either because they are God Himself, or because they have an ordering toward God as Principle and End."[240] As we now know, the I-II (and II-II, as well as in a special way, III also) take up the aspect of God as "End" of all creation.

According to Saint Thomas in his introduction to his *Exposition of the*

[240] "Omnia autem pertractantur in sacra doctrina sub ratione Dei, vel quia sunt ipse Deus, vel quia habent ordinem ad Deum, ut ad principium et finem." ST 1, 1, 7, in corpore; t. 1, p. 7a, ll. 10-14.

*Nicomachean Ethics* "the subject of moral philosophy is human operation ordered to an end, or also, insofar as one is acting voluntarily for the sake of an end."[241] Substitute, in this definition of moral philosophy, for the word "end" the word "God," or replace "end" by "ultimate end of eternal beatitude." By this substitution, you have ⟨defined⟩ the subject of the "moral Part" of the *Summa theologiae*. Do not think that by this operation, which is easy to perform, you have left the former definition almost intact. In reality you have retraced the immensely laborious and important step from a world without Christ to a world with Christ, from heathendom to Christendom. You have repeated the transition in history which came about when humanity entered the "fulness of time."

Aristotle did not make that step and yet, Aristotle's formula may be transposed and transplanted into Christian soil where it receives a new meaning. What is Aristotelian here is, at the same time, and under different aspects, very much and very little. "Very much," namely the Aristotelian teleological orientation of ethics; ethics to be built on the rock of the principle of finality, and not all types of ethical system do thus build up their systematization. "Very little" because the concrete teleology of the *Nicomachean Ethics*, namely, the immanent, the this-worldly, teleology subsists no longer. Let us say a merely abstract moral principle, as such, is taken over into the *Summa theologiae*; there its complete and concrete meaning is totally changed.

The contribution of Article 3 to this general topic is easy to perceive. What is especially worthy of note is Saint Thomas's strong emphasis on *interiorizing* morals. The formal element of a moral act consists in something interior, not in something exterior. The exterior act is what one does; this *is* visible to everyone, or it *might be* visible to everyone; the interior act is your intention, not exactly what you do, but *for what* you do it. Your moral personality is woven together and built up with your interior acts. They count *morally*. The intention is that for which we are fully responsible morally. What counts here, in the moral order, is (to use an old and Christian expression) the "pure heart," the *cor purum*, in the eyes of God.

The interior act is also that about which we are sure as moral agents. It is that which completely and in every respect depends upon us. Our choices—they also belong to the category of "exterior" acts to which belong all acts that are not the intention of an end—are uncertain by definition since they have to be made in the unintelligible domain of concrete,

241 "...subiectum moralis philosophiae est operatio humana ordinata in finem, vel etiam homo prout est voluntarie agens propter finem." *In decem libros ethicorum Aristotelis ad Nicomachum expositio* 1, 1, par. 3, p. 3a, b.

individual realities; "the individual is inexpressible," *individuum est ineffabile,* as the scholastics say. Once an exterior act is done, it is, so to speak, thrown outside us, it becomes a part of an exterior world over which we have no longer any power. You do some good to a person with all you have and with the best of intentions. This intention is yours and remains so for all eternity; the act of helping is no longer yours: it is done. Anything might happen to it. It might be twisted around and flung back in your face. It might have consequences, not only of which you never dreamt, but also ones which you simply could not have foreseen, for which, therefore, you cannot be held accountable. "Actions exist among the particulars," *actiones sunt in particularibus* and there is that "ineffability," that mystery about them; while doing them, one cannot know all they imply.

This is behind the phrase often repeated by Christian moralists: "God looks into your heart and God weighs your intentions." Nothing less is expressed in Article 3. This Article, however, like all the ones we have read, must be considered as it were, a sketch, a first draft. The Articles are all complete and perfect in themselves, but they are such as sketches, as drawings, the essential lines of which must be filled in through time: they are "metaphysical blueprints"! So it is that Saint Thomas will later work out, for example, a certain synthesis between the moral aspect of these things, so sharply emphasized here, and their juridical aspect, a conciliation between ethics and law. The human judge cannot look into the heart. What counts with him must be our exterior and visible actions, Between morals and law, however, no radical, essential, and perpetual tension or contrariety can or ought to subsist. All this will be a matter of later discussions. Here we deal with the first and most essential aspect of our human acting, which is also its theologically most relevant aspect: our actions under the eyes of God in that "human community under God, the Ruler of the universe."

# PART TWO

## *ESCHMANNUS AEDIFICATOR*

I know of no theology that is more free and more daring than is that of Saint Thomas; neither do I know of any other which those who lay claim to it as their own have domesticated more severely.

— Etienne Gilson

...but the 'Thomists' are unwilling to take risks.

— Domingo Bañez

# Saint Thomas Aquinas O.P., the *Summary of Theology* I-II: The Ethics of the Image of God

## A. ⟨Prudential Ethics⟩

*a. The Text*

As we have seen above, Saint Thomas opens the "moral Part" of his *Summa theologiae* with a "Prologue." The whole preceding "First Part" of the *Summa* has treated of God, His nature, the Blessed Trinity, and of creation. To this treatise naturally there now succeeds a treatise on that creature which is modelled in a special way after the divine pattern. This is the human person, the "image of God." Appealing to the words of Saint John of Damascus saying that "...the human being is made to the image of God," Saint Thomas continued,

> ...after what has been said on the Exemplar, that is, on God and on the things which come forth from the divine power in accordance with the divine will, it remains that we ought to consider that His image, the human precisely as human, is also the principle of that being's own actions...as having free arbitrament and power over those works....[1]

The theme of the image of God has received careful attention in Christian tradition, especially with the Greek Fathers. In our text, the mention of Saint John the Damascene (ca 675-ca 749) bears witness to this tradition. The similitude between God and humanity, or rather the similitude which is called "image," consists in the fact that both God and the human being, the human subordinated to God, are intellectual in nature: it is intellectuality which founds liberty. God, the supreme Intellect, is the Principle of

[1] "...postquam praedictum est de exemplari, scilicet de Deo, et de his quae processerunt ex divina potestate secundum eius voluntatem; restat ut consideremus de eius imagine, idest de homine, secundum quod et ipse est suorum operum principium, quasi liberum arbitrium habens et suorum operum potestatem." ST 1-2, Prologus, t. 2, p. 710a, ll. 8-15.

His works, works which He created as having the freedom of discretionary decision and mastery over what He did. God did not create from necessity, ⟨not from⟩ a necessity imposed upon Him, nor ⟨from a situation in which⟩ He Himself is ⟨that⟩ necessity; He created from liberty.[2] Likewise and proportionally is the human person (whom the Greek Fathers were wont to exalt as "God on earth," an intellectual nature, the principle of actions as having free arbitrament over the works ⟨each⟩ one performs. Precisely as human, we do not act from necessity, ⟨from⟩ a necessity imposed upon us, but from liberty. This is the theme of the "moral Part" of the *Summa theologiae*. It treats of the image of God which we humans are, principles of our own actions, free, responsible agents; in one word, "moral" agents. In the words of Etienne Gilson, "As God creates the world, a human being constructs his life."[3]

*b. The Subject Matter of Ethics*

We should be entirely wrong if we read this very short and very unassuming declaration of Saint Thomas as a merely ornamental phrase for which a number of others could be found, replacing it, and just as adequately decorating the frontispiece of the II Part of the *Summa*. Aquinas is not the writer to indulge in merely decorative fancywork! He means what he says. He is not a preacher, but a theologian. The "human being like God," "the human as the image of God, being the principle of ⟨one's own⟩ actions and life," is Aquinas's original and comprehensive statement of his whole ethical thought; it is its resumé. It contains virtually all, ⟨each⟩ and every affirmation which we find in the 1535 Articles composing the II Part of the *Summa theologiae*. Technically speaking this "human-like-God" is the definition of the subject of the moral Part of the *Summa*.

Science is a movement, the movement of the mind toward the object. The use of the notion of "movement," of course, must be handled analogi-

[2] The sentence from "God did not create..." to "...created from liberty" is a handwritten addition from the facing page with a caret for insertion at this point; one is authorized to think Eschmann saw this as a necessary warning against the notion that God as the Good is necessitated by nature and not freely choosing, by the divine will, to be "diffusive of Itself."

[3] This text (and the following one from T.S. Eliot) are on the reverse of the facing page in Eschmann's hand, the first with an imprecise (2), presumably an indication of where he wanted it to be inserted, that is, at the title of this section which in his notes is marked "2." He cited Etienne Gilson in French: "Comme Dieu crée le monde l'homme construit sa vie" (*L'Esprit de la philosophie médiévale* [Paris: Vrin, 1948], p. 173).

cally; let no one imagine science to be a local movement toward an object lying about in some place on campus! The principle of a science is that proposition whence the science starts. This, in technical, scholastic terms, is the definition of the subject, the term "subject" here again used analogically and in the original meaning of the word: "that which is subjected" (that which lies under) the sciential inquiry. Generally speaking the movement of a science is a circular one:

> We shall not cease from exploration
> And the end of our exploring
> Will be to arrive where we started
> And to know the place for the first time.
>
> — T.S. Eliot, *Little Gidding*[4]

In other words, science "turns about" its subject, always staying with it, always clinging to it. Science begins with an as yet vague definition of the subject, a definition which, however, is comprehensive and correct: it hits the point. Science then moves on toward greater and greater precision, toward fuller and scientifically justified knowledge of this same subject. Science follows the natural movement of our intellect, from more universal to less universal, from simple to composite notions. This is the movement, the work of synthesis and construction: the material of a science is found and collected by analysis; its sciential form and shape are the work of synthesis.

Evidently, the definition of the subject is of decisive importance to a science. By it the science establishes and defines itself. Every movement is that which it is thanks to the term toward which it moves. In other words, when defining the subject, a scientist indicates what in that discipline one talks about, what, through such discourse, one *will be* talking about. It is highly recommendable, to anyone about to open the mouth, to make such a declaration and, not only to make it, but also to abide by it!

The starting point of a science may in fact be taken at entirely different points. Since this starting point is at the same time the lever to pry up the whole science, differences at the beginning will bring about entirely different results. It is the initial step which determines everything that is to be said in a science, including its very organization and its method. The definition of the subject in a science is the source of intelligibility for everything that is said in the body of the science. The declaration of our Prologue will be understood in its proper significance if we consider it as

[4] Eschmann has not given a caret for insertion of these lines of Eliot; handwritten below the Gilson text of note 3, its location at this point is an editorial decision.

the source, pouring forth the light of intelligibility upon the whole "moral material," the whole *materia moralis*. Human acts, human life, are "human" as well as "moral" (which means one and the same thing!) because, and inasmuch as, they are the actions and the life of a human creature, the principle of ⟨that creature's⟩ actions, of the human being as image of God. That is why Saint Thomas says and repeats that the moral genus (we might translate: "the area where we speak of 'morality'") begins where we first discover ourselves as principles of our actions, as humans, ⟨as⟩ images of God. Take another starting point of moral consideration, say for instance, with our modern ⟨scholastic⟩ moralists: the area of morality begins with submission to law—and the absolutely *first* ethical intelligibility will be different. This means that another notion of what a human being is, an entirely different anthropology, is now the foundation of your discourse. I have no qualms in stating that the difference between Saint Thomas and "the Thomists" is a different notion of the human being, which of course at the same time springs from, and leads back to, a different notion of God, an entirely different philosophy and theology. If you take a starting point other than his, you may fill up your discourse, or the pages of your book, with quotations of Thomas Aquinas; this will not conceal the fact that indeed you are talking about something different from that which Saint Thomas is talking about. It would have been easy for Saint Thomas to say *something like this* at the beginning of his Moral Part:

> After, in our First Part, we have considered God, the cause of all creatures that proceeded from His power through the free decision of His will, it now remains for us to study the human being inasmuch as that being depends on God for the ruling and direction of that being's life and actions, just as, and because, a human being depends on God for existence.

A text of Holy Scripture, or of a Father of the Church, could easily be found to decorate this declaration. This would have been a prologue of Moral Theology. I can, if you wish, show you that it, or something like it, has been written a hundred and more times by way of a prologue or preface to works of Moral Theology or ⟨to works⟩ of a moral-theological character and outlook.

Most certainly there will be, in Aquinas's ethics, talk about the dependence of the human being on God and on His representatives on earth, in the right place, in the right manner, and to the right extent. But an *ethics* which is *founded* upon the fact that the human being is God's image, and is the self-causative principle of that being's own actions, has nothing in common with an *ethics founded* upon the idea and the fact of human dependence. The former ethics will say that the human being has a moral vocation (which is also the total *human* vocation) because a human being is great; the other because a human being is small. We must choose, if not between the grandeur and the smallness of the human being—there is no "choice" here—but certainly between one or the other type of ethics. In the ethics of smallness and dependence, evil will be defined as an infraction of the constitutional charter of servitude; in the ethics of grandeur and liberty, it will be, in the first place, an evil direction which the agent voluntarily gave to that agent's own actions. In one type of ethics morality will be human perfection and the imperfection will be seen, and consequently mastered, in the light of that perfection. In the other, morality will be human imperfection and the perfection is left to the "professor for free mortifications." In one type we shall meet with the mature person, corporally and spiritually, but we shall also meet with the child who *by definition* is *growing up*. In the other type we shall deal with children only and such as *by definition never grow up*! If they did, this "ethics" would lose its meaning and its bread and butter. In one type, a human person tends to the maximum; in the other, is satisfied with the minimum, but does not even see what the minimum really is since the line cannot be drawn without the whole surface being there on which to draw a line. When[5] someone makes an error, you will not put that person straight by simply saying, "You are mistaken." You must tell the one who has made the mistake what the truth is. When we are on a wrong road and someone tells us, "You are on the wrong road," this is good and serviceable, but less good and less serviceable than if we are told what the right road is and how to get to it. The ethics of the maximum *includes* the minimum, the ethics of the minimum, "of itself," *per se*, excludes the maximum and often it does so for all practical purposes also.

### c. *"Moral" and "Morality" in Thomas Aquinas*

It will be useful at this point strongly to insist on the complete difference of the notions of "moral" and "morality" in Thomas Aquinas from that of our usual "Thomism." To illustrate this difference I could (as I first had in mind to do) introduce the prologue written by the so-called "Salamantine theologians" for their treatise on the goodness and the badness of human action, a prologue found in a commentary on the I-II. But I think I can make things clearer when, instead of reading a text of the baroque age speaking a baroque language, I turn to a text of the twentieth century, written in our own language. I take W.G. De Burgh, "From Mora-

[5] The text from "When someone makes..." to "...for all practical purposes also" is written by hand on the reverse of the facing page with a caret for insertion.

lity to Religion," the author's Gifford Lecture delivered in 1938.[6] De Burgh used to be Professor of Philosophy in the University of Reading; he is a Protestant and a philosopher steeped in the ethics of Kant.

The author contrasts (p. 86) the action done from a desire of good as such, and the action regulated by the consciousness of obligation. In the first, there clearly is "the aspect of spontaneity, aspiration, harmonious self-expression"; in the second, whatever there is, or may be, of desire is "the desire to obey a constraining authority." The first is an aspiration after an ideal. The author says of it,

> If this aspiration after an ideal were present everywhere in full measure, and if it were capable of unbroken sustainment, there would be no place left for **moral** [!] action. Morality, in the modern sense, is not to be found here. Morality "is a form of practical experience," and it is essential to grasp it in the making by placing ourselves in the position of the man acting or about to act. Hence the terms that most fitly express moral experiences are "ought" and "duty" rather than "good." A man about to act does not naturally ask himself, "What is it good for me [!] to do in the present situation?" but "What ought I to do? What is my duty?" [Note this carefully: the "for" containing the utilitarian aspect of the good is smuggled in; and what the author is really talking about is the "useful good," the *bonum utile*, not the good as such.] The terms good and bad imply a certain indirectness and detachment from the immediate practical issue or, to put it more positively, a contemplative, theoretic interest that is **foreign to moral** experience in the strict and proper sense. We use them in speaking of a man's life and character as a whole, or of his general course of conduct when we quit for the moment the standpoint of direct moral judgment and adopt the attitude of a spectator contemplating what is already done. To say of a man that he is a good man, really is a theoretical judgment, it is not a practical and therefore moral judgment since it does not concern the actualized acting....

In an Appendix to some of the chapters, the author speaks of his personal experience:

[6] William George De Burgh, *From Morality to Religion,* being the Gifford Lectures, delivered at the University of St. Andrews, 1938 (London: MacDonald & Evans, 1938). This work is not available to us, but Eschmann's two long citations are undoubtedly accurate.

> A life worth living has always presented itself to me as a task to be faced rather than as an ideal end to be desired and enjoyed. The thought of good has not, of course, been wholly absent, especially in later years, but the dominant principle before my mind has been, and still is, that of duty. Even in religion, a sense of duty towards God is always in evidence. This, of course, is not to claim that I habitually followed duty rather than inclination; the reverse would be far nearer the truth. But even when inclination has been on this side of duty, the distinction has always been present to consciousness.... This explains why I have always felt a strong leaning towards the moral doctrine of Kant...rather than that of Aristotle.

This last remark can lead us back to Thomas Aquinas for there is no doubt but that Thomas Aquinas had a strong leaning indeed toward Aristotle. Kant, on the other hand, depends, in the general statement of the moral question and consequently in his fundamental notion of morality, on the religious, Protestant, tradition. This tradition in turn, as to this precise point, namely, the statement of the moral problem, is identical with the religious Catholic tradition of the Counter-Reformation period. That morality begins with obligation and the consciousness of obligation is a conviction universal in modern times where more and more we have forgotten the old Greek tradition of Plato and Aristotle. It is this conviction which simply does not work in Saint Thomas, neither in the Kantian "autonomous" form of duty for duty's sake, nor in the older, heteronomous, theological form of duty *because commanded.* Stick to this conviction?—you will not be able to understand one single word in the II Part of Thomas Aquinas! I have had the experience myself; I have been sitting over the II Part for many years and it has been a book sealed with seven seals (Revelation 5:1) to me until I got rid of this conviction in which I had been educated, like (I suppose) everybody else. With Saint Thomas, the first thing in ethics is the desire for good as such, which is the desire for human natural and supernatural perfection, that is, the perfection of the moral agent, the moral personality, the image of God. We shall have ample occasion, I hope, to develop this idea more and more distinctly. Here I wanted to put a strong emphasis on the difference. Every time I use the words "moral" and "morality" from now on, unless otherwise indicated, they are identical with human perfection, the ideal, the perfection of the human as human, the maximum realization of the human being's human virtualities.

#### *d. The Scriptural Foundation of Aquinas's Ethics*

The scriptural foundation of Aquinas's ethics, as you can see, is the first chapter of the Bible where, in the recital of creation, it is written,

> And God said, "Let us make man in our image, after our likeness" (Genesis 1:26)

The prologue of the II Part is the result of accurate theological reflection; it expresses nothing but the very idea of "the human" as revealed to us in Holy Scripture.

But does not Holy Scripture also, and often, insist on God's absolute sovereignty and authority to which absolute submission and obedience are due? (I seem to have seen this question many times in your eyes!) Did not, therefore, Saint Thomas make a more or less arbitrary selection from among the texts of Holy Scripture? Did he not simply suppress those that urge obedience, and stress, or even overstress, those that exalt liberty?

I do not think so; I for one am satisfied that a strict and convincing theological proof can be, and has been, presented (a) that no arbitrary selection, but a deep understanding of *all* the texts of Holy Scripture, is at the bottom of this prologue and (b) that, not the theologian on his own human authority, but Holy Scripture itself and thus divine authority, indicate this understanding.

The proof of this is given by Thomas Aquinas in his theology of the three laws, namely, the natural law, the divine positive law of the Old Testament, and the divine positive law of the New Testament, laid down by our Lord Jesus Christ. It is in view of precisely this proof that later on we shall study Aquinas's teaching on law and on the laws. I shall, therefore, postpone the proper discussion of this point until later.

Here only a few remarks. Why is it, and what does it mean, that in Saint Thomas's ethics we have to wade through 97 Questions with well over 500 Articles before God, the Legislator, is introduced to us? But did not humanity also go through a history of God only knows how many thousand years, from the creation of Adam until the legislation on the mountain Sinai in the time of Moses, till God laid down the law? Saint Thomas (II-II 98, 6) divides with Saint Paul, the history of humanity into three periods, (a) the times of Natural Law when all humans (like the "gentiles" to whom Paul preached) had "no law, but did [in principle] by nature the things of the Law" as is written in Romans 2:14; (b) the times of the Old Law, especially, but not only, of course, the Decalogue which in the main is a codified part of the Natural Law, a writing down of a part of the unwritten law, and a writing down which was necessary for specific historical reasons, as we learn from the Bible; and (c) the New Law, an unwritten Law again, revealed by our Lord Jesus Christ.

Now the point for us here is to see and to keep in mind that Natural Law is an *unwritten*, that is, a non-codified, law. It is not a code of law, but a vital principle. It is nature itself that is, more precisely, rational nature; it is reason understood as the power of reasoning. We must get rid, once and for all—I have pointed this out already, I repeat, it and I will repeat it over and over again hoping, perhaps against hope, that the point may finally get across—we must get rid of a sort of myth which may linger in our minds, but surely would be a crude and clumsy disfigurement of the truth. The first human, we might think, or rather imagine, was at first free, that is, under no law; roaming about in the woods and having a grand time. Then, thereafter, God grabbed him by the neck saying, "This cannot go on forever; You have got to be moral or else!" And God imposed the Natural Law upon him. From that day on the fun was over and morality started; Adam was bound and gagged. Reading certain moral theologians and ethicians of our schools I am not sure whether this is not, after all, the myth they do have in their minds, whether they know it or not. It has certain affinities with certain ideas widely held in the seventeenth and eighteenth centuries which were the times of the origin of moral theology.

Natural Law is nature. Natural Law is not an established, a posited law, not even a law posited by way of nature if by this we mean to say that there was a first nature (first either genetically, in the order of time, or even logically, in the order of essentialities) and then, thereafter (again, either genetically or even logically) there came the law of nature. We are under a typical puerile illusion if we imagine the origin of morality to have taken place in the meeting of a lord and a vassal, an authority and a subject, as though for morality to be it would be necessary to have first, a nature, and then, thereafter, either genetically or even logically, an authority ruling and commanding its movements. I am not speaking of my own fancy-work; we read, black on white, in a book published in the year 1960, this sort of apple-tree-ethics which is presented to us as the authentic thought of Thomas Aquinas. The Creator did not create a heavy body and then, thereafter, either genetically or even merely logically, command it to gravitate toward the center of gravity! The Creator did not first create plants and animals, and then, thereafter, either genetically or even logically, establish for them the law to reproduce their species. The Creator did not create Adam and then, thereafter, either genetically or even logically, command him to do the work of man. All this is an illusion and it is an illusion coming about when lawyers (incompetent lawyers at that) get hold of the notion of "natural law." ⟨Positive law⟩, Law as something "posited," even posited by the divine Lawgiver, is posterior to the creation of natures, especially the creation of rational natures. Posited law, even the divine posited law, the act of God the sovereign Lawgiver, cannot be conceived or made intelligible unless it is seen as a law given to rational creatures, and according to their created, rational, nature. Even grace does not destroy nature; it perfects nature. *God is Legislator as Creator and His being Creator is presupposed to His being Legislator.* God's legislation is given to the *image of God* to instruct, to help, to guide us, especially to our supernatural end. There we have the explanation why Saint Thomas's ethics is that of the image of God and not, right at the beginning and throughout, the ethics of subordination and obedience.

As a theologian brought up on the Gospels, Saint Thomas recognizes in God our Father. This does not attenuate the fact of God's legislative authority and the fact of our submission, but it puts the emphasis elsewhere, namely, on the relationship between father and child, on the communication of life, and on the dwelling together of friends. This evangelical idea is primary in Aquinas's ethics and causes it to be an ethics that does not start from obligation. It also is the reason why Thomas succeeded in washing the pure gold of ethics clean of gangue, the worthless rock that had accumulated around it through primitive juridical and sociological associations. Surely, God is Sovereign, Master, and King, but He is all this *as* Creator, which means that He is someone other than, and infinitely more than, what we think a sovereign, a master, or a king to be. Saint Thomas does not indulge in any puerile fancies in his theology. Surely God, better than any other master, may hold us in servitude, but this supposes that we exist and, existing as He created us, we are His image. Then, in His mercy, He might conclude a covenant with us. This, philosophically speaking, is possible. The reality of it, however, and the terms under which it is made, are a matter of our sacred history. Meanwhile, no matter whether there is, or there is not, such a covenant (which the theologians will have to study by having recourse to revelation) meanwhile, I say, morality is founded. It is there at the very moment, and through the very fact, of creation as Holy Scripture says, "Let us make man in our image after our likeness" (Genesis 1:26).

*e. The Teleology of Human Life*

At this point of our considerations, my first plan for these lectures implied a section on the blueprint, so to speak, of the whole II Part, that is, the moral Part of the *Summa*. This study was to be undertaken with the intention of showing that every step taken in this work was indeed an unfolding and development, a deepening precision, of what Aquinas in the present Prologue had announced to be the subject of his investigations, namely the human image of God, the human master of what that human does. I have given up this plan. Too many things would need explanation and this explanation could not be given in a few words. My intention now is to take a plunge, as it were, into the very midst of Saint Thomas's ethics, which is his doctrine on prudence.

One preliminary note, however, is necessary. The doctrine of prudence, like the whole of Saint Thomas's ethical thought, is founded on, and every detail of it is intimately connected with, the metaphysics of the end, the *finis*, and that which is for the end, in one word, with the metaphysics of final, teleological causality. Now great misunderstandings have from olden times surrounded this metaphysical doctrine. I am not the one to say that it is the easiest thing in the world to understand; it is not. Right at the beginning of the II Part when Aquinas affirms that the human act is for an end, and for *the* end, that is, the last end which fully realizes the notion of end—right here lies one of the most difficult problems of all metaphysics. My remarks will as far as possible abstain from professional analysis.

I wish in the first place to protect notions and teachings from a misunderstanding which easily creeps into our mind when we read Saint Thomas's texts. What we have to guard against is a merely materialistic, an "industrial," understanding of the teleological relation between the end and that which is *for* an end. This misunderstanding has its origin in the world of technique and industry where, indeed, the teleological relation is most obvious, but at the same time most confusing, if we try to transpose it onto a field which is not ⟨a field of⟩ technical or industrial practice. In the field of this practice, means are nothing but tools, lying about in a chest. We take one because it is best adapted for "achieving," "obtaining," the end we intend. We use this screw, or this hammer, because it best fits the work we are doing. Means and ends are purely external one to another. No inner, natural and necessary connection obtains between the hammer and the nail that is to drive it in the wall. We can obtain this effect by other means. Moreover, means, in this technical, industrial, context are something in themselves indifferent. They derive all their value, all their good, from the end they further, as the builder's scaffolding does from the value of the building to be erected. Means here are useful and all they are is to be useful. Let us not pretend that, when thinking of the teleological nexus, even in a religious way, we are at once innocent of the fault of this kind of materialistic and, to use the ⟨most precise⟩ word, "utilitarian" thinking. The last end is, let us say, to go to heaven or even (here again I am looking at my friends, the moral theologians!) to keep out of hell. The means are to perform certain actions, or rather (and mostly) to omit the performance of certain actions. If, in our mind, more or less the *only* connection between this end and these means is the fact of reward or punishment, we are indeed in the midst of a merely materialistic, utilitarian, industrial, technical trend of thinking. I do not say that this sort of motivation is bad, morally speaking. Morally, it too has its place, its function. But surely it is not a way of thinking on which to found ethics.

Now what we must learn and keep in mind is that this understanding of the teleological nexus is wrong. There is no philosopher worth his salt who would have limited his metaphysics of the end, and that which is for the end, to this vulgar understanding. This I say in spite of certain appearances. By this I mean the fact that our great philosophers, Plato, Aristotle, Augustine, Thomas Aquinas, and others, sometimes speak a language which to the uninitiated would appear to be the language of the technical, industrial, practice. Let us consider Thomas Aquinas.[7] In ⟨his⟩ philosophy we distinguish between "transient" and "immanent" actions. Transient actions are such as pass over into matter; immanent actions are such as remain in the agent. Transient actions are a perfection of the matter; immanent actions are a perfection of the agent. Sawing a piece of wood is a transient action perfecting the matter, that is, the wood; knowing, loving, seeing, and so on, are immanent actions perfecting the agent, that is, bringing about an entitative perfection in the agent, an increase in the agent's very being.

Now ethics deals exclusively with immanent actions. Even if ethics should deal with a transient action, for instance, with economic activity, it deals with it, not inasmuch as it is a transient action, but inasmuch as it is a human action, it too is an immanent action. It follows from this that every time I use the example of a transient action in order to clear up an ethical truth, I expose myself to misunderstanding because I fix the students' attention on a field in which there is no moral, human action at all, or I fix their attention on a merely useful thing or good, which also does not fully contain the idea—I indulge in coarse utilitarianism. The end, then, as it is understood in ethics, is not something to be done, like putting a nail in a wall, nor are the means a tool with which to do this, for instance, a hammer. The end is rather to be something and the means are constituent parts of this being.[8] They participate in the very nature and dignity of the end (the *per se* good) which is that *it* is sought after for its own sake, and not for the sake of something else. The means are the end

[7] At this point Eschmann has included a few words in handwriting: "Here I am again at the job of criticizing. The cat doesn't seem to be able to quit catching mice. But I'm glad..." In his typed lecture material there follows a full page controverting the views of a modern writer whose "Thomism" seemed wrong-headed to Eschmann. This page has been omitted from the present section, "Eschmann the Builder"; the pugnacious side of Eschmann has been presented sufficiently in the first set of texts by "Eschmann the Warrior."

[8] Here the sentence, with a caret for insertion, has been written by hand on the page facing this typed material.

*in fieri*, "in the process of becoming," of being realized, actualized, brought into existence. The end is a perfection, a form of that for which it is the end; only here this form is considered, not in its static condition, but in its dynamic function.

It is always the perfection of philosophical thinking to take account of analogies. What I miss in not a few of our current works on ethics is an almost complete lack of the art of moving through the infinite richness of reality with refined, formal, and analogous thinking. If I am not mistaken, the reason for this is that the authors address themselves to the millions.[9] The millions do not think with formal precision nor with analogical differentiation. It is, I suspect, a wrong idea perhaps to want to make accessible to the millions the thought of Thomas Aquinas who excels in the perfection of philosophical thinking.

The teleological idea should be conceived in the way the Greek word *telos*, "end," leads us for, from the word *telos* is derived *teleios*, "marked by having reached the end, the goal" which means "perfect." Human actions are not tools whereby we "acquire," "obtain," something else, as we obtain for our money the goods, hats, and shoes we desire or need. They are rather realizations of our human perfection and in this human perfection consists our beatitude, the beatitude of the image of God. Human actions are, I say, realizations of our beatitude and I must add, they are *partial* realizations, not total realizations. Still, even being partial realizations, they are realizations nevertheless. Saint Thomas expresses this in the important notion of "participation" as he uses it in Part I-II, 2, 8.[10] All created goods are participations in, shares of, the Uncreated, Subsistent, Good which is God, our perfect beatitude.

Hence, good human actions, good human life, which it is incumbent

[9] Here Eschmann's "authors" who "address themselves to the millions" seem to be the modern ethicians including, and even especially the "Thomist" ethicians with their manual text-books. The "millions" doubtless coincided in Eschmann's view with the *polloi* of the ancient Greek philosophers, incapable of following elevated philosophical discourse.

[10] This is discussed above in the first set of Eschmann's class lectures; see above the presentation of the last (the 8th) Article of the first Question of ST 1-2; it has been suggested that a perhaps more pointed reference might be to ST 1-2, 2, 8: "...nihil potest quietare voluntatem hominis, nisi bonum universale. Quod non invenitur in aliquo creato, sed solum in Deo, quia omnis creatura habet bonitatem participatam. Unde solus Deus voluntatem hominis complere potest." Here it may be remarked that in Eschmann's first set of lectures he was concerned to show the content of ST 1-2, 1, 1-8 in its role as introduction to the "moral Part" of the great *Summa*.

on us to live, is not in the utilitarian and industrial sense of the word a means to, but a constituent of, beatitude. If it were simply such a means, it would have no value in itself and this, clearly, would be diminution of the dignity of the human being as the image of God. Good human life *is* our beatitude, as much of it as we can expect in this life!

It is one of the most astonishing and the most marvellous achievements of Thomas Aquinas under a historical, as well as under a philosophical, point of view to have shown that the otherness and the absolute transcendency of God, as Christian doctrine teaches it, are perfectly compatible with this idea of beatitude which, in its far-away origins, is Greek. Aquinas does this in his teaching about the beatific vision which is an intellectual union with God, the highest and most intimate type of union, a fusion, but not a confusion, of God and the intellectual creature. Even Saint Thomas's doctrine has been criticized as some sort of utilitarianism. It is true that many commentators of Aquinas are utilitarians pure and simple. To say that human actions are "tools for making beatitude" is utilitarianism, and I would say that it is even a worse species of this very bad and primitive philosophy than, for example, the utilitarianism of Bentham or John Stuart Mill. We must get rid of the idea that our last end is something we "get out of" something else. When Saint Thomas says that the end is the "good" life, and that this is a *finis debitus* (we ought to live this life), he does not mean we ought to do this because we shall get something out of it. He means just what he says, that it is itself its own reward. If morality could be destroyed by converting right action into the clever choice of means to an another end, a non-moral end such as pleasure or, for that matter also, power, physical existence, and so on, then I am afraid practical reason will have abdicated in favor of some irrational will, and "right," in the last instance, is pronounced to be independent of moral good. This "ethics" is indeed a purely utilitarian ethics!

Another point, connected with what I have just said, must be mentioned. It belongs to the query as to what Saint Thomas means when he insists in the first Question that a human being acts, not only for *an* end, but for *the* end, namely, that last end which fully realizes the notion of "end." What is wrong with the utilitarian is also that such a philosopher is a believer in what we may call an "atomic" conception of life, meaning a conception wherein the agent's human and moral life is pulverized into a succession of momentary acts with no inner connection between them. The value of each act, being a mere utility, is to be measured by itself and its momentary usefulness in view of that which we expect to be its result. That is why we have a world of difficulties in trying to understand Aquinas in the first thesis of his ethics, namely, that a human being always acts for the last end. ⟨As seen in the first section⟩ our moralists have gone to work on this and came out with long dissertations on exactly what intention is needed in order to conform to this law (for they interpret everything in ethics as "law"). Explicit or implicit? Habitual or merely interpretative? In the thought of Saint Thomas the problem does not arise in these terms.

What he really means may be clarified by an example taken from the field of aesthetics. The "industrial" conception of ends and means which are purely external to one another is as much out of place in ethics as it is in aesthetics. Take a poem. The mastery of Milton over the rhythms of his verse is, of course, not a mere "means" to the production of poetry; it is a constituent of the poem's beauty. For all that, a great poem is a typical example of the actualization of one end, of one conscious and coherent purpose. It is not only that the poem, when contemplated as a whole, is felt to form a unity in which every part but the *finale* has a forward-looking reference to that which is to follow, but further, that the poet, to do the best work, must be profoundly conscious of this reference and be controlled by it throughout the poetic procedure. If the poet loses sight of it (as a poet sometimes does) then there is a fall into over-elaboration of parts in the poem on their own account; the work becomes episodic. A well-wrought poem is, from the first to the last, a realization of one end, an embodiment of one purpose.

Now the same is true of a really well-lived life. It is a life in which every interval looks before and after. A great work of art, and likewise a nobly lived life, have a sort of forward-looking unity, a meaning, which is more analogous to the functioning of a living organism than to the construction of a dwelling house or of an airplane. Let us not overdo the example. It is, I think, better than any example taken from the realm of technical activity. Still, it is only an example. Saint Thomas's doctrine, especially in that first Question of Part I-II, which lies like a roadblock before the uninitiated reader, cutting off understanding, is one of the most difficult pieces in the whole *Summa theologiae*. Saint Thomas's doctrine really goes deeper. It proceeds on the metaphysical level of a "transcendental" notion, namely, the notion of "Good" as such, which is coextensive with the notion of "Being" as such. It is indeed in regard to the will and the practical intellect exactly what being as being is in regard to the speculative intellect. Here, however, I must stop. It was sufficient for my purpose at the moment to remove as well as possible some misunderstandings which, in the long run, might have proved fatal. The discussion of the metaphysical foundations of this ethics will at any rate be easier, I think, after we are better acquainted with some of its substantial doctrine. Let us proceed to Saint Thomas's teaching on prudence.

## B. The Philosophy of Prudence

### *a. A Semantic Note*

In classical Latin and Greek, the word *prudentia*, "prudence," and the corresponding *phronesis*, designate an intellectual moral virtue. In our languages certain traces of this intellectual moral character are still preserved. Our words "prudent," "prudence," "prudential," originally Latin words have undergone the same semantic devalorization which was, and is, generally the lot of the whole vocabulary of intellectual terms. "Intelligence," the "intellect," in the philosophical sense of those words have not much currency among ordinary people. The only use these people normally have for these things is to admire their technical proficiency. According to the *Oxford English Dictionary* there are two meanings of the words "prudent," "prudence," "prudential."

First, they signify the ability to discern the most suitable, politic, or profitable action, sagacity in adapting means to an end. There is in this description an element which, as we shall see, also appears in Aristotle's and Saint Thomas's definition, namely, the ability, the sagacity in adapting means to an end. The relation between means and end is fundamental in teleological and axiological ethics, but it ought not to be understood in any pragmatic and materialistic fashion. In ethics, means are not tools nor is end the purpose for which such tools are used. Nail and hammer in putting the first into a wall is the popular idea of the relation between means and end. This is not wrong absolutely, but is a very rudimentary and primitive idea, an idea missing the philosophical level which is that of analogous differentiation. The common usage of the words "prudent" and so on reflects this limited idea, as does also the moralists' usual notion: "end"—keep out of hell; "means"—don't commit a mortal sin!

Here are a few of the examples given in the *Oxford English Dictionary*, the "OED." From the year 1642: "What is prudentially and politickly fit for the good and the preservation of the whole"—the vicinity of "prudent" and "politic," of "prudently" and "politically" is noticeable. Politics, of course, all through modern times, is a mere technique. In fine, it is the cleverness, the smartness to get no matter what for no matter what purpose. From 1652: A book was published with the title *Arcana aulica*, or *Manual of Prudential Maxims for the States-man and the Courtier.*[11] From 1770: ⟨*Junius Lett.*

[11] The 1971 edition of the work Eschmann cited (from an earlier edition, of course) does not present the 1642 illustration; and the last word of the alternative title for the 1652 work is as given here, not as Eschmann copied it, "Courtesan" with its current derogatory meaning.

xii (1820) 217⟩ "Here, too, we trace the little prudential policy of a Scotchman." "Prudentialism" was (and, perhaps, still is) a word designating either Utilitarianism pure and simple, or some of the worst features of it. From 1866 a critic says, "I have called utilitarianism superficial because it rests so much on prudentialism." (That is, we may say, on prudential considerations.) "Prudentials" in New England were matters that could be dealt with on a lower level of the given administration without need to go to the summit (to use a word familiar to us). In 1646 (from Massachusetts): "Every township, or such as are deputed to order the prudentials thereof, shall have power to present to the Quarter Court all idle and unprofitable persons." In 1774: "Agreed with Frederick Earnest to take care of the kitchen and inspect and conduct the prudentials thereof." (That is, the pots and pans!) Still, in 1891 it was said, "The condition of the College is such as well might have led anyone to hesitate to take the helm." (Presumably, on a "prudential" motive.)

The second meaning of these words is the ability to stay out of trouble or danger. Prudent rules are safety rules. Prudence is cautiousness. This is a signification frequently employed by the moralists as might be expected. From 1850 the Dictionary quotes: "Prudence, the soul's stern sacristan" (It would be easy to confirm this usage by a dozen or so quotations from modern moralists: "Mathematical prudentials—the cautious mathematicians"; I suppose these moralists have been working against all the moral prudentials in these lectures by standing up to Saint Thomas's uncloaked *appetitus naturalis intellectualis*!) And from 1898: "It is better far to have the hero with all his drawbacks than to have nothing in human life that rises above prudentialisms, commonplace and humdrum."

*b. How Is Prudence Introduced in the* Nicomachean Ethics?

In the *Nicomachean Ethics,* Aristotle begins speaking about virtue in the First Book. Of virtue, The Philosopher says, we cannot speak unless we know first how the human soul is constituted. The soul is represented as consisting of two parts, a rational and an irrational. The first part, which is reason, will get attention later in the work. As regards the irrational part, Aristotle here suggests a subdivision. There are two parts of it; the first of these is the vegetative which has nothing rational about it at all. It is that which does not and cannot partake of reason. Vegetative growth and the functions of nutrition cannot, in themselves and directly, receive a rational imprint. The second is that from which spring the appetites and desire in general; and this part does in a way participate in reason, seeing that it is submissive and obedient to it.

To this division of the soul corresponds a parallel division of the virtues. There are intellectual virtues, that is, those which are in the reason and concern reason, and there are moral virtues, that is, those which concern the appetite. This division is important: it governs the whole Aristotelian doctrine on virtues.

Moral virtues are greatly esteemed by Aristotle. They are properly human values. They are even a constituent of *eudaimonia*; from Book Two to Book Five Aristotle describes a great number of these virtues and his elucidations are the best treatise on human values in mankind's universal literature. Aristotle's absolutely unique attempt to set up and carefully to analyze a complete table of human values has been exploited by many ancient philosophers and, of course, very fully by Thomas Aquinas. After Thomas the learned world got interested in obligation and rudimentary ethics. Only in the present century, the interest in Aristotelian axiology has been revived by a philosopher whom I mentioned on another occasion, namely, Nikolai Hartmann. Aristotle was the first to discover that moral virtues consist in a "mean," in Latin *medium*, whence the old saying, "Virtue stands in the middle," *virtus in medio*, "Virtue is in the 'mean'." This means neither the mediocre average nor has it anything to do with a mathematically or statistically computed middle point. Take whatever virtue, you will notice two extremes contrary to it, corrupting it, the one an excess, the other a defect. Too much and too little alike destroy the perfection, as it is in an artistic masterpiece. Goodness, therefore—and Aristotle adds moral goodness which is more exact and of a higher character than art—is the action that hits the mean.

Here prudence is mentioned for the first time in the *Nicomachean Ethics* (2, 6). Virtue, Aristotle says (1106b 36) is a disposition of the soul in reference to our deliberate choices (that is, the act of choosing, the election). It hits the mean relative to us (that is, that which in the circumstances of our concrete, personal acting is the mean, avoiding both excess and defect. *This mean is determined by reason and according to how a prudent person would establish it.* Reason and the prudent person are not two criteria, but one and the same, differently envisaged, once in the abstract, the other time in the concrete. Saint Thomas fully agrees with Aristotle and often repeats his statement. However, as we shall see, on the basis of post-Aristotelian philosophy, and especially the philosophy of Saint Augustine and the Christian tradition, Saint Thomas goes deeper, even to the core of the matter. Saint Thomas never took the characteristic turn of interpretation which was to come to the fore in the sixteenth century.[12] In cases

[12] Here Eschmann permitted himself a few lines on his sixteenth- (and twentieth-) century *bêtes noires*; they have been dropped from this section in which our author is a "builder," but their omission deprives the reader of nothing not seen

such as this I am inclined to think that our vital question is not, perhaps, so vital a question of the philosopher we read. Neither Aristotle nor Saint Thomas are in the habit of avoiding vital questions that spring from the terms and the essential situation of their problems. We ought to know and to keep in mind that they state *their* problems, not ours, and answer *their* questions, not ours. They do not try to found ethics; they do not start from a *tabula rasa*, a "tablet on which nothing is written,"[13] a clean-swept tablet *à la Descartes* upon which then, by hook or by crook, they have to convey a thing or things in order to be able to start talking about them. The prudent person is just as easily recognizable as good bread; and, it may be, that *we* have difficulties in this recognition *because* we also seem to be poor at discriminating good from bad bread. At any rate, *reason* is the distinguishing mark of the prudent person. While we characteristically are here in a hurry to add and to specify right reason, Aristotle and Thomas are not in that hurry. Of course, the addition is correct, and sometimes made by both these thinkers. More often they just say "reason" without any addition. Saint Thomas once explained this in a text buried, as it were, in his early work, the so-called "Commentary" on the *Sentences* (Book 3, distinction 24, 3. to the 3rd:

> A corrupt reason is no reason, just as a false syllogism properly speaking is no syllogism. Hence the rule of human actions is reason which, of course, is not every reason, but right reason. Hence, Aristotle says that the prudent person is the measure of acting.[14]

Reason is a first notion in the ethics of Aristotle and Thomas Aquinas. By definition, these notions cannot be elucidated by something which would be "first-er than first"; there is no such thing. But we must continue our analysis of the Aristotelian doctrine on prudence. Prudence concerns active, practical life, just like moral virtue; this is the starting-point of the Aristotelian doctrine.

---

already in the first section, where he was a "warrior"; nor does its omission interrupt his thought.

[13] "...a writing-tablet on which as yet nothing actually stands written...." *De anima* 3, 4; 430a 1, 2.

[14] "Ad tertium dicendum, quod corrupta ratio non est ratio, sicut falsus syllogismus proprie non est syllogismus; et ideo regula humanorum actuum non est ratio quaelibet, sed ratio recta.... et ideo Philosophus...dicit quod homo virtuosus est mensura aliorum...." *Scriptum super libros Sententiarum*, Liber 2, Distinctio 24, Quaestio 3, Articulus 3, Ad 3; t. 2, p. 624.

*c. Practical Knowledge*

Prudence is a virtue of reason. Its act and its acts consist in knowing. All human activity depends on knowing as its principle and rule. The human act, Saint Thomas formulates, proceeds properly speaking from reason. This is the Socratic tradition to which Aristotle also remains faithful inasmuch as its essence and principal intention are concerned. Aristotle's task is now to explain what this type of knowledge or knowing is, which is specially adapted to moral virtue and life and which thus is very different from the speculative type of intellectual knowledge to which the philosopher's life is so much attached.

## C. The Moral and Intellectual Context of Prudence

The doctrine of Aristotle on prudence is the philosophical frame of Saint Thomas's respective doctrine. Saint Thomas meditated on it and penetrated its meaning. Questions 57 and 58 of the I-II are outstanding witnesses to this endeavor. Aquinas judged the Aristotelian doctrine sufficiently true and secure to constitute the philosophical sinews of his respective theology. As always in similar cases, he does not simply repeat it: he works it over, he elaborates it, even corrects it in the light of his theology and Christian tradition on which theology rests.

Prudence was conceived by Aristotle as a virtue intimately connected with other qualities or dispositions of the soul. If these bonds are disrupted, prudence disintegrates and is lost. It is significant in the highest degree to be a prudent person in the ethics of Aristotle and Thomas Aquinas, since this notion involves other qualities apart from the one which is immediately designated by this word and notion. I insisted on the Aristotelian point that prudence is distinguished from art. Art does not imply anything else but what this notion indicates. An architect, a logician, an ethician, might excel only in their specialties and for the rest be numbered with the rest of ordinary, mediocre people. Their human mediocrity would not make them less competent and excellent architects, logicians, ethicians, and so on. We today make a great fuss about specialization and special competencies in all sorts of endeavors or activities. Could it be that we have become less sensitive to the beauty of the person, harmoniously and universally developed and cultivated as human, as a human being? Prudence represents exactly this quality and excellence of a person, universally and totally developed as human. Such as conceived by Thomas Aquinas, this virtue is *the* human, moral excellence. To be prudent is to be human, to be moral; the moral human being is the prudent person. Let the disillusioned lover of Nirvana be the moral ideal of Buddha, and the stoically unperturbed bearer of misfortune that of Epictetus, the successful tradesman that of Jeremy Bentham, the believer in unlimited progress that of John Dewey, the television announcer selling every soap that of Bertrand Russell; Saint Thomas's ideal is the prudent human being. Such as conceived by Thomas Aquinas, prudence is connected on the one hand with the virtues residing in the will and on the other hand with certain dispositions residing in the intellect or reason. Prudence will not work unless it functions within this context. We do not have prudence alone. Prudence is the quality of an integrated personality. When Saint Thomas says that prudence does this or that, moral virtue is this or does that, we should always be aware that these are abbreviated formulas. I do not think they are meant as usual in English as they are in other languages. There is, of course, nothing in us by way of a detachable mechanical device called "prudence" which works when we push the button. It is always the person as a whole who acts. We use these formulas, and I am afraid that in explaining Saint Thomas it is impossible not to use them, in order more clearly and more sharply to put into relief what precisely, *formally*, is involved in an action. The same applies to will and to reason and to the other faculties of the soul. Will produces the action as its effective cause, reason as its formal and forming cause. These are abstract propositions. Will and reason are distinct faculties. Still, they are not two *things* that either are at peace or fight each other; and *we* are the more or less interested spectators of the drama. It is hardly necessary to mention this to students who are somehow initiated into philosophical language, but it is better, perhaps, to mention it all the same. In Saint Thomas, as in Aristotle, prudence has two terms of reference; one, the moral virtues and second, other dispositions or habits of the intellect. We shall study these two references in distinction.

*a. The Connection of the Virtues*

On the relation between prudence and moral virtue, Aristotle established the decisive doctrine. I have shown what, according to the Philosopher, belongs to moral virtue, and what to prudence. Neither one can be without the other. Saint Thomas insists on these Aristotelian teachings in I-II, 58, 4 and 5. It follows from this that, as Aquinas puts it, prudence and the moral virtues *are connected.* This "connection of all the virtues" is the formula with which Thomas Aquinas presents this doctrine; and as to this formula he relies immediately on Saint Ambrose. The text of this Father of the Church is quoted in I-II, 65, 1, in the "But on the contrary," the *Sed contra*: "The virtues are connected and linked to each other so that whoever has one, must be seen to have the others."[15] Several other authorities are quoted in this context: Saint Augustine, Saint Gregory the Great, Cicero. The connection of the virtues is a capital and very characteristic point in Saint Thomas's ethics. In short, our moral personality, our moral life has that forward-looking unity of purpose which is analogous to the functioning of a living organism. Either it grows and unfolds itself organically or it will not really grow at all. It will be an infinity of actions which all may be good in themselves, taken in isolation, but they are scattered about and, in the end, are squandered and wasted. Remember[16] that atomic conception of life of which we spoke of on another occasion, characteristic of ethical legalism as well as utilitarianism. Life is pulverized, conceived as an unconnected succession of momentary acts, and the whole attention is directed upon either their utility or legality, that is, their licitness. Both utility and licitness are the same quality of this action today and of that action tomorrow. That these actions are intrinsically, essentially, connected, that they are parts of one organically structured movement, is not considered in this merely materialistic way of thinking. Do not think that I am speaking here of a materialism or nominalism which we have overcome, which does not concern us. I am speaking of course of our own primitive and puerile ethical convictions which also have found their way into our schools.

Many right-feeling people know this. They ask themselves, is to do this good action and that good action really all that is needed? What is the good of this and that? Saint Thomas gives the answer and it is easy to see that among professional Catholic ethicians he is the only one to give an answer. Our aim in moral life is not to be "do-gooders" in this respect and in that respect, but to be, with our total spiritual and corporeal being "present" in, and committed to, the good as such, for its own sake. In our Christian and Catholic language this means to be committed to God Who is the Highest Good, the value of all values. I cannot leave this subject of the connection of all virtues in prudence without at least opening up the theological perspective.

In the supernatural order this connections operates too. Charity, the virtue proper to our supernatural end is, as Saint Thomas says, the *form* of

[15] "Connexae sibi sunt, concatenataeque virtutes, ut qui unam habet, plures habere videatur." ST 1-2, 65, 1, Sed contra; t. 2, p. 1047a, ll. 8-10. St. Thomas cited this from St. Ambrose's Gospel exegesis, *Super Lucam* Lib. 5, (Luke 6:20); PL 15 1738.

[16] Here a handwritten insertion on the obverse of the previous page has been marked for insertion; it ends, and the typed page resumes with the words "Many right-feeling people know this."

all virtues. "Infused" prudence, then, is a prudence connected, in the way described a minute ago, in the first place with charity, and through charity, with all the other virtues. Prudence is the driver-seat-virtue in regard to charity too and it will be especially important that we keep away the popular and miserable notion of *prudence, cette sotte vertu,* "prudence, that stupid virtue."[17] In the supernatural order prudence is inspired by charity, and through charity, by the other virtues. Its intention is our reaching our last supernatural end, union with God, through all our activities and life. Even here prudence is not deprived of its characteristic privilege to be the driver-seat-virtue, that is, to construct, to build up, to actualize, to bring into existence, into the concrete existence of concrete human life, that charity which is diffused in our hearts by the grace of the Holy Spirit.

*b. The Intellectual Context of Prudence*

We are now to study the place of prudence in its intellectual context, in other words, the connection of prudence with the other intellectual habits. We shall see that here Saint Thomas goes far beyond Aristotle. He corrects The Philosopher or, if this word is perhaps too strong (Thomas himself would not have used it!) he integrates other elements into the Aristotelian teaching, elements due to the Christian tradition, especially to Saint Augustine.

I made it a point, in the former topic on Aristotle's doctrine on prudence, to stress the fact that the Stagirite's prudence is entirely turned toward the concrete, the particular, the ever-changing situations in human life. Something akin, therefore, to what we today call "Situational Ethics," the ethics of the situations, a trend of modern existentialist ethical thinking against which Rome some years ago expressed a strong warning. Something which is akin to this thinking, although it proceeds from different presuppositions, comes to the fore in Aristotle. There is, of course, in this philosophy a certain knowledge of general principles or rules, but Aristotle insists, with definitely more energy, on the knowledge of the particular situations which, according to him, is the proper characteristic of prudence. Moreover, he somehow belittles the importance of such general knowledge. He refuses to attribute to the general principles an invariable certitude. One of the characteristic features of the Aristotelian ethics is again the stress on the *relative* validity of general principles in ethics. Let us read just one significant text from Book 2, Chapter 2, ⟨of the *Nicomachean Ethics*⟩:

[17] This remark Eschmann later (and correctly) will ascribe to Voltaire; see below, note 36.

> We must begin the study of Ethics with the admission that any theory of conduct must be content with an outline without much precision in details. We noted this when I said at the beginning of our discussion (Book 1, Chapter 3) that the measure of exactness of statement in any field of study must be determined by the nature of the matter studied. Now matters of conduct and considerations of what is to our advantage have no fixity about them any more than matters affecting our health. And if this be true of moral philosophy as a whole, it is still more true that the discussion of problems in ethics admit of no exactitude. For they do not fall under any science or professional tradition, but those who are following some line of conduct are forced in every collocation of circumstance, to think out for themselves what is suited to these circumstances, just as doctors and navigators have to do in their different matters.[18]

John Dewey could not more vigorously insist on this peculiar aspect of ethics which, surely, is one *true* aspect. However, it is not the whole truth. If the Aristotelian prudence rather turns its face forward, so to speak, to the concrete, situational experience (without of course indulging in pragmatism in Dewey's style), Saint Thomas's prudence keeps a very attentive eye backward to the general principles by which it is constantly nourished. Prudence is, of course, in Saint Thomas too a practical knowledge. It is never to be confused with theoretical knowledge. The philosophers, the metaphysicians, by the very fact that they are metaphysicians, are not kings in Aquinas, as they were in Plato's ideal Republic, although, as we shall see later, some integration of the "theoretical" and the "practical" will also belong to Aquinas's full doctrine on prudence. With manifest emphasis, the Thomasic theology scrutinizes the connection of prudence with what is prior to it in the very intellect, with what is its intellectual principle within the total organization and development of our intellectual life. Saint Thomas is a dedicated Aristotelian, but he is not dedicated to the extent of slavishly taking the oath on the words of the Master.

*c. Synderesis*

Saint Thomas links prudence up with the so-called "synderesis." The origin of this notion is found in a text of Saint Jerome[19] upon which the

[18] *Nicomachean Ethics* 2, 1; 1104a 1-11.

[19] "...quam Graeci uocant *suneídêsin*—quae scintilla conscientiae in Cain quoque pectore, postquam eiectus est de paradiso, non extinguitur, et, uicti, uoluptatibus uel furore, ipsaque interdum rationis decepti similitudine, nos peccare sentimus...."

whole scholastic doctrine was constructed. Saint Jerome used the word "synderesis" (the text probably has come to us in a corrupt form) in order to designate "that scintilla of conscience which was not extinguished even in Cain after he was chased out of Paradise, that sparklet of our soul which makes us feel guilty when we have been overpowered by lust or anger or even when we have been seduced by counterfeit reason"

In Saint Jerome synderesis is identical with conscience. Saint Thomas, on the contrary, distinguishes between synderesis and conscience; he assign to the former a special meaning which will become clear from the following summary of pertinent texts (*Super Sententiarum libros* 2, 24, 2, 3; *De veritate* 16, 1, 1, 79, 12):

> Human reasoning is a certain intellectual movement starting from principles which are naturally known, without any investigation. Now always that which is moved begins to move at an immovable point; hence, (to begin with the speculative reason) we see that our speculative knowledge starts with certain principles such as the principle of ⟨non-⟩ contradiction or the principle that the whole is greater than the part, which are naturally known and, in order to be understood, need no reflection.

Let us pass to the domain of practical knowledge. Here, too, there is reasoning, that is, intellectual movement. This movement also begins with naturally known principles. These principles are called "synderesis." Is synderesis a special power of the soul? It needs hardly to be said that it is not; it is simply a *habitus*, that is, the entitatively fixed ability of knowing the first practical principles. The three texts in which Saint Thomas sets forth this doctrine prove the fact that the word synderesis, and its curious history, especially in early scholasticism, are not really of any great importance. What Saint Thomas wants to show is the truth of the doctrine of Saint Augustine and an old conviction in Christianity. The classical text of Saint Augustine is the following, taken from the Dialogue *De libero arbitrio*, (*On Free Arbitrament*) 2, 10. Encountering, in the course of this dialogue, these first principles, Augustine, the leading dialogist, says to his companion, "There is no need to ask any more questions. It is enough to come to these propositions which are first rules, true and invariable lights of the virtues. You see them just as well as I do and you can-

---

Jerome's use of the term in his commentary on the Prophet Ezechiel has been noted above (note 98 of Part I) and will be noted again. His words are translated immediately below by Eschmann; see *S. Hieronymi presbyteri opera* 1, 4; *Commentariorvm in Hiezechielem Libri xiv*, CCLS (Turnhout: Brepols, 1964) p. 12, 11. 218-222.

not but agree with me: these principles, taken singly or all together, are there to be contemplated by those who have come to the use of their reason. There are no questions about them."

Whatever, therefore, be the truth and, as I insinuated, the controversial meaning of the word "synderesis" in Saint Jerome, it is clear as far as Thomas Aquinas is concerned that this word merely furnishes him with the occasion to incorporate into his own doctrine an Augustinian datum and so makes it possible for him to join, through Aristotle and beyond Aristotle, a capital point in all Christian ethical teaching, namely, the immutability and invariability of first, practical principles, the eternity of *moral* truth. A reliable source on "synderesis" is V.J. Bourke.[20]

*d. Natural Law*

Synderesis is the natural habitus of the naturally known principles which are the first principles of our human acting, that is, our acting as a human, as a human being. We might also say, and this is an equivalent formula often used by Thomas Aquinas, that synderesis is the natural habitus of the ends of all the virtues. These ends, Aquinas affirms, are the "connatural ends of the human being," *fines connaturales homini*, the ends *connatural* to the human as human. Now these principles and these ends constitute the NATURAL LAW. Hence, and note this very carefully, in Saint Thomas's ethics we come to the notion of Natural Law by a simple analysis of prudence which is a personal virtue, a personal perfection of a human being. It is one of the foremost characteristics of the ethics of Thomas Aquinas, especially if we compare it with any and every type of obligationist ethics, to reach the notion of Natural Law, not from above and from outside, that is, finally through the divine Legislator, but from below and from inside, that is, from an analysis of the practical reason. Natural Law is a constitutive element of practical reason: it designates the natural part of this reason, that is, the practical principles naturally known to it, naturally formed by it. The notion of Natural Law, again, is deeply anchored in Christian doctrine: remember Saint Paul. It is no specific invention of Christianity; it was present in post-Aristotelian Greek philosophy. As to the relation at this point, between Saint Augustine and Saint Thomas, something special will have to be said presently. I shall first read a text of Aquinas which summarizes well his thinking on Natural Law: Part I-II, 91, 2. This Article, in view of the post Tridentine development of

[20] *History of Ethics*, Vernon J. Bourke (Garden City, N.Y.: Doubleday, 1968), pp. 91 and 96. Eschmann, of course, cited an earlier edition of this very successful work; see above, Part I, note 98 and Part II, note 19.

Catholic ethics,is one of the most important texts in the authentic ethics of Aquinas:

> All things subject to divine Providence evidently partake in some way in Eternal Law, namely, insofar as from its being impressed upon them, they have their respective inclinations to their proper acts and ends. Now among all others, the rational creature is subject to divine Providence in a more excellent way, inasmuch as it itself partakes of Providence by being provident, both for itself and for others. Therefore, it has a share of the Eternal Reasons, whereby it has a natural inclination to its proper act and end. And this participation of Eternal Law in the rational creature is called the Natural Law.
>
> Hence the Psalmist, after saying (Ps 4:6), "Offer up the sacrifice of justice," as though someone asked what the works of justice are, adds, "Many say who showeth us what is good?" In answer to which question he says, "The light of Your countenance. O Lord, is signed upon us." He thus implies that the light of natural reason, whereby we discern what is good and what is evil, which is the function of Natural Law, is nothing other than an impression on us of the divine Light. It is, therefore, evident that Natural Law is nothing other than the rational creature's participation in Eternal Law.[21]

This text, I repeat, is one of the principal texts of authentic Thomasic ethics, worth our most attentive consideration. It joins up with the Prologue of the I-II. The human being as intellectual is God's image. The

[21] It is notable that here (and he will follow this practice several times in this Part II) Eschmann gave this text in English; the Latin is as follows: "...manifestum est quod omnia participant aliqualiter legem aeternam, inquantum scilicet ex impressione eius, inquantum scilicet ex impressione eius habent inclinationes in proprios actus et fines. Inquantum cetera autem, rationalis creatura excellentiori quodam modo divinae providentiae subiacet, inquantum et ipsa fit providentiae particeps, sibi ipsi et aliis providens. Unde et in ipsa participatur ratio aeterna, per quam habet naturalem inclinationem ad debitum actum et finem. Et talis participatio legis aeternae in rationali creatura lex naturalis dicitur. Unde cum Psalm. IV:6 dixisset: 'Sacrificate sacrificium iustitiae,' quasi quibusdam quaerentibus quae sunt iustitiae opera, subiungit: 'Multi dicunt Quis ostendit nobis bona?' cui quaestioni respondens, dicit: 'Signatum est super nos lumen vultus tui, Domine,' quasi lumen rationis naturalis, quo discernimus quid sit bonum et quid malum, quod pertinet ad naturalem legem, nihil aliud sit quam impressio divini luminis in nobis. Unde patet quod lex naturalis nihil aliud est quam particpatio legis aeternae in rationali creatura." ST 1-2, 91, 2, in corpore; t. 2, p. 1210b, ll. 3-28.

human being is "God on earth," as the Greek Fathers were wont to say. Man is not only subjected to God's Providence, but takes part in it. A human is, in a real sense, God's Providence on earth, "providing" for self and for others. We ought not to have any qualms in saying this and we ought to say it loudly and clearly. We may note that the Latin word *prudentia*, "prudence," is contracted from the Latin *providentia*, "providence." The one who is prudent is in a special way God's Providence on earth. There is no objection either against the notion of *autonomy* applied to us, although it would seem, according to run-of-the-mill ethics, that no word is more dreadful, more horrifying, than this word autonomy applied to us—which, of course means "to you" and "to me"! We are autonomous in a relative, but true and authentic sense. Morals is not an order that originally comes to us from the outside, not even as a ready-made set of rules, a prescriptions from heaven; we have to make it, it comes to us through the voice of our reason which we recognize to be the voice of God. There is no canned morality which could be bought cheaply at the spiritual grocer's and which would spare us the trouble of cooking, on our own account and responsibility. And note very carefully in this text the notion and the analogy of light, which is used by Saint Thomas in order to say, or to convey, what Natural Law is. It is the *light* of our reason by which we discern what is good and what is evil. It is the "light from light," namely, from the "Light" of God's countenance which is signed upon us. This is good and sound, scriptural and traditional theology. Saint Bernard, for instance, in the twelfth century speaks of the "light of discretion which is the mother of all virtues and the consummation of perfection."[22] There is not a Father of the Church who would not stress the intellectual aspect of morality. Try to find the notion of light and of its analogates, namely, "intellect," "intellectuality," "intelligibility," in our current moral theology. Your search will be in vain and this experience alone may be sufficient to make you grasp the difference. Did you ever hear a sermon on these words "The light of Your countenance, O Lord, is signed upon us?" But then, did you ever hear a scriptural, theological sermon about the dignity of the human being? In the "Oration" of the Third Sunday after Easter the Church prays, "God, thou showest the erring the *light of truth* that they may return to the

[22] "...illuminari necesse est lumine discretionis, quae mater virtutum est et consummatio perfectionis." Sermo tertius In Circumcisione Domini, Sermon 3, in *S. Bernardi Opera*. Vol. IV, Sermones I, edd. J. Leclercq O.S.B., H. Rochais (Rome: Editiones Cistercienses, 1966), p. 290, ll. 17-18 (PL 183 142A).

way of justice."[23]

This whole doctrine of Aquinas about Eternal and Natural Law rests firmly on reason and tradition. Yet it should be noted that Saint Thomas had to sift the tradition and to separate the wheat from the chaff, for there was chaff in the tradition. There is an Augustinian definition of Eternal Law which, although justifiable if rightly understood, could (and did) give rise to certain misunderstandings. It is found in Saint Augustine's writing *Against Faustus the Manichee*: "Eternal Law is God's reason or (!) God's will commanding to preserve, or prohibiting to disturb, the natural order."[24] This definition is obviously liable to be understood in an anthropomorphic and legalistic sense; it was so understood and constantly brought up and stressed in the Augustinian schools of the Middle Ages, especially in the surroundings of Aquinas, namely, the Franciscan schools of the thirteenth century. Clearly it is far below Saint Thomas's understanding of Eternal and Natural Law. Because Aquinas hated controversy, instead of laboriously refuting or even straightening out the Augustinian definition, he did something else. He used an innocent trick; he simply did not mention this definition. Franciscans, post-Tridentine theologians or philosophers, up to our own day, find Augustine's anthropomorphism still a support for their legalistic thinking. On the other hand, read Saint Thomas's pertinent Questions in Part I-II (91, 93, etc.). Augustinian quotations are liberally spread all over the pages, but this legalistic escapade of the great Saint Augustine is conspicuously absent; a good example of Thomas Aquinas on how to handle tiresome and useless controversies! This one is useless once it is understood that Natural Law is not a statute enacted by the divine Legislator, but is the self-same act by which the Creator brought into being our rational nature.

I, for one, am inclined to think that the expression (not the reality!) "Natural Law" would better be dropped from our philosophical and theological vocabulary. A legalistic thinker can put all the "laws," Eternal Law, Natural Law, the Ten Commandments, the Sermon on the mount, Ecclesiastical Law, Civil Law, Traffic Law, and so on, into one big kettle, and merrily go on his way as a lawyer and casuist. Saint Thomas explains Na-

[23] Needless, perhaps, to mention, Eschmann here refers to the Roman Catholic liturgy current in the years when he spoke; his point was to reinforce his claim that his view of basic morality is, in fact, scriptural, theological, and ecclesial.

[24] "lex vero aeterna est ratio diuina uel uoluntas dei ordinem naturalem conseruari iubens, perturbari uetans." *Contra Faustum Manichaeum*, 22, 27, CSEL 25.1, ed. J. Zycha (Prague, Vienna: F. Tempsky, Leipzig: G. Freytag, 1891), p. 621, ll. 13-15 (PL 42 418).

tural Law more fully as to what it contains. In order to clear up the intellectual background of prudence, we now must turn to:

*e. The "Golden Rule" of Natural Law*[25]

In the philosophy of Saint Thomas a proposition, in order to fulfill the conditions of Natural Law, must be an "analytical" proposition of such simplicity and evidence that, without investigation, it is known and approved by all humans. An analytical proposition is one in which the predicate is contained in the subject, for instance, "The part is less than the whole." The predicate, "part," is contained in the very definition of the subject "whole" for a "whole" is that which contains "parts." This definition and its analysis are immediately evident to anyone who is capable of conceiving the notions in question, namely, "whole" and "part." If anyone doubts this proposition, he cannot be argued into accepting its truth; he is best advised to take a cup of tea, or some stronger concoction, which it is hoped will straighten up his spirits.

In the Part I-II, 94, 2, Saint Thomas undertakes to describe the essential structure of both the speculative and, especially, the practical reason. In speculative reason the immovable starting point from which the whole movement of reason begins in the order of nature is the "principle of identity" or, inversely, the "principle of contradiction": Being *is* being, or, Being *is not* non-being.

In practical reason there is analogously a "principle of practical identity," or a "principle of practical contradiction," as simple as the former one. Saint Thomas presents it with the famous formula of the Gold Rule of Natural Law: "Good is to be done" (*Bonum est faciendum*) and, inversely, "Evil is to be avoided" (*Malum est vitandum*). This proposition, because it is a "first principle" needs no explanation; it is analytically evident.

Still, some moralists have introduced damaging equivocity into the first principle of practical reason. "Obligationalists" have smuggled their

[25] Eschmann's qualification "of Natural Law" distinguishes his present "golden rule" from the traditional one derived from the Gospel according to Matthew, 7:12. A handwritten addition seems more appropriate at this point than where Eschmann located it (just before his heading "6. The procedure of practical reason"). Eschmann's commendation of an article on this issue is unreserved: "On Saint Thomas's Golden Rule, the Benedictine G. Stevens has written a solid doctrinal note 'The Relations of Law and Obligation' in the *Proceedings of the American Catholic Philosophical Association* 29 (1955): 195-205; he denies the principle *Bonum est faciendum* to have anything to do with obligation. We salute this brother-in-arms and hope that there are more to come who see the light!"

counterfeit money over the borders of Thomas Aquinas's philosophy. For they make this principle a container for the first judgment, whence all ethical discourse takes its starting-point and whither it returns, and it contains the first obligation, the first moral necessity from which all other moral necessity is suspended and into which every obligation, imposed by any law whatever, is resolved. If this theory were true, the first practical principle would be neither first nor immediately self-evident. Not first, because it would presuppose the evidence of obligation, which is that legitimate authority must be obeyed by its subordinates; it would not immediately self-evident because it would have to made evident through the construction of the order of authority and all its essential elements. The idea of "good" does not immediately and "of itself," *per se,* contain all this. It contains for Saint Thomas, nothing but the idea of good which is that it is "something everyone desires." Hold a beautiful apple out to a small child who is beginning to stammer out the first words: here, that word will be "good" and the child's out-stretched hand is "doing this good," materializing it, giving it existence. There are moralists who are suspicious of the idea of "good" and "value" because, apparently, they cannot rise to the philosophical level of the "good as such," which corresponds to the philosophical precision the "human as human." Hence they cannot understand that, in spite of what Tom, Dick, and Harry usually do desire, there is an insuperable "natural desire," *desiderium naturale,* in the human being, precisely as human, to live the life for which we have been created and constructed by God.

In the rest of this Article, Saint Thomas goes on to put in sharper relief the principle, "The good is to be done." He does so by having recourse to our natural inclinations in more detail, the inclination to preserve one's own life and that of the human species, the inclination to live in society, the inclination know the truth about God. These natural inclinations cannot be, as such, the object of obligations, since obligation is a necessity imposed from without whereas these are natural, inner, and spontaneous, "like the fire which necessarily gives heat." Still, they are not physical necessities; rather, they are moral necessities because they are the inclinations of a human, and therefore moral, being. In the subsequent Article 3 Saint Thomas couches the same doctrine in different terms:

> As has been stated, to natural law belongs everything to which we are inclined according to our nature (as human). Now each reality is inclined naturally to an operation that is suitable to it according to its form (which makes a thing to be what it is); for instance, fire is inclined to give heat. Therefore, since the ration soul is the proper form of the human being, there is in every human a natural inclina-

> tion to act according to reason, and this is to act according to virtue.[26]

This brings us back to prudence. Natural Law is not prudence, but the inner-most depth and foundation of prudence according to Thomas Aquinas, a doctrine which is not "Aristotelian," but was incorporated into Aristotelianism from post-Aristotelian, philosophical and theological sources. Through this contact with the divine Light, our moral life takes on a grandeur and a gravity which is not in Aristotle.

*f. The Procedure of Practical Reason*

The principles of natural reason are *general* principles. Prudence, on the other hand, intellectually directs the *particular* actions to be performed within the total concretization of actual human life. Between that general and this particular, there is a sort of intermediate space, a vacuum, if you like. A general principle such as "Good is to be done" is no *immediate* guide; it points to no definite action to be performed or omitted; it does not tell us where to begin nor does it tell us where to finish. The general principles of natural reason are *ultimate* criteria; they are not involved in action straightaway, without any further elaboration. We might say that they are constitutional law, supreme directives, defining the fundamental form and the spirit of our inner, spiritual, or moral organization rather than its more immediate, more practical outlines. Natural reason thus will have to be more and more particularized, given more and more definite and concrete shape. Saint Thomas uses the following example:

> The human being is a social animal; now social life would be impossible without respect for the other's life and property; therefore, this life and this property ought to be respected; murder and stealing ought to be avoided.[27]

The major proposition in this syllogism is natural reason or law; the conclusion, more definite and more practical, is human reason or law, ob-

[26] "Dictum est enim quod ad legem naturae pertinet omne illud ad quod homo inclinatur secundum suam naturam. Inclinatur autem unumquodque naturaliter ad operationem sibi convenientem secundum suam formam, sicut ignis ad calefaciendum. Unde cum anima rationalis sit propria forma hominis, naturalis inclinatio inest cuilibet homini ad hoc quod agat secundum rationem. Et hoc est agere secundum virtutem." ST 1-2, 94, 3, in corpore; t. 2, p. 1226b, ll. 21-31.

[27] Eschmann has given no reference as to where precisely Saint Thomas proffered this example; he may have considered it implicit in the doctrine of the Articles on natural law.

tained by a certain elaboration of the major as is evident in the minor proposition of the syllogism. This elaboration which, as it were, fills out the space between the general and the particular, again belongs to practical reason; it is an element in its essential structure which Saint Thomas takes so much care to describe. It is one of the presuppositions on which prudence does its work as the immediate conductor-virtue of our actions here and now to be performed.

The procedure of this elaboration is philosophically described by Saint Thomas in Part I-II, 95, 2. It is achieved in two ways: (a) by logical deduction; and (b) by practical determination, that is, contraction, limitation, "specification." The first way, Saint Thomas says, is like that by which in the sciences conclusions are demonstrated when they are drawn from principles; the second is like the determination by which in the arts a general form is "determined" and receives a particular shape and style. The architect, for instance, is charged to build a house or a church. House and church are general forms, general ideas. Nobody can build, as it were, a Platonic idea of a house or church. Such an idea cannot exist in reality although, thereby, it is not an empty abstraction; "house" as an idea has rooms and a roof and windows and doors and the rest, else it would not be a "house." The[28] architect who in the delightful German legend forgot the windows in his building and urged the workers to fill a number of big bags with air and light and carry them into the thing ⟨he had built⟩, did not build a house. Yet the house to be erected must have its particular layout, its size, its style which are the determination of the general idea, the "creation" of the artist or craftsman.

We have seen some elaboration (by deduction) of the principle that human beings live in society. The way of practical determination will concern the concrete, livable form of society and its particular institutions: how the essential order of authority should be set up, whether our society should be organized along monarchic, or aristocratic, or democratic lines, and so on and so forth. There are "a thousand thousand" problems of this sort which cannot be solved by logic, but "in the way in which in the arts general forms are determined to a concrete shape or style."[29]

The *agencies* filling out that space between the general and the parti-

[28] This illustration is written by hand on the facing page and its place for insertion marked.

[29] "Secundo vero modo simile est quod in artibus formae communes determinantur ad aliquid speciale, sicut artifex formam communem domus necesse est quod determinet ad hanc vel illam domus figuram." ST 1-2, 95, 2, in corpore; t. 2, p. 1232a, ll. 38-43.

cular up to the point where prudence will be necessary are mainly two: human law and moral science. (Custom and tradition should also be mentioned, but we leave out treatment of them for brevity's sake.) The particularization of which we are speaking here is not yet that of the concrete act or action to be performed. Let no one tell Saint Thomas to hurry up: he has time for refined analysis! Both agencies, human law and ethics use the two ways of elaboration indicated, although human law will insist upon practical determination by preference while ethics, being philosophical, naturally prefers logical deduction. Both human law and moral science are placed by Saint Thomas within the realm of the intellectual connections of prudence, on the soil in which prudence is to be planted and from which it is nourished.

Each of these two agencies has its own task, specifically different from that of the other. Saint Thomas expresses this at the beginning of his exposition of the *Nicomachean Ethics* most significantly and vigorously. To moral science it belongs to bring the order of reason downward, in the direction of human life and action through *consideration* and *investigation*. To human law, the, the same task is incumbent through *command* and *active obligation*. Here one must insist that neither moral science, nor still less human law, can rule human life totally and in every concrete detail; neither one can pretend to master all our situations. Claims to do so have not been lacking in history, neither from the side of legislators nor, especially, on the side of ethicians, for instance the Scribes and Pharisees and other casuists. But life always spilled over; Blessed be life!

Another big problem needs mention here. The tendency in the history of ethics has been to extend the limits of natural law and reason, to qualify as natural law whatever logical conclusion may have been drawn correctly from the first principles. This tendency was especially strong in the so-called "Jusnaturalism" of the seventeenth and eighteenth centuries and is clearly traceable in the Catholic ethics of the same time. There is doubtless considerable truth in this for conclusions are not exactly added to, but rather contained in, their principles. Yet here Saint Thomas makes a very noteworthy observation. Deduction is a movement of reason, while first principles, inasmuch as they are first, are characterized by immobility, that is, by their incontrovertible and immediate evidence. Principles are the firm ground on which we stand; conclusions are obtained by our moving about, be it ever so slightly. First principles are evident of themselves; conclusions are evident by the principles. I give the floor to Saint Thomas himself on this delicate problem in ethics which is also a problem of burning actuality, Part I-II, 94, 4:

The speculative reason is in a different condition in this matter ⟨of

> principles and conclusions⟩ from practical reason. For, since the speculative reason is concerned chiefly with necessary things which cannot be otherwise than they are, its appropriate conclusions, like the universal principles, contain the truth without fail. The practical reason, on the contrary, is concerned with contingent matters which is the domain of human actions; and consequently, although there is necessity in the first general principles, the more we descend towards the particular, the more frequently we encounter defects. Accordingly, therefore, in speculative matters truth is the same in and for all humans, both as to principles and conclusions; although the truth is not known to all as regards the conclusions. But on the contrary, in matters of action, truth which here is identical with practical rectitude ⟨rightness⟩ is not the same for all as to what is particular ⟨as to what regards concrete life⟩, but only as to the common principles; and, moreover, where there is the same rectitude or rightness in relation to concrete life, it is not equally known to all.[30]

Clearly this is approval by Aquinas of what is sound in Aristotelian ethical relativism. A code of concrete ethical rules set up in, say, Washington cannot be expected to be both *right* and *understood* in Timbuktu! Let Aquinas draw his principal conclusion on the absolute or relative validity of natural law in the wider sense of the term:

> It must be stated, consequently, that natural law as to the first general principles is the same for all humanity both as to rectitude and as to knowledge. With respect to certain specifications, however, which are as it were conclusions from those general principles in most cases it is the same in all, both as to rectitude and as to knowledge. Still, in a few cases, it can fail as to rectitude owing to some particular

[30] "Aliter tamen circa hoc se habet ratio speculativa, et aliter practica. Quia enim ratio speculativa praecipue negotiatur circa necessaria, quas impossibile est aliter se habere, absque aliquo defectu invenitur veritas in conclusionibus propriis, sicut in principiis communibus. Sed ratio practica negotiatur circa contingentia, in quibus sunt operationes humanae; et ideo, si in communibus sit aliqua necessitas, tanto magis ad propria descenditur, tanto magis invenitur defectus. Sic igitur in speculativis est eadem veritas apud omnes tam in principiis quam in conclusionibus; licet veritas non apud omnes cognoscatur in conclusionibus, sed solum in principiis, quae dicuntur "communes conceptiones." In operativis autem non est eadem veritas vel rectitudo practica apud omnes quantum ad propria, sed solum quantum ad communia; et apud illos apud quos est eadem rectitudo in propriis, non est aequaliter omnibus nota." ST 1-2, 94, 4, in corpore; t. 2, p. 1227b, ll. 8-30. Eschmann has given this text in English.

> obstacles, as it happens, too, in a few cases that things of nature, subject to generation and corruption, are defective owing to obstacles. So too with respect to knowledge and this because some people have a depraved rationality owing either to passion, or to evil custom, or even from an evil of their nature. Thus it was that, as Julius Caesar reports in his book *On The Gallic War*, at one time robbery was not thought to be evil among the Germans, even though it is expressly against the law of nature.[31]

In short, conclusions are "natural law," not in the strict sense in which the notion comprises principles only, but in an extended sense, implying a movement of reason and fallibility. Although conclusions are clear to some, they are not clear to others. Finally, conclusions may not be even morally right if the concrete cases are of a nature that changes the whole general condition of a given moral problem. Implacable logic has no currency in ethics!

This doctrine, surely, is worthy of the greatest attention, but I cannot discuss it in detail. It reveals an eminent and rare good sense, a feeling for, and a sympathy with, human life; these are astonishing in a man who passed his life in seclusion and solitude. He is, in truth, as a contemporary said of him, "That most prudent Brother Thomas," *prudentissimus ille frater Thomas*. He does not mount the high horse, pretending to master the whole world, to answer all questions and more, to decree left and right what is sin and what is not, what is to be done and what not. More often than not, in vital problems he would say, "I do not know the answer; reason it out for yourself; take your responsibility!" The notion many people have of Saint Thomas is a distorted imagination. It is a copy of the portrait not infrequently presented to them by so many popular speakers and writers: a school master with a narrow, closed *system* where everything is in

[31] "Sic igitur dicendum est quod lex naturae quantum ad prima principia communia, est eadem apud omnes et secundum rectitudinem, et secundum notitiam. Sed quantum ad quaedam propria, quae sunt quasi conclusiones principiorum communium, est eadem apud omnes etiam ut in pluribus et secundum rectitudinem et secundum notitiam; sed ut in paucioribus potest deficere et quantum ad rectitudinem propter aliqua particularia impedimenta, sicut etiam naturae generabiles et corruptibiles deficiunt ut in paucioribus, propter impedimenta, et etiam quantum ad notitiam; et hoc propter hoc quod aliqui habent depravatam rationem ex passione, seu ex mala consuetudine, seu ex mala habitudine naturae; sicut apud Germanos olim latrocinium non reputabatur iniquum, cum tamen sit expresse contra legem naturae, ut refert Iulius Caesar in libro *De bello Gallico*." Ibidem p. 1228a, ll. 11-32. Eschmann has provided the translation given in the text.

place, once and for all, and nothing spills over. I met not a few students who hated Thomas Aquinas for this, as he might well be hated if such were the truth. This picture *à la* Christian Wolff is not the truth; it is a caricature drawn up by those who have neither the courage nor the intelligence to speak out for themselves and who must run for cover: *prudentissimus ille frater Thomas de Aquino*!

*g. Prudence and Contemplation*

Saint Thomas's ethics, as regards the central chapter on prudence, is a work both confirming Aristotle's philosophy and going beyond it. Aquinas goes farthest beyond Aristotle in a splendid effort to connect prudence and contemplation.

In Aristotle's ethics not one idea of human life, but in reality two are set forth as the perfect human achievement, the life of action which is that of the development and organization of moral virtue through prudence, and the life of contemplation (as we translate his *theoria*), which is the life of a philosopher. On one hand the *politikos*, the man of human moral action whose supreme work is the *polis*, the "city," ⟨the basic political organization for the ancients⟩ on the other the *philosophos*, ⟨the one who loves wisdom⟩, who is not a part of the *polis*, but stands outside and above the "political" life. There is, in Aristotle, no attempt to unify these two lives, there is no attempt, in other words, at a total integration of the human personality.

Saint Thomas at first went along with Aristotle. The philosophical expression of this companionship is the relation between the speculative and the practical intellect. They are not only distinguished, they are separated. Prudence, then, in Saint Thomas—and this is already an improvement on Aristotle—is connected with, and founded upon, other habitus of the practical intellect, synderesis and moral science; but up to the time when Aquinas had finished his Part I-II, he saw no necessity even of asking the question whether or not a connection of prudence with certain habitus of the speculative intellect could be found. In the Part II-II only he begins to broaden his perspective and even to correct certain of his own former views on this point. Far from being a schoolmaster with a narrow and closed system, Aquinas is a thinker constantly working on his own positions and intuitions, constantly deepening them and trying more completely to grasp their virtualities. From the Part II-II on, on the basis of a new penetration.of the theology of faith, a new vision of the profound unity of human, Christian life, an integration of action and contemplation begins to take more definite shape in this great man's subtle and plastic mind. Even the speculative, contemplative intellect now belongs to the presuppositions of prudence which it did not yet in the Part I-II. The reason is that in Christian, theological understanding there is no mere theorizing about God. The knowledge of God, whether it be "pre-sciential," as in faith, or sciential, as in theology, is not a detached, a purely objectified, a merely theoretical cognizance. Rather it is a personal relationship from the beginning. It is, as we would say today, a meeting of Thou and I. Saint Thomas had known this and explicitly affirmed it when he sat down to write the very first page of his *Summa theologiae* if not earlier. But in his Aristotelian fervor he seems to have overlooked this point in some of the rather peripheral elucidations of his ethics. The study of the virtue of faith at the beginning of the Part II-II seems to have made him more actually aware of what he had been after for a long time. The treatise on prudence immediately benefits from this insight in the way I have indicated. The Christian prudent person is dedicated to contemplation and to action, but dedicated to each one because of the other. The chief inspiration for action itself comes from contemplation which is a perfection of the speculative, not of the practical, intellect.

All this can only be seen and appreciated from a theological point of view. Philosophically speaking there are no connections between prudence and any habit of the speculative intellect, wisdom and science. Saint Thomas states this in Part I-II, 58, 4. In philosophy the theoretical and the practical, metaphysics and ethics, are not only distinguished, but separated. In theology, and only in theology, they are connected and united.

Here I cannot go into details. Father Deman has written some of the finest pages in modern theology about this aspect of the Thomasic theology of prudence in his Notes to the French translation of the treatise on prudence (*Revue des jeunes*).[32] Reading these pages one gets the feeling of how inexhaustibly rich Saint Thomas's ethics is, and of how incredibly poor and miserable our current so-called moral theology is. It would be time for us, I think, to stop going, like the Pharisee in the parable, to the front of the temple and boasting about the merits of the Golden Age. It would be time for us to stand back and blame ourselves for what, through our negligence and stupidity, we have lost. There is no greater harm ever done to any fine and noble thing in history than the harm done to

[32] Eschmann refers to the esteemed, pocket-sized edition (with a French translation) of the *Summa theologiae* first published by the Éditions de la Revue des jeunes in 1924. Here he specifically means the second edition of the volume containing ST 2-2, 47-56 and entitled *La prudence*, translated, with notes and appendices, by T.-H. Deman O.P. (Paris, Tournai, and Rome: Desclée, 1949). The relevant notes of Father Deman, praised so highly here, are contained in two Appendices: "Notes explicatives" (pp. 247-343) and "Notes doctrinales thomistes" (pp. 375-523).

theology when the ⟨theorists of the⟩ "Golden Age" declared that it was to be divided, as though it were a piece of cake, into speculative and practical theology, the latter being so-called moral theology.

### D. ⟨THE DRIVER'S-SEAT VIRTUE: PRUDENCE AND TRUTH⟩

*a. Auriga virtutum*

Under the direction of the various kinds of knowledge which we have just seen and on the basis of those rectifications which the virtues accomplish in the appetitive and volitive part of the soul, prudence proceeds to its proper work. This work is "the things which are: with respect to the end, in view of the end, and for the sake of the end," as Saint Thomas says in the well-known, philosophically abbreviated, formula. Prudence arranges and measures the action which is to be performed in such a way that the good and the value be found in it, that is, really and truly in our own concrete, whole, human life. A good and right intention, which is the act of the will in willing the end, is no sufficient preparation for the action to be good and right in every respect. The task of prudence is to establish the concrete equivalence between virtuous intention and the action we perform, the life we live. It is the virtue of moral, human, *realization.*

In the present topic I intend to present first, Saint Thomas's doctrine on the three acts of prudence, showing prudence in the driver's seat and secondly, always with Saint Thomas, to examine the question, "How good a driver is prudence?" The expression "driver's-seat virtue," translating the Latin *auriga virtutum,* is used by Saint Thomas;[33] it comes from Saint Bernard's "Sermons on the Song of Songs"[34] and is founded upon Saint Augustine's *De moribus ecclesiae.*[35] It is a beautiful, very expressive simile, especially

[33] "Omnibus autem virtutibus moralibus motor est ipsa prudentia quae dicitur *auriga virtutum." Super libros Sententiarum* Lib. 4, Dist. 17, Quaest. 2, Art. 2, Ad Quartam Quaest., num. 250; t. 4, p. 868.

[34] "Est ergo discretio non tam virtus, quam quaedam moderatrix et auriga virtutum, ordinatrixque affectuum, et morum doctrix." Sermones super Cantica Canticorum, edd. J. Leclercq, C.H. Talbot, H.M. Rochais, in *Sancti Bernardi opera* (Rome: Editiones Cistercienses, 1958) 2: 76; text available also in PL 183 1018.

[35] "An uero, si mihi auriga obtemperans equos quibus praeest alit ac regit commodissime atque ipse quo mihi est obedientior, mea liberalitate perfruitur, negare quisquam potest non solum quod auriga, uerum etiam quod equi sese optime habent, mihi deberi?" *De moribus ecclesiae* 1, 5; cited in a variant form, ST 1-2, 56, 4, Arg. 3; t. 2, p. 1001b, ll. 5-10. See CSEL 90, ed. J.B. Bauer (Vienna: Hoelder-Pichler-Tempsky, 1992), p. 11, ll. 4-9; PL 32 1314.

if the object of our imagination is the ancient chariot. If you cannot get the image of an automobile out of your head, take care at least to avoid the connotation of "safety first"—no rule in ethics! That may be the rule of what Voltaire called "la prudence, cette sotte vertu,"[36] whereas the rule of prudence and of ethics is not safety, but truth. Paul Claudel said that "prudence is to the North of my soul, it is the knowing prow that leads the whole ship."[37]

*b. The Acts of Prudence*

Analyzing the steps which, from the intention of the end, the work of moral virtue, lead down to the actual action, that is, the actual performance of the action, Saint Thomas sets forth three steps: counsel, judgment, and precept.

"Counsel" here means the act by which one deliberates within oneself, something which must be done if the action is to be a completely human action. In important decisions, of course, one can take counsel from those who are able to give it; if one acts *with* counsel the perfection of one's work will not be impaired. If one acts *from* counsel, the action at any rate will not be morally perfect-- it may be on the lowest level of morality if it is one's laziness, according to the rule "Let George do it," which prompts one to perform the action. Counsel is research. Committed to the end, one looks around for the means to realize the end. The end being good and right (this is our supposition since prudence depends upon the rectitude of the will brought about by moral virtue) one will be careful to find good and right means. Certain people excel in the goodness of their intentions but are incapable of discrimination when it comes to the question of what actually to do, that is, how to translate good intentions into real life. Saint Thomas, a lover of refined analysis, describes very exactly the one who possesses good counsel in Part II-II, 49, and that in several Articles—including virtues supplementary to prudence of which you prob-

[36] "Il y en aurait eu beaucoup ⟨de traits hardis⟩ si on n'avait été obligé, à quatre-vingt et un ans, de sacrificier à cette sotte vertu qu'on appelle prudence..."; words in a letter from Voltaire, dated 31 mars, 1775. This information has been provided graciously by a colleague, Professor Charles Principe, of the Department of French, University of Saint Michael's College, Toronto.

[37] "La prudence est au Nord de mon âme comme la proue intelligente qui conduit tout le bateau," Paul Claudel, *Cinq grandes odes* Ode 5, "'La maison fermée,' in the section on the four cardinal virtues. For this line, which is inspired by Saint Thomas, I ⟨Eschmann⟩ give the whole moral-theological literature of the last three centuries, the four volumes in folio of Alphonsus of Liguori included...."

ably have never even heard the names, but are required of the one of good counsel.

Good counsel, however, is but one step toward the goal, although it is the first. It must bring forth the "judgment" by which we adopt one definite way of action. The judgment is, "This should be done." It is already a certain decision; its function is to announce the truth, that is, the moral rectitude of the action to come. For a good action possesses the quality of being a true action: moral goodness is *practical* truth.[38] When Saint Thomas insists on this, he aptly underscores the importance of the intellectual element in human actions. Counsel and judgment are intellectual acts, acts belonging, not to the theoretical, but to the practical intellect.

Of intellectual character is again the third and last act, the "precept" "*Do* this which has been decided in the judgment." This precept, Aquinas insists, is the most proper, the most important act of prudence. Some may have good judgment, but they can be curiously hesitant about "making up their minds" definitely and irrevocably. This act of the precept is here so conceived that it is immediately translated into the action actually performed. The conclusion of prudence is the actual action. Nothing would be farther from the mind of Aquinas than to construe at this point a sort of pure precept, a precept, if I may say so, hovering somewhere in the air, fluttering still above the action which then would be yet to come. Such a "precept" would leave the action still in the state of possibility, that is, of a thing which may, or may not, come into existence; at some time the procedure finds an end: we act.

Prudence is the intellectual preparation of this end and the precept, therefore, is the chief act of prudence. It is an intellectual act upon which and from which the action actually performed follows with necessity. It is an act of the practical reason, the last act rationally determining the action itself. This precept which one formulates within oneself and addresses to oneself most clearly reveals the presence of the intellect, the practical intellect or reason, *within* the very act of the will. For the action actually performed is a product, an effect, of the *will* speaking of efficient causality, but an effect of *reason* speaking of formal causality. We act as humans inasmuch as we act voluntarily, willingly, but the will is "in reason."

So it is that from counsel, through judgment, to precept, there is a progressive growth and maturation of an activity which in its several moments bears the mark of that rational being which is the human *image*

[38] This perception has been expressed forcefully by Saint Anselm in his *De veritate* in which he added to the "truth of enunciations," a "truth of things," and a "truth of actions"; this last is the "truth" echoed here.

*of God.* Some of the hardest and deepest problems of philosophy and theology are involved in all this, especially the problem of intellect and will and freedom. Although I cannot go into this now, let it be noted that every difference of doctrine, even every fluctuation, even the slightest retouching, of Saint Thomas's philosophy of the intellect and the will, must needs result in a different ethics.

Such differences are not just insignificant, peripheral opinions, but entirely different philosophies and theologies of the human being and of God. The relations between intellect and will are a highly debated matter and relatively few there are who follow Thomas Aquinas. No wonder that his ethics, with this absolutely central piece on prudence, is not admitted either. The Counter-Reformation ethics rests, in fine, on a totally activist, anti-intellectual, and therefore authoritative notion and appreciation of the will of God as well as that of the human race. The philosophy of will and intellect would be the proper seat of discussion if one would want to develop our present ethical problem from the bottom up, along strictly professional lines by talking shop! This was not, and is not, my intention.

*c. Prudence and Truth*

Prudence is an intellectual, rational virtue. It represents the intellectual and rational element in human actions, their guide, their management, which is necessary in order that there be human actions. The intellect is the faculty of truth. If truth is taken away from the intellect, the practical as well as the speculative intellect, no intellect remains. The proper value of prudence is that it is a virtue elaborating truth, the true good, in all our actions and life. The evaluation of prudence stands and falls with this. If one is declared to be incapable of truth, either the speculative or the practical truth, prudence has no meaning any longer. If one is held to be too foolish, too childish, or too rotten to elaborate this truth—and therefore must be given over to the authority which does this for that unfortunate—then prudence again has no meaning any longer. The shape of ethics is decided at this point. There is an ethics acknowledging prudence and another suppressing prudence. These two types are clearly distinguished, but they are, moreover, opposed to each other in such a way that no combination is possible. The prudential ethics will be at least as *realistic* as the other type pretends to be. Saint Thomas said, and often repeated, that the majority of humankind are fools and only a few are marked by wisdom: *pauci sunt sapientes*, "the wise are few"! The majority follow their passions; only a few rise above the level of sensuality and greed. Saint Thomas is not therefore ready to suppress prudence in ethics. On the contrary, and rightly so: how could he even give his rather pessimistic factual judgment on humankind a proper justification if not by urging the idea and the necessity of prudence? Aquinas is not marked by empty rhetoric. He shows that prudence is a rare value and this is exactly the reason why the ethician should elaborate a treatise on prudence with the greatest care. Instead of abiding by the fact of childishness and immaturity or, even worse, instead of making these facts the greatest "virtues" of all, Saint Thomas indicates to us the proper remedy by showing us exactly what our foolishness is and where it lies.

Here I should like to show some small, but extremely significant, examples of the way Aquinas appreciated truth in ethics and, therefore, what in him lies behind all his insistence on prudence, what the characteristic mentality, the *ethos* as we say, of this thinker may be.

In the medieval schools a certain controversy arose about whether a certain action is or is not a mortal sin. The action here is the consent, limited to our mind, to certain sensual stirrings or emotions which it has always been very difficult for the theologians accurately to qualify and explain. Saint Bonaventure holds for the opinion (against Saint Albert the Great) that this consent is a mortal sin. Apparently, however, he was unable to show a convincing argument pointing up the true merits of the case. He concludes his explanations by saying, "Whatever be the *truth* of the matter, the *safer* opinion is to be held and this is that this action is a mortal sin."[39] Saint Thomas had read this text and his answer is to be found in Part I-II, 74, 8: "Some say that this consent is a venial sin, others that it is a mortal sin. The latter opinion (supported by Saint Augustine) is more common and is more like the *truth*, is *verisimilior*."[40] In these two statements by two of our really outstanding theologians, you have two very different mentalities, two different worlds. Saint Bonaventure says in so many words, "What do we care about truth when something else is the really important point, namely, safety. "Safety first"!

Saint Thomas says, "Truth first, truth is the safest form of safety!" In this controversy "truth," in the full meaning of the word, is difficult to establish, but there is an opinion which comes near the truth and this, sometimes, in practical problems is all we may expect. Saint Bonaventure is here a Pragmatist (without, of course, making a profession of faith in this); Saint Thomas is not, decidedly not, not even in the most casual of

[39] "Sed tamen securior via tenenda est, quidquid sit rei veritas." *In Sent*. 2, 25, 2, 2, 2; (manual edition), t. 2, p. 602b.

[40] "Respondeo. Dicendum quod circa hoc aliqui diversimode opinati sunt. Quidam enim dixerunt quod consensus in delectationem non est peccatum mortale, sed veniale tantum. Alii vero dixerunt quod est peccatum mortale; et haec opinio est communior et verisimilior." ST 1-2, 74, 8, In corp.; t. 2, p. 1123a, ll. 19-25.

his remarks. You may be tempted to call him an Intellectualist; I have no objection at this moment. It is very interesting to study the texts of these great men and to pay careful attention to what they say, to how they speak inadvertently as it were; then they reveal something of the core of their thinking.

Here is another example from my collection. The question now belongs to the big matter of the treatment of the Jews by the medieval Church. A certain measure taken against them by Canon Law in order to protect the Christians and the Christian faith, looked like an expropriation without indemnification, thus a punishment to which the Church is not authorized because the Jews are outside the fold. Hence there appeared to be a conflict between divine justice forbidding unauthorized punishment and human, ecclesiastical justice making it imperative.

The Franciscan *Summa* ascribed to Alexander of Hales has this to say about the case. "The Catholic Church has no intention of doing injustice to anyone. The law in question, however, has been enacted in order that no injury be done to God. It would be an injury to God should anyone's faith be put in danger for no other reason than that temporal justice be preserved."[41] In other words, what do we care about human, temporal justice; the main thing is that divine justice, faith, be made safe. Again, "Safety first"! Safety is preferred to the practical truth of justice. Of course, to Saint Thomas who, again, knew this text, this is unacceptable. Saint Thomas is not satisfied with the good intention to safeguard the glory of God, coupled with an action of injustice. This is imprudent, and prudence is the virtue which realizes good intentions by good and appropriate, that is, by *true* means. Never mind Aquinas's solution in detail.[42] We are here interested in the problem of prudence and truth and let no one say that this problem does not daily occur in our lives! Injustice is untruth. No injustice to the Jews can *truly* serve the cause of faith or the glory of God, nor even our safety, temporal or eternal. In the Franciscan theology of the thirteenth century a pragmatist, activist, mentality comes to the fore which is not the mentality of Aquinas. It was destined to have a considerable success in this beloved Church of ours.

The author of *The Imitation of Christ* (fifteenth century) is an anti-intellectualist because, apparently, he has never been acquainted with

[41] *Summa thelogica* Inq. 3, Tract. 8, Sect. 1, Quaest. 1, Tit. 3, De haeresi; (Quaracchi: Collegium S. Bonaventurae, 1930), t. 3, pp. 737-752.

[42] See I.T. Eschmann, "St. Thomas Aquinas on the Two Powers," *Mediaeval Studies* 20 (1958): 177-205, especially p. 201, n. 77 on the sources of Thomas's position on this very issue, the *Summa fratris Alexandri* included.

good and sound intelligence; he knows only the decadent intellectuality of Nominalism. He says at the beginning of his work, "I much prefer to feel contrition rather than to know its definition."[43] Saint Thomas surely is incapable of writing down such imprudent nonsense. The definition of contrition answers the question "What is contrition?" obviously necessary in order that certain feelings may be identified correctly. The author of this book apparently has another technique of knowing that he feels contrition and not something else—perhaps a phantasmagoria or a diabolic illusion. Probably he "goes to teacher" who is expected to tell him; but this would be shifting the problem around, not solving it. Since there must be someone who *knows* the *definition* of contrition, would it not be a good idea that the author study some sound theology. This *Imitation* may contain some good advice, but one who loves Thomas Aquinas will find it difficult to get over its first page: it is pragmatism, and Saint Thomas is not a pragmatist!

*d. Pragmatism in Ethics*

In the common, colloquial, sense of the word, a pragmatist is a fussy, officious fellow, a busy-body. As usual in common speech one feature of the thing is pointed to and somewhat distorted. Pragmatism is a mentality and in America especially, but by no means in America only, it has become a philosophy. This philosophy identifies all knowing, all thinking, under the aspect of utility. "What is the use of your thought?" "How do your ideas stand up when their practical consequences are brought about?" These are the pragmatist's questions. Truth is not something in itself, something having its own value and significance. The old philosophical principle that truth is thinking in conformity with being makes sense in pragmatism only if being is understood as functioning. True, one being is indeed functioning (or also, sometimes being is functioning), but it is not true that all being, or being simply, is functioning. This would, and in fact does, lead in a large part of modern philosophy to empty *functionalism*. We are not talking, however, about modern philosophy; our subject is ethics and our own ethics. The pragmatist's problem is, "What is the efficiency of our actions and, more generally, of our life?" Moralists of a very primitive sort answer, "It is to be safely in heaven, or rather, to stay safely out

[43] This aphorism occurs in the first chapter of *The Imitation of Christ*, a work generally, but not universally, ascribed to Thomas à Kempis of the Brothers of the Common Life and translated in the form: "I had rather feel compunction than know how to define it," a formula often cited, as here, by those who judge this classic work of the *devotio moderna* to be "anti-intellectual."

of hell!"

You will realize at once how handsomely the principle may pay off here which says that "all humans want to be happy." The way to heaven (or, in their view, better) the way to stay out of hell is to keep the commandments, the characteristic short-cut of our run-of-the-mill moralism. Keeping the commandments is like using tools; a nail in the wall and a hammer probably is the only simile by which most are able to understand the relation between an end and that which is for the end, a primitive conception which substantiates their pragmatism. It is easy to find this pure pragmatism in almost any manual of moral theology. On the one hand, a moralist may be hesitant to declare an opinion stands the test of *truth* and yet, on the other hand, will say that this same opinion is *safe* and that, apparently, is quite enough. The definitions we find most of the time in our moralists are functional and pragmatic, not definitions of moral essences so much as safety rules. A typical safety rule, for instance, is the proposition which is presented as the definition of matrimony: matrimony is a contract by which the exchange of qualified rights and duties, between one man and one woman, is perpetually established. As has often been observed, a contract referring to an exchange of goods does not establish a community. The justice of exchange (we say "commutative justice") does not bring people together; rather, it keeps them at a certain distance one from the other, a distance protecting their peaceful co-existence and making it possible for them to enjoy themselves and their goods without disturbance. Fences, in a way, "make good neighbors,"[44] but they are no means of communication; they are means of separation!

Saint Thomas never attempted to show that the foundation of a community as such, or of any particular community, consists in "commutative justice." The definition of matrimony by the idea of contract does not say what matrimony is, rather it says how certain disputes, intimate disputes, may and must be settled in matrimony. It is a safety rule for the times of conflict and crisis. In the typical lawyer's manner, this conception at once envisages the situation of conflict in which and by which lawyers from time immemorial have made their name and their money. Clearly it is not

[44] "Good fences make good neighbors," a formula used twice by the poet Robert Frost, lines 27 and 45 (the last) in his poem "Mending Wall," an account of two Vermont farmers replacing fallen stones in a wall between their properties, each walking on his own side of the wall, after hunters or the winter frosts had damaged it. Eschmann may have only heard the line he cited without reading its context in which the two neighbors are literally brought together by their common wall.

conflict that brings a man and a woman to the altar!

Clearly, again, it is not precisely the marital relation which of itself, *per se*, causes conflicts. This relation is one, not of conflicting but of complementary tendencies. Conflicts may arise, but they arise outside the essence of matrimony; they come up *per accidens*, that is, through the deficiencies, the lack of understanding, in one word, the lack of *prudence* in the persons concerned. The pragmatist will object that it is highly advisable to think a little ahead of time and, of course it is, but sober advice is not an essential definition.

The most obvious, and a very frequently encountered form of pragmatism, is the opinion that "good intentions" are all that counts. We have seen this extremely (and shockingly) popular form of pragmatism in the medieval legislation against the Jews. "The Catholic Church has no *intention* to do injury to anyone. The laws against the Jews were enacted lest injury be done to God...." I leave it to you to judge how hypocritical this declaration is; in this context, the Catholic Church has no *intention* to do injury to anyone! This is exactly what we have been looking for, a bad realization covered by a good intention. The realization, the unauthorized punishment of the Jews, is unjust. The apologist says so, but adds that it does not matter; the good intention was to protect the Christian faith! The good intention belongs to the order of ends, the bad realization to that of the actions which are for the end. The total ethical structure of intention and realization, which should be organically integrated, is split up into two incoherent and even contradictory pieces.

As Saint Thomas says on this occasion, "The faith of Christ never destroys, rather it strengthens, the order of human justice." Ask yourself how often you have had to say, "What I did was foolish, but I had the best of intentions!" How often did you think that this was really sufficient? It was not! God protect us from all the "good intentions" and all the precipitate and inconsiderate, in one word, all the *imprudent* realizations, let alone those that are morally bad in other regards. Saint Thomas elaborated the virtue of prudence precisely for this reason, that there might be an intelligent guide directing the order of our realizations so that they may, together with the good intentions, constitute one organic, truly moral, truly human structure. This brings us to the consideration of three "integral parts of prudence" by which Saint Thomas shows how serious he is about prudence and truth.

### *e. Expertness, Docility, and Ingenuity*

With the word "expertness" I try to translate the word *memoria*, literally "memory," which Aquinas in Part II-II, 49, holds to be the first integral part of prudence. This is to say that "expertness/memory" is a part forming

⟨with other parts⟩ the whole of this virtue and, as it were, helping it to accomplish its task of finding and expressing the truth in our actions. Memory, of course, has nothing to do here with any sort of mnemonics, the art of improving the technical efficiency of our memory, the technical ability not to forget. It is experience and expertness, sense of reality, sympathetic talent for recognizing facts and persons, for admitting them and basing our conduct upon them.

Many people who do not possess this are apt to call it "cold and calculating intelligence"; it is neither cold nor calculating. Young people are not prudent, no one expects them to be; morality, I insist again, is not a schoolboy's homework well-done, but an arduous task which, in principle, can be achieved only with our complete maturity in spirit as well as in body; morality *is* human maturity and perfection. Expertness is based on true memories. True memories are those that preserve true facts. True facts are such as are not distorted by prejudices or resentments, but really correspond to reality. We often are given to falsifications ⟨which are⟩ due to our unreal and unrealistic egoisms; egoism is always unrealistic and untrue. Nothing is more dangerous than these falsifications, even if they are only slight. We retouch the facts, we give them a twist, we color them, we add to them or subtract from them, shift the emphasis, and so on and so forth. It is clear here how much prudence on which depends all moral virtue, depends in its turn on all moral virtue, but especially on justice, on the inner justice of the just person. All this, you will note, is not psychology: it is ethics. Our notions of ethics and morality are so perverted that in order somehow to grasp the meaning of all this, we might have recourse to some such notion as "the metaphysics" of the moral personality. "In things belonging to prudence" Saint Thomas says in the same wonderful Question, Article 3, "no one is sufficient unto himself." Docility is not the simple, not-yet-intelligent zeal of a schoolboy, the manageableness of a gentle child. What Saint Thomas has in mind may be best described by the opposite attitude: the absurd self-sufficiency of narrow-minded, headstrong people, who know everything better—no one can ever tell them! This docility of Aquinas does not originate in a vague modesty, but in the love of truth which, indeed, implies an authentic humility. If one is wayward and stupid (stupidity is the common denominator of all vices contrary to prudence) one resists the truth, is incapable of silencing egoistic interests within; their silencing is the indispensable condition of true prudence, of human truth.

By "ingenuity" I translate the Latin *solertia* (which, I think, is not quite correctly rendered by "shrewdness" in the usual English translation). I prefer "ingenuity," which connotes a free-born person with connatural high-mindedness, with nobility of character and disposition, but also with a distinguished intellectual capacity. Prudence in Saint Thomas is a virtue of heroic *noblesse*. It bears all the characteristics of distinction, of nobility, of reservedness, as well as open-mindedness, but also of human warmth and understanding which are such outstanding features of Aquinas's ethics. How far is Saint Thomas from that intrusive and officious rigmarole, from that indiscreet and breathless pedantry, of so many of our books on ethics and moral theology, our apple-tree ethics! What Saint Thomas means with this *solertia*, this ingenuity, is also a certain quickness of moral wit which grasps human situations, even complicated human situations, in an inkling and accurately, instinctively as it were, by connatural perception, unhampered by the temptations of injustice, of cowardice, of immoderation. There is more to this than meets the eye; at bottom it is spiritual and *vital* soundness. It is vital soundness especially in that realm of soul in which our neuroses originate, the nocturnal realm of the unconscious. If it is not exactly an inferno thronged with monsters, the seat of pure bestiality crouched in the depth of the human being, that realm is the source of many of our falsifications and distortions, our repressions and our complexes. Prudence will not be found in psychopathological patients; it should be found in their doctors! Psychoanalysis, however, does not speak about it. The doctrine of prudence calls for vital sanity. It reveals the high and severe claim made on the well-trained, spiritual and corporal soundness which is the hallmark of the classical and Christian ethics of virtue.

Prudence is the virtue of true realizations: it guides us and makes us do truly good actions. Those actions are individual realities. The truth of an action, that is, an actually performed action, is not that of a general principle. It is neither that of the speculative intellect, for instance the truth of "two plus two are four." It is that of the practical intellect, of the practical reason. Here again it is not that of the general practical principles and of their correct deductions. The truth of prudence is the mobile, the perpetually changing truth of concrete situations and actions: prudential ethics is a situation ethics.

*e. "Uncertain are our foresights"*

The problem is aptly stated by Thomas Aquinas in Part II-II, 47, 3. I read first the main part of this Article, then the statement of the problem, and finally the solution:

> To prudence belongs not only the consideration of reason, but also its application to action, which is the end of practical reason. No one, however, can conveniently apply one thing to another without knowing both that which is to be applied and that to which it is to be applied.

> Now actions fall among singulars; it is therefore necessary for one who is prudent to know both the universal principles of practical reason and the singulars with which actions are concerned.[45]

Now, the problem:

> Singulars are infinite; but infinites cannot be comprehended by reason; therefore, prudence, which is right reason, is not about singulars.[46]

In other words, the situations in which we act are composed of an infinite number of circumstances and reason cannot comprehend an infinite number of anything: where should it start? Where should it finish? Hence the position of prudence is indeed a metaphysically impossible position. Prudence is assigned a work which no reason can ever perform. To this Saint Thomas gives a brief, concise, and sufficient answer:

> Hence it is that, as is said in the Book of Wisdom 9:14, 'Uncertain are our foresights'. Nevertheless, experience reduces these infinite singulars to certain finites which come to pass in most cases and a knowledge of these suffices for human prudence.[47]

This is one of those most exact and exhaustive answers, in a few lines, of which Aquinas knew the secret! Note right away that theologians here speak of human *reason*. There is, of course, divine reason or intellect comprehending the infinite number of singulars. There is also infused prudence, and there is the gift of the Holy Spirit, the gift of counsel, specifically given for the right solution of *this* problem. But let us remain with human prudence, the ethical problem, as Saint Thomas does. In principle,

[45] "...ad prudentiam pertinet non solum consideratio rationis, sed etiam applicatio ad opus quod est finis practicae rationis. Nullus autem potest convenienter alteri aliquid applicare nisi utrumque cognoscat, scilicet et id quod applicandum est et id cui applicandum est. Operationes autem sunt in singularibus. Et ideo necesse est quod prudens et cognoscat universalia principia rationis, et cognoscat singularia, circa quae sunt operationes." ST 2-2, 47, 3, in corpore; t. 3, p. 1666b, ll. 29-40.

[46] "Singularia sunt infinita. Sed infinita non possunt comprehendi a ratione. Ergo prudentia, quae est ratio recta, non est singularium." Ibidem, Argument 2; p. 1666b, ll. 15-18.

[47] "...inde est quod sunt 'incertae providentiae nostrae,' ut dicitur, *Sapientia* IX 14. Tamen per experientiam singularia infinita reducuntur ad aliqua finita quae ut in pluribus accidunt, quorum cognitio sufficit ad prudentiam humanam." ST 2-2, 47, 3, Ad 2; t. 3, p. 1667a ll. 3-8.

Aquinas concedes the point of the problem. Here his whole theory of intellectual knowledge and of the possibility of knowing singulars is involved. In intellectual human knowledge the individual is "ineffable." There is a depth in the concrete human being and its concrete situation which is not translatable into thought and language. Therefore, speaking this strict language of the classical theory of knowledge, our foresights are indeed uncertain. Should this prompt us to give up every effort to strived after prudence? By no means! In fact, Saint Thomas says, a reduction of this infinity is possible, a reduction achieved through experience, through expertness. We know from experience (or rather, we might know from experience if we are truly experienced people in the full sense which is meant here) what most of the time happens or will happen. This is sufficient for human prudence.

Not a few, I suppose, will disagree with this solution. Walter Winchell (if I am not mistaken) once wrote something like this: "The expert is the one who most accurately knows how everything will happen and, who afterwards, most exactly explains why it all happened differently." The State Department too, I guess, could offer some interesting comment on this text of Thomas Aquinas. We should try to understand Saint Thomas correctly. The second remark in his answer surely does not imply a sort of cheap optimism by which a serious objection would be disposed of with an easy gesture; he is given neither to rhetoric nor to empty dialectics. There is, and there always will be, a problematic remainder in human foresight and counsel, a remainder which will remain unpenetrated and impenetrable. The metaphysical constitution of our intellect cannot be changed.

No such remainder is left in prudence. Prudence is infallible. If errors and mistakes are made, we obviously did not act prudently and the failure, not infrequently, will have to be put down to our debit. The accurate understanding of why things went wrong, and how, and to what extent this depended upon ourselves, is an enrichment of our experience and will profit the growth of our prudence.

We must, of course, get rid of our usual notion of morality and be especially careful at this point in keeping that notion out. Morality is not something "punctual," but something "linear." It is not a "point" without extension or duration, not a "monad," not a single performance without any context, to be subsumed under formal, juristic, logic. Rather it is a line leading to perfection, a way, *the* way, to perfection. Morality, in other words, is not static, but dynamic. It does not consist in conformity, that is, not *only* in conformity, but also in collaboration with the rule of reason. Morality is the human perfection which can never be realized at once, in one invariable and fixed point, as it were, but is a perpetual development and a perpetual striving. It is *life*. It would mean foisting a really miserable view of human life on Aquinas if we supposed him to have anything to do with our common notion of morality which is that of a schoolboy's homework, well done and finished. Saint Thomas's answer, I think, simply translates his idea of morality and perfection into the language of the particular problem which he set out to solve.

From the standpoint of Saint Thomas we must say that there can be no failure of prudence because a failure of prudence is "imprudence" and imprudence is no-prudence or not-prudence! There are failures in our lives and a lot of them. For some, we are responsible, for instance, when fools, as the saying goes, "rush in where angels fear to tread" or when we behave like the bull in a china shop—as do those who urge marriage on immature youngsters. No good intention will wash their foolishness clean. Foolishness, stupidity, precipitation, inconsideration, and such like are indeed sins.

For some other failures we are not responsible, namely, when and if in truth we are up against the "uncertainty of human counsels" of which Holy Scripture speaks. These are not failures of *prudence*; rather they are lessons in prudence. For we are the *image* of God, but we are not the omniscient God. Humility, docility, are as much necessary dispositions of prudence as are charity, justice, temperance, and fortitude. The human world will never be as full of the prudent as it is relatively full of the well-meaning. The human world does not consist of undifferentiated, merely co-existing, individuals. Prudence is a "distinguishing" virtue, a virtue of differentiations entailing a differentiated society as Aquinas points out in the Articles 10 to 12 in Question 47.

Now the "rectification" of the will, in respect of the end of the virtues, is the first thing in morality. As long as this first thing is not settled, we cannot even begin to talk about prudence. After the ordering of the field of *ends* there remains the ordering of the field of *the things which are for the end*. This is to say that after our intentions are made good, our realizations need to be made good. Is it such a rare thing in life to find a chaste person "rectified" as to the end of this virtue, and not rectified as to the means by which it can be brought into existence? Truly intending to be chaste, such may be prudish, squeamish, fastidious, straight-laced, pathologically scrupulous, and a nuisance to themselves and to others. A whole people may be lead by a puritanical oligarchy and the persons responsible will not even notice that this imprudence as to realization brings about the most dangerous obsessions and the most unbridled licentiousness. Are these rare phenomena, unheard-of exceptions? Is it really so hard to admit that the order of human, moral realizations presents its own specific difficulties? Those difficulties are of an intellectual-moral nature which need precisely the intellectual-moral virtue, namely, prudence! Or are people afraid that by introducing the intellect into our human, moral life, they make this life dependent on shrewdness, smartness (smart aleck-ness!) and the like? Or are our people so preoccupied with the education of children and youngsters that they are afraid to speak of prudence because children are notoriously *not* prudent? Who would want them to be "prudent"? Who would want precocious children?

## E. Law and the Liberty of the Christian

### *a. Natural and Positive Laws*

In this topic we are not discussing natural law. Natural law is not law in the plain and obvious sense in which people usually speak about law. I have warned several times in these lectures not to put Natural (and for that matter Eternal) Law in the same pot in which we find the other laws. The characteristic of law, as we talk about it here, is that it is "posited." The word "to posit" whence is derived "positive" is here to be understood in the technical meaning of legal philosophy and jurisprudence. It means to make, to establish, and promulgate law. Positive, used to qualify law, is not opposed to "negative," but to "natural." Natural law is not posited since it is nature and nature is not legislatively established and imposed, but created. It is not an extrinsic, but an intrinsic principle. With regard to natural law, therefore, Saint Thomas, who is very careful about his language, does not say that it is "a given law," *lex data* but it is "an inserted law," *lex indita*. Law generally is *given*, it supposes the lawgiver; natural law is not given, but inserted, implanted. Not even this is a quite correct expression; in truth, natural law simply *is* rational nature or natural reason, in principle as accessible to us, to you and me, as a thing can be, because a human being *is* the nature that makes one human.

Our question, then, is about positive law. I shall try to read and annotate a few pertinent texts of Aquinas, in the first place the very original and historically important Article 1 of Question 95, Part I-II about "legis-position" or, as we prefer to say, "legislation."

Why are there laws? Montesquieu gave his famous book, published in 1748, the title *De l'esprit des lois*. It is a treatise on the spirit of the laws, on the ideology of legislation, which we are going to study in Aquinas. A thinker worth his salt usually reveals his mind on human life both completely and characteristically when he comes to this problem. Aristotle did so in the last chapter of his *Nicomachean Ethics* (10, 9) in which, at the same time, he recapitulates his whole ethical thought and prefaces his work on *Politics*. This chapter is an important source of Aquinas's teaching, but it is not the only one. In fact, Saint Thomas takes care at the outset, as he often does, to show his agreement with the Christian tradition. He quotes Isidore of Seville (who, in turn, speaks the language of Saint Augustine who, in his turn, speaks the language of Aristotle and the whole Greek and Roman tradition). Laws are made, Isidore says, that in fear thereof human activity might be held in check, that innocence might be safeguarded in the midst of wickedness, and that the dread of punishment might prevent the wicked from doing harm.[48]

*b. De l'esprit des lois*

Let us read the text of Saint Thomas:

> The aptitude for virtue is in the nature [and indeed is the very nature] of the human being. The perfection, however, of virtue is not a natural gift, but acquired by discipline. An example taken from the domain of our technical, industrial doings will illustrate this. A human being needs food and clothing. The beginnings of these is all one has from nature which gave both reason and hands. But the achievement is not a gift of nature. One who is human has to prepare food and clothing oneself. We are different in this from other animals to whom nature itself gives all they need in the way of food and clothing.[49]

In other words, the animals grow furs and feathers, we have to make our clothes. Animals do not cook; we have to prepare our food. This statement comes directly from Avicenna, but it is rooted in the famous argument with which Aristotle proved the social nature of humans. In his work *On Kingship to the King of Cyprus* we find this same reasoning in a more developed fashion:

> ...For all other animals, nature has prepared food, hair as a covering, teeth, horns, claws as means of defence or at least speed in flight,

[48] See ST 1-2, 95, 3, a discussion of whether Isidore had "suitably" or "unsuitably," *convenienter*, or *inconvenienter*, described the quality of positive law in his *Etymologia* Lib. 5, Cap. 21; PL 82 203.

[49] "...homini naturaliter inest quaedam aptitudo ad virtutem; sed ipsa virtutis perfectio necesse est quod homini adveniat per aliquam disciplinam. Sicut etiam videmus quod per aliquam industriam subvenitur homini in suis necessitatibus, puta in cibo et vestitu, quorum initia quaedam habet a natura, scilicet rationem et manus, non autem ipsum complementum, sicut cetera animalia, quibus natura dedit sufficienter tegumentum et cibum." ST 1-2, 95, 1, in corpore; t. 2, p. 1230b, l. 45–1231a, l. 3.

> while the human being alone was made without any natural provisions for these things. Instead of all these, the human being is endowed with reason, by the use of which one could procure all these things for oneself by the work of those hands.... Moreover, all other animals are able to discern, by inborn skill, what is useful and what is injurious, even as the sheep naturally regards the wolf as enemy. Some animals also recognize by natural skill certain medicinal herbs and other things necessary for their life. A human, on the contrary, has a natural knowledge of the things which are essential for life only in a general fashion, inasmuch as one is able to attain knowledge of the particular things necessary for human life by reasoning from natural principles.[50]

With these indications we are in the midst of human history and the growth of civilization which is the human way toward all-around and properly human perfection. In technical as well as in moral matters this history starts from nature, but is a work of human industry and ingenuity, In the field of technique we have our reason and our hands to do the work, the hand an instrument shaped according to reason; a human hand is also one of the most perfect expressions of an individual human's reason and personality. In the field of morality and moral realizations we have again our reason directing us. The beginnings of virtue, *seminaria virtutum*, lie in natural reason and its principles. These are but the beginnings; the key word in Aquinas here is "discipline." Discipline is a matter related to disciples, to their instruction and education. Since we are in ethics, not so much instruction, but rather education is the thing designated by the word *disciplina*, "discipline" in our text. Discipline is a method of forming character, a way of training disciples in virtuous conduct, the not-yet mature pupil or child or youngster. That these notions of maturity and immaturity have to be taken formally is clear. We are not talking about age differences which can be counted and fixed by the years, but of real conditions in human individuals. There might be, indeed there are, "young" and "old" children. The "old" ones are ridiculous; the young ones, the authentic children or youngsters, are not ridiculous. Saint Thomas's judgment about the real conditions of human individuals should here be re-

[50] This is a slightly modified excerpt from Eschmann's revision of the English translation by G.B. Phelan of the *De regno ad regem Cypri* by Saint Thomas Aquinas, under the title *St. Thomas Aquinas. On Kingship to the King of Cyprus* (Toronto: Pontifical Institute of Mediaeval Studies, 1949), I, 5 and 6, pp. 4, 5; the source in Avicenna is there identified as *De anima* V, 1.

membered. Most people are morally and spiritually immature however old in years they may be. Most people follow their senses and not their reason. To continue with his text from the *Summa theologiae*:

> Now, no one will easily be found to suffice himself or herself in regard to this discipline, for the perfection of virtue consists chiefly in being free from the power of those undue pleasures to which humans are prone to yield; and most of all are so inclined the youngsters, *iuvenes* who are more receptive to discipline. Hence, concerning this discipline which aims at making virtuous people of us, we need to receive it from others.[51]

Whenever Saint Thomas speaks of "others," of "the other," he means society and its institutions. Society itself, in Aquinas, and its various forms, are things ethical, that is, organizations of and for human life, institutions brought into existence not only for merely economical purpose, but chiefly for the purpose of, what Aristotle called and Saint Thomas often repeated, "the good life," good in the sense of human, moral perfection. Society in this conception, helps one to be virtuous. Its necessity results from the various differentiations found, not in the human being as such, but in the various human individuals. We are not an undifferentiated mass of people with one face and physiognomy, or rather with no face and individual shape at all. We are different. There are men and women (*vive la différence!*), there are grown-ups and youngsters, the prudent and the fools, intellectuals and practitioners, contemplative natures and those more inclined to activity, and so on and so forth *ad infinitum*. Society is not built upon a total egalitarianism which would even think it to be an advantage to obliterate and confuse the most natural and permanent differentiations.

Society is here seen in the service of human perfection, that is, moral goodness in the full sense of the word. Saint Thomas now goes on to describe in greater detail the moral discipline which is the business of society in its various forms:

> As to those youngsters who are prone to perform acts of virtue because they are naturally gentle, well-born, and well-reared, or also distinguished by the grace of God, paternal discipline will suffice

[51] "Ad hanc autem disciplinam non de facili invenitur homo sibi sufficiens. Quia perfectio virtutis praecipue consistit in retrahendo hominem ab indebitis delectationibus, ad quas praecipue homines sunt proni, et maxime iuvenes, circa quos est efficacior disciplina. Et ideo oportet quod huiusmodi disciplinam, per quam ad virtutem perveniatur, homines ab alio sortiantur." ST 1-2, 95, 1, in corpore; t. 2, p. 1231a, ll. 3-12.

> ⟨discipline⟩ which is given through counsels and admonitions. But some are of a different kind. They are a saucy baggage, cheeky as a cocksparrow [this is my own paraphrase of the text; Saint Thomas says, "insolent and prone to vices and not easily amenable to words"]. They then must be restrained from evil by force and fear. In such a way, they might at least desist from evil-doing and leave the others in peace; and, by being habituated in this way to doing what is good, they might be brought to do willingly what hitherto they did from fear and thus become virtuous.[52]

Now the way is cleared for the conclusion:

> Now this kind of discipline, compelling through fear and punishment, is the discipline of laws. Hence, it is in view of peace and virtue that laws are posited. For, as The Philosopher says, as the human is the most noble of all animals, if perfect in justice, so also the lowest of all, if severed from law and justice (*Politics* 1, 1, 1253a 31). For a human uses reason to devise means of satisfying lusts and evil passions, which other animals are unable to do.[53]

The Article of Saint Thomas contains more than meets the eye. To understand it correctly, we must especially guard against the danger of thinking that Aquinas is here speaking about age differences. He is speaking formally, as a philosopher and a theologian. The opposition which he means to discuss is that between moral and spiritual maturity as against moral and spiritual immaturity, an opposition which runs across biological ages. Maturity consists in virtuous acting, immaturity in the lack of it.

[52] "Et quidem quantum ad illos iuvenes qui sunt proni ad actus virtutum ex bona dispositione naturae, vel consuetudine, vel magis divino munere, sufficit disciplina paterna, quae est per monitiones. Sed quia inveniuntur quidam protervi et ad vitia proni, qui verbis de facili moveri non possunt; necessarium fuit quod per vim et metum cohiberentur a malo, ut saltem sic male facere desistentes, et aliis quietam vitam redderent, et ipsi tandem per huiusmodi assuetudinem ad hoc perducerentur quod voluntarie facerent quae prius metu implebant, et sic fierent virtuosi." Ibidem, p. 1231a, ll. 12-26. It will have been noticed that Eschmann has referred to his own words as "paraphrase."

[53] "Huiusmodi autem disciplina cogans metu poenae, est disciplina legum. Unde necessarium fuit ad pacem hominum et virtutem, quod leges ponerentur, quia sicut Philosophus dicit in I *Pol.* ⟨1; 13⟩ 'sicut homo, si sit perfectus virtute, est optimum animalium; sic, si sit separatus a lege et iustitia, est pessimum omnium,' quia homo habet arma rationis ad explendas concupiscentias et saevitias, quae non habent alia animalia." Ibidem, t. 2, p. 1231a, ll. 26-36.

Normally the distinction between maturity and immaturity corresponds to that of the grown-up and the growing-up persons. A grown-up is *per se*, "essentially," mature. It is this *per se* language which Saint Thomas speaks. The opposite, *per accidens*, "accidentally," is infinite and ineffable. "The spirit of the laws," according to this philosophy is, in one word, that they are *pedagogical* institutions. They are means and methods of instruction and discipline in view of the ethical education of humanity. The Aristotelian philosophy is behind this teaching to be sure, but the decisive authority for Saint Thomas is here The Apostle, Saint Paul, who said that the Law (meaning the Old Law) is *pedagogus in Christum*, "the pedagogue ⟨the slave who takes a child to school across the dangerous streets⟩ unto Christ" (Galatians 3:24). We must here investigate a little further Aquinas's teaching on law.

*c. The Pedagogy of the Laws*

The intention of the lawgiver, Saint Thomas repeats over and over again (after Aristotle), is to make a good human being, "good" in the Thomasic sense of human perfection through virtue. The lawgiver can only make us perform virtuous acts, that is, acts which objectively conform to the rule of acting established by the laws. The lawgiver cannot force us to act virtuously. Here we confront the distinction, of great importance in Aquinas's ethics, between an act of virtue and a virtuously performed act of virtue. Let us read a brief text in which this distinction is used:

> A virtuous act may be considered in two ways. First [objectively] inasmuch as a person does that which is virtuous. Concerning justice, for instance, one does what is just [pays what is owed], or, concerning fortitude, does that which is brave. Acts to be performed [in accordance with the objective demands of the virtues] are the objects of the precepts of the laws. Still, fully understood, an act of virtue is [not only to do what is virtuous, but] to do it virtuously [that is, in such a way that the act proceeds from the inner center of our fully-grown moral personality]. Considered under this second aspect, the act of virtue always comes from [the personal] habit of virtue [while, on the contrary, no habit of virtue is needed to perform a virtuous act according to the merely objective aspect of virtuous acting. Understood in this way] virtuous acting does not fall under the precepts of the laws, but is the end to which the legislator intends to lead those subjects.[54]

[54] "...aliquis actus dicitur esse virtutis dupliciter. Uno modo, ex eo quod homo

In other words, the legislator (we should add the *human* legislator) is satisfied with mere objective conformity. We have seen that a legalistic moral teaching is thus satisfied too; it cannot demand more on account of its characteristic starting point.

Conformity itself, however, is only half of the business—if it is "half" at all! We learned from Saint Thomas how he makes the laws work and what he expects of them in the case of those "immature youths" who cannot be restrained from evil-doing by admonitions, since their individual nature is somehow corrupted. They are forced by fear, or also by the application, of punishment to do what is right, to conform, so that other people may have peace. The penal sanction is the "last resort," the *ultima ratio*, of the legislator, his last and most effective means and that in which the pedagogical nature of legislation shows up in the clearest light. Legislation is an effective, a categorically decisive, inducement to the ethical minimum, namely, the conformity of the action to the rule, not the collaboration of the person with the rule and with the ruler. Those immature youths are not forced to act virtuously; no one can be so forced, since acting virtuously is in the first place acting spontaneously, acting from an inner, natural, principle and in the second place, it is acting in the total, unified context of a morally formed, a spiritually mature, personality. Those immature youngsters, then, are not forced to act virtuously, but it is hoped (more or less piously) that, by being forced to conform, after a time they might possibly come to collaborate.

The inner tendency of this philosophy which emphasizes the pedagogy of legislation and integrates the laws into an ethical analysis, is to make laws superfluous. Education, of itself, is an activity of transitory character. The better and the more successful education is, the sooner it will have educated the pupil, made a mature person, and will have withdrawn. We shall see how boldly Saint Thomas pursues this idea when we consider his theology of the New Law, the New Testament, for Aquinas is a theologian whose object in this whole treatise on law is to prepare a theological explanation of the two Laws in which consist the Holy Scriptures of the Church.

These few traits of Saint Thomas's teaching on positive law have been insisted upon for two reasons: first, in order to prepare the answer

---

operatur virtuosa sicut actus virtutis iustitiae est facere recta, et actus fortitudinis facere fortia. Et sic lex praecipit aliquos actus virtutum. Alio modo dicitur actus virtutis, quia aliquis operatur virtuosa eo modo quo virtuosus operatur. Et talis actus semper procedit a virtute, nec cadit sub praecepto legis, sed est finis ad quem legislator ducere intendit." ST 1-2, 96, 3, Ad 2; t. 2, p. 1238a, ll. 13-24.

to our question "Where do we find the prudent person?" or rather, the justification of the answer already given, namely, that we—you and I—are in principle that prudent person. I shall come back to this at the end of the present discussion. The second reason, however, was to show how a treatise on *obligation* may be integrated into the ethic of Saint Thomas.

*d. Obligation in the Ethics of Saint Thomas*

Obligation must be inserted here and in no other place. As you will remember, obligation is a necessity imposed by another, namely, by the legislator. It is, we learn here, a necessity imposed for pedagogical reasons, for instruction and for discipline. Obligation is clearly involved in positive law (not in law as such, according to Saint Thomas). This is self-evident, so much so that Aquinas does not even discuss it. He only states the question, "Whether this is an obligation in conscience?" The imposition, as far as good people are concerned, is always for *instruction*; every time the wicked are concerned, which is the case of us all, saints perhaps the only exceptions, although to be sure they would be the first to proclaim loudly that they too (and even in the first place!) need the other role of law, its *discipline*, the *disciplina legum*. This discipline shows most clearly the specific necessity in which obligation consists. For, I repeat, it is a coactive and effective discipline, as effective as anything can be among human beings. There we have a real "categorical imperative."[55] With this I do not mean to say that penal sanction is part of the very meaning of obligation. All that penal sanction does is to bind more tightly, with a chain of a different material, if the chain in which obligation consists, should prove to be too weak. I leave it to you to reconsider the essential features of obligationism and to find my criticism verified by the considerations of Thomas Aquinas which we have just studied.

Of course, Saint Thomas's ethics is not an "obligationist" ethics. The reason for this is that the very notion of obligation introduces a perspective which, although essential and important in ethics, nevertheless is

[55] Eschmann here refers to the Kantian construction called by its author "the categoric imperative" and formulated in a number of varied expressions of which the first is, "Act only on that maxim through which you can at the same time will that it should become a universal law" ("handle nur nach der jenigen Maxime, durch die du zugleich wollen kannst, dass sie ein allgemeines Gesetz werde"); see *Kant's Gesammelte Schriften* (Berlin: G. Reimer, 1911), Bd IV, S. 421, ll. 6-8; English translation, *The Moral Law or Kant's Groundwork of the Metaphysic of Morals*, translation, introduction, notes by H.J. Paton (New York, Melbourne, Sydney, Cape Town: Hutchinson's University Library, ca 1947), p. 88 at no. 421, 52.

secondary and limited. If elevated to the rank of *the* perspective in ethics, the perspective *par excellence*, it can only bring about all the distortions and failures, all the false problems and false answers which we have seen. Ethics becomes a teaching profitable to children, if not downright a teaching to be addressed to those youngsters who cannot be restrained from evil-doing except by the fear of hell whaled into them. The fear of hell is salutary if it be a reverential fear, as Saint Thomas says—which it is not with those "youngsters" (old and young!). With them it is a servile fear. No matter—even servile fear may count in ethics as a faraway beginning of virtue. It counts in an ethics for slaves, and with Saint Thomas we are indeed far from overlooking the fact that many people *are* slaves of their passions. Still, if an ethics is exclusively focussed on this aspect, it is bound to miss the real problem of ethics which is that of human perfection.

*e. Divine Legislation: The "Imperfect" and the "Perfect" Laws*

In the treatise on the two divine Laws, the old and the new (I-II, 98-108), Saint Thomas's ethics reaches its culmination, its zenith. It is regrettable that this treatise is never taught in our schools. In philosophy it is not mentioned because it is thought to be too theological, as though it were not precisely Aquinas's philosophy which, in a theological setting, comes to light in its most profound meaning, its very ultimate intentions. In moral theology, of course, they teach the ten commandments, but they hardly see them in their biblical, theological context, within the total economy of our salvation.

The intelligibility of Aquinas's theology of the two laws is given through the notions and the opposition of the "imperfect" and the "perfect." The Old Law is imperfect, the New perfect. This implies no criticism of the Old Law, nor is it Saint Thomas's own invention; it is biblical, especially Pauline doctrine and it is sound Patristic theology, especially the theology of Saint Augustine. The meaning of this distinction, as applied to these Laws, may best be seen and studied in a text like the following:

> Just as in the speculative sciences people are led to assent to conclusions by syllogistic means so, in every law, they are led to observe its precepts by the threat of punishment or the promise of reward. Now, we see that in the speculative sciences the means of our proofs are presented to the disciple according to that disciple's mental conditions. Teaching these sciences must proceed in an orderly fashion; we begin with things the student knows, and go on from there to the things the student does not know. So, likewise, the one who would induce people to observe the laws, will move them first by presenting to them an object which is dear to their hearts; just as

children are brought to do something by means of little gifts that appeal to them. [Obstinate children must be tactfully brought to reason by dangling before their eyes the bribe of a new toy.] Now, the Old Law prepared people for the advent of Christ, just as the imperfect prepares for the perfect. It was indeed given to a people as yet imperfect in comparison to the perfection which was to result from Christ's coming. This is, why The Apostle, Galatians 3:24, compares the Jews to whom the Old Law was given, to a pupil who is still under a pedagogue, a tutor: "The Law has been our tutor to bring us unto Christ." True, our perfection, our maturity consists in this, that despising temporal goods, we adhere to things spiritual for their own sake and value. But those that are yet imperfect, desire temporal goods. They do so with God in view, for it would be a perversion to place the last end in these goods. Hence the Old Law, being a Law for the imperfect, promised temporal rewards and threatened temporal punishment [as it is written in Isaiah 1:19, "If you be willing and will hearken to Me, you shall eat the good things of the Land. But if you will not, and will provoke Me to wrath, the sword shall devour you.] These were the means by which the lawgiver in those times took the people by their hands, as it were, and led them to God. [They were not yet grown up to the stature of Christ].[56]

[56] "...sicut in scientiis speculativis inducuntur homines ad assentiendum conclusionibus per media syllogistica, ita etiam in qualibet legibus homines inducuntur ad observantias praeceptorum per poenas et praemia. Videmus autem in scientiis speculativis quod media proponuntur auditori secundum eius conditionem; unde sicut oportet ordinate in scientiis procedere, ut ex notioribus disciplina incipiat, ita etiam oportet eum qui vult inducere hominem ad observantiam praeceptorum, ut ex illis eum movet incipiat quae sunt in eius affectu; sicut pueri provocantur ad aliquid faciendum aliquibus puerilibus munusculia. Dictum est autem supra quod lex vetus disponebat ad Christum sicut imperfectum ad perfectum; unde dabatur populo adhuc imperfecto in comparatione ad perfectiorem quae erat futura per Christum; et ideo populus ille comparatur puero sub paedagogo existenti, ut patet *Ad Galatas* III, 24. Perfectio autem hominis est ut, contemptis temporalibus, spiritualibus inhaereat, ut patet per illud quod Apostolus dicit. *Ad Philippenses* III, ⟨13, 15⟩: 'Quae quidem retro sunt obliviscens, ad ea quae priora sunt me extendo. Quicumque ergo perfecti sumus, hoc sentiamus.' Imperfectorum autem est quod temporalia bona desiderent, in ordine tamen ad Deum. Perversorum autem est quod in temporalibus bonis finem constituant. Unde legi veteri conveniebat ut per temporalia, quae erant in affectu hominum imperfectorum, manuduceret homines ad Deum." ST 1-2, 99, 6, in corpore; t. 2, p. 1257b, l. 40-p. 1258a, l. 25. The translation given is that of Eschmann.

Thus far Saint Thomas. We know where these considerations come from and where they lead: to the central theme in Aquinas's ethics, the virtuous action virtuously performed, which is the privilege of the prudent person. Now let us see.

*f. Fear and Love*

The same view on the two Laws which we just read in Aquinas may be expressed in another way (or even in other ways). Saint Augustine did this by using the notions and the dialectics of fear and love. The Old Law is the Law of fear, the New Law is the law of love. Here is how Saint Thomas, in I-II, 107, 1, To the 2, discusses the Augustinian doctrine:

> All the differences which are assigned [i.e. which Augustine assigns] between the Old and the New Laws are expressions of the same fundamental difference, namely, that between imperfect and perfect. Every law establishes precepts about the acts of virtue. Now the imperfect do acts of virtue differently from the perfect, the difference consisting in this that the former have not the habit of virtue which the latter have. This habit consists in an intrinsic principle, an entitative perfection making us do with ease and mastery the things which belong to the habit. The imperfect then need an extrinsic cause to do an act of virtue. They therefore need the threat of punishment or the promise of certain rewards such as honor, riches, and the like. These sanctions are added to the acts of virtue themselves and different from them.
>
> For this reason, [said Augustine] the Old Law is called the Law of fear. It was indeed given to the imperfect, that is, those that had not yet received the spiritual grace of Christ, and sanctions consisting in either temporal punishment or temporal promises were essential to this law. On the other hand, the perfect do acts of virtue from an intrinsic principle, that is to say, by themselves, for the very love of virtue, not motivated by some added punishment or promise. Therefore the New Law *which consists in that very spiritual grace infused in our hearts* is called [by Augustine] the Law of Love. Its promises are spiritual and eternal; they are the objects of virtues themselves, and especially of charity [whose object is God]. Hence we have here the situation [not of act of virtue *plus* something else as reward working as motivation, but] simply of the act of virtue itself which is its own reward. [Note in this very enlightening passage how Aquinas is always arguing from the midst of his ethical thought which he has taken right at the beginning, in the Question on beatitude!] Therefore [Augustine says that] the Old Law was a law "restraining the

> hand rather than the will" [in other words, like Moral theology today, it did not go to the center of the moral personality, is satisfied with our "hands" and a minimum of morality. When one refrains from sin because of the penal sanction, one's aversion against sin is not absolute nor total, as it is in one who abstains from sin for the love of justice itself. This is meant when [Augustine] says that the New Law restrains the will: [it strikes through to the center of our moral personality].[57]

It is clear that this doctrine cuts across the lines drawn by the historical development of the economy of our salvation. Saint Thomas observes this explicitly:

> There were of course some people in the state of the Old Testament who had that charity and the grace of the Holy Spirit. They were looking forward to the spiritual and eternal promises and so belonged indeed to the New Law, under this respect. And, on the other hand, in the state of the New Testament [in which we are and live] there are certain people who have not yet attained to the perfection

[57] "...omnes differentiae quae assignantur inter novam legem et veterem, accipiuntur secundum perfectum et imperfectum. Praecepta enim legis cuiuslibet dantur de actibus virtutum. Ad operanda autem virtutum opera aliter inclinantur imperfecti, qui nondum habent virtutis habitum; et aliter illi qui sunt per habitum virtutis perfecti. Illi autem qui nondum habent habitum virtutis, inclinantur ad agendum virtutis opera ex aliqua causa extrinseca; puta ex comminatione poenarum, vel ex promissione aliquarum extrinsecarum remunerationum, puta honoris vel divitiarum vel alicuius huiusmodi. Et ideo lex vetus, quae dabatur imperfectis, idest nondum consecutis gratiam spiritualem, dicebatur lex timoris, inquantum inducebat ad observantiam praeceptorum per comminationem quarundam poenarum. Et dicitur habere temporalia quaedam promissa. Illi autem qui habent virtutem, inclinantur ad virtutis opera agenda propter amorem virtutis, non propter aliquam poenam aut remunerationem extrinsecam. Et ideo lex nova, cuius principalitas consistit in ipsa spirituali gratia indita cordibus, dicitur lex amoris. Et dicitur habere promissa spiritualia et aeterna, quae sunt obiecta virtutis, praecipue caritatis. Et ita per se in ea inclinantur non quasi in extranea, sed quasi in propria. Et propter hoc etiam lex vetus dicitur 'cohibere manum, non animum,' quia qui timore poenae ab aliquo peccato abstinet, non simpliciter eius voluntas a peccato recedit, sicut recedit voluntas eius qui amore iustitiae recedit a peccato. Et propter hoc lex nova, quae est lex amoris, dicitur 'cohibere manum, non animum'"; ⟨the formula "comprimere manum et non animum" is to be found in Peter Lombard, *Sent.* Lib. 3, Dist. 40, Cap. 1, no. 300⟩; ST 1-2, 107, 1 Ad 2; t. 2, p. 1339a, l. 33-p. 1339b, l. 20. It may be noted that this somewhat free translation by Eschmann includes justifiable expansions, "Augustine says," not included explicitly in the text of Saint Thomas.

> of the New Law [and let us add, at some time and on some occasions we all are carnal, let nobody feel exempt!] These must, even in the era of the New Testament, be led to virtuous living acting by the fear of punishment and the expectation of temporal advantages.[58]

Our quarrel with Moral Theology was not and is not, I repeat for the last time, that account be taken of the many "carnal humans," *homines carnales*, living ⟨now⟩ in the age of Christ and of the Holy Spirit, but that this is regarded as, and called, "Moral Theology" which it is not; it is neither moral nor is it theology!

*g. On the Liberty of the Christian*

Now the New Law is called the "law of liberty." This is not a theologoumenon (a theological conclusion or doctrine), but straight and explicit revelation in the Epistle of James, 1:25: "He that looketh into the perfect law, the law of liberty...."

In opposition to the law of liberty, the Old Law is the law of servitude. Christian ethics, consequently, is the ethics of liberty, Jewish ethics is the ethics of servitude. Or, inversely, if an ethics insists on servitude (and conformity), it is Judaistic and Talmudistic; Christian ethics as such insists on liberty and the image of God. There is no Christian ethics without a chapter on the liberty of the Christian, *Von der Freiheit des Christenmenschen*.

Saint Thomas, whose Prologue to Part I-II at once put this point into relief, strongly and repeatedly emphasizes it in his Questions on the two laws. Let us begin with a text (Question 108, Article 1, To the second Argument) where the foundations and the doctrinal synthesis appear in the clearest light:

> As The Philosopher says in the First Book of the *Metaphysics*:
>
> Liberty consists in self-causation. Hence one acts freely who acts from oneself, the cause of one's own action. Now if one acts from that entitative strengthening of one's nature which we call a natural habit, one will act from oneself: the habit inclines in the fashion of

[58] "Fuerunt tamen aliqui in statu veteris testamenti habentes caritatem et gratiam Spiritus Sancti, qui principaliter expectabant promissiones spirituales et aeternas. Et secundum hoc pertinebant ad legem novam.— Similiter etiam in novo testamento sunt aliqui carnales nondum pertingentes ad perfectionem novae legis, quos oportuit etiam in novo testamento induci ad virtutis opera per timorem poenarum, et per aliqua temporalia promissa." Ibidem, p. 1339b, ll. 21-31. The text is Eschmann's translation.

> a nature. And if, on the other hand, the habit were contrary to nature [as indeed is the habit of a sin or of sins] one having such a habit cannot act of oneself, one acts in virtue of an added corruption. [Now this being so, let us apply this to the matter in hand.] The New Law [as was said] is the grace itself of the Holy Spirit. This grace is an inward habit infused in us; it is a new nature, a new being, inclining us toward right acting. Therefore it is clear that it makes us to act freely [that is, spontaneously], and self-causatively, the things that correspond to this new being, just as, spontaneously and self-causatively, that is, freely it makes us avoid the corresponding evil.[59]

In other words, the principle of the New Law is grace which is a second, a supernaturally added, nature. Grace is as much, if not more, a vital principle than is nature. Hence, if we act from grace, we act spontaneously and "self-causatively," just as if we act from nature, because nature is something inward and intimate in us. We *are* our nature. Nature is our being. Likewise, in the supernatural order grace is our being. The New Law, again, just like natural law, is not a body of law, it is not a codification, but it is a "law implanted," a *lex indita*, a vital principle, the source of a free dynamism. It is not a book, at least not a law-book, but the Holy Spirit, the Third Person in the Blessed Trinity, dwelling in us. And that is the reason why the New Law is called the "law of liberty."

If we look closer at the law of liberty, we find, Saint Thomas continues in his text that,

> The New Law is called the law of liberty in two ways: first, because it does not bind us [obligation!] to do or avoid anything but that which is absolutely necessary for salvation [it binds us to faith, hope, and charity and, of course, to the sacraments]. Neither does it bind us to avoid anything but that which is absolutely contrary to our salvation. [Saint Thomas finds the specific characteristic of the New

[59] "...secundum Philosophum in I *Metaph.* ⟨2, 9; 982b 26⟩: 'Liber est qui sui causa est.' Ille ergo libere aliquid agit qui ex seipso agit. Quod autem homo agit ex habitu suae naturae convenienti ex seipso agit, quia habitus inclinat in modum naturae. Si vero habitus esset naturae repugnans, homo non ageret secundum quod est ipse, sed secundum aliquam corruptionem sibi supervenientem. Quia igitur gratia Spiritus Sancti est sicut interior habitus nobis infusus inclinans nos ad recte operandum, facit nos libere operari ea quae conveniunt gratiae, et vitare ea quae gratiae repugnant." ST 1-2, 108, 1, Ad 2; t. 2, p. 1345a, ll. 22-36; Eschmann's translation.

> Law in its counsels rather than in its precepts while on the other hand, the specific characteristics of the Old Law, the law of servitude, is that it had no counsels: everything in it was precept, or prohibition. The New Law is the law of the Father who counsels and admonishes rather than commands those that are His children (*filii Dei*) rather than his servants (Question 108, Article 4).] The New Law is called the law of liberty: secondly because it makes us to observe its precepts and prohibitions [including the Decalogue which has not been abolished] freely, inasmuch as we keep them from the inner instinct of grace.[60]

The very illuminating parallelism between Natural Law and Evangelical Law is set forth by Thomas in Question 106, Article 1, To the second Argument.[61] Neither law is written, codified law, he says. Both, principally, that is at their root, consist in a living, vital principle. Natural Law is the order of reason, Christian Law the order of faith. Natural Law, principally, is not objective, codifiable, and codified reasonableness, but the subjective power of reasoning, not a dead letter, but a living thing, a seed to whose growth we all must contribute constantly.[62] Christian Law principally is not an objective, codified collection of propositions regarding faith and discipline, but the Holy Spirit dwelling in our souls, grace intrinsically given to the faithful. Natural Law is the light in us lit up by the Creator; Christian Law is the light of faith lit up in us by the Holy Spirit. I am quoting Saint Thomas; who would dare saying such things today? No precept of the natural Law could ever be encountered without its being formulated by the power of reasoning, nor can any such precept be observed without reason and prudence. No precept of the Christian Law could even be enounced which is not formulated by faith, nor can there be any obser-

[60] "Sic igitur lex nova dicitur lex libertatis dupliciter. Uno modo, quia non arctat nos ad facienda vel vitanda aliqua, nisi quae de se sunt vel necessaria vel repugnantia saluti, quae cadunt sub praecepto vel prohibitionis legis. Secundo, quia huiusmodi praecepta vel prohibitiones facit nos libere implere, inquantum ex interiori instinctu gratiae ea implemus." Ibidem, p. 1345a, ll. 37-45; Eschmann's translation.

[61] "Dicendum quod dupliciter est aliquid inditum homini. Uno modo, pertinens ad naturam humanam; et sic lex naturalis est lex indita homini. Alio modo est aliquid inditum homini quasi superadditum per gratiae donum. Et hoc modo lex nova est indita homini, non solum indicans quid sit faciendum, sed etiam adiuvans ad implendum." ST 1-2, 106, 1, Ad 2.

[62] From "not a dead letter" to "contribute constantly" is a handwritten addition on the facing page; that it be located here is an editorial decision since Eschmann did not include a sign for insertion.

vance of such a rule without faith and supernatural prudence. Both these Laws again are laws of liberty. Reason is the root of natural human liberty; "The whole root of liberty is constituted in reason," *Tota radix libertatis in ratione est constituta*, Saint Thomas says and faith, likewise, is the root of supernatural, human liberty. Both laws are structured alike and we have here a wonderful application of that harmony of nature and grace, of reason and faith.

These considerations on the liberty of the Christian constitute that lesson in Metaphysics which Father Deman suggested a certain moral theologian should have taken, but did not take. Law and liberty, in modern ethics are conceived antinomically. They are two principles both of which are true and at the same time contradictory! There is law, thus there is no liberty; likewise, there is liberty, thus there is no law. The more moral law —that much the less liberty; the more liberty—that much the less law. Hence ethics consists in accurately drawing the line, and it is left to the temper of the moralist whether he restricts the area of law or that of liberty. Moralists are either "laxists" or "rigorists" or something in between and this is their essential division. The discussion always proceeds on the same level, namely, that of legalism which, as Saint Thomas teaches us, is the level of the Judaic Law. A good law, I repeat with Saint Thomas, but an imperfect one, a law tailored to the measure of an "imperfect" People but (except for the Decalogue, which is codified natural law) unworthy of the Christian. Here ⟨with Aquinas⟩, for once we disregard the pettifoggery ⟨of professional religionists⟩ against which our Lord Jesus Christ had to fight all His life. A law of liberty, that is, a law constituting, forming, vivifying, liberty itself, is inconceivable on the level of this legalism. That is its *proton pseudos*, its "first" and radical "falsehood."

Saint Thomas teaches us to transcend this level. We can do this only if we transcend the level of merely "juristine" thinking and go up to the heights of sound philosophy and theology. The contradiction then, between law and liberty appears to have been a superficial contradiction. At the root, the dialectical tension between law and liberty on which moralism so tenaciously lives is non-existent, or rather it disappears the deeper we go into the matter; it is, to use an untranslatable German word, *aufgehoben*, which means that at the same time it is "put away" and "put in good keeping." We can now conquer and master this contradiction which, as I have said on another occasion, may be the cause in us of many, even of psychopathological troubles. For all this, of course, is not an academic matter, good for merely speculative and intellectual discussion. It is a vital matter, regarding our lives, yours and mine, directly and intimately. Sound, morally sound people, know these things by a connatural knowledge; they need not be elaborated for them in academic, technically refined fashion.

But if an ethics does not pierce through to these truths it is, in my opinion, a failure.

Tears may come to our eyes when we read Thomas Aquinas on the law of liberty and consider what we have lost. It has been observed, and correctly so, that ever since the sixteenth century a significant silence on the part of Catholic theologians is predominant when it comes to the subject of the "liberty of the Christian." Only in our own present day is this topic being unearthed here and there and spoken about again. I wonder how long it will take our moral theologians to speak about a subject which they, in the very first place, should never have abandoned, but which they had to abandon once they decided that moral theology was to be what they pretend it is. Otto Karrer, a Catholic theologian living in Switzerland some years ago wrote a small book with the title I have given to this present section, *Die Freiheit des Christenmenschen*. This, of course, is the title of Luther's famous book. Otto Karrer is a Catholic priest, of a certain age and with many outstanding merits; his little book has the *imprimatur*. Since there is no English translation to my knowledge, I shall read a small extract from the Preface:

> This book is an attempt to present in a synthesis the doctrine of the Gospel on the liberty of the Christian. In spite of its pastoral importance, this doctrine is rarely made the object of discussion in our religious writings, and this is significant. I shall try to remedy this failure and to apply the doctrine on liberty to a number of questions which today are a source of anxiety and doubt to not a few religiously-minded people. It seems a duty to me not to leave these people alone with the doubts from which they suffer, and keep suffering, until in their own way they have found a solution. Unfortunately this solution, most of the time, is a make-shift, leaving the truth still obscure and, more often than not, leading those people away from the Church. [The author here has in mind our Protestant brethren to whose theological enlightenment and conversion he has dedicated his life]. Often the opinion may be heard [again, of course, expressed by our Protestant brethren] that the Church would rather not have these questions asked, that the Church would even tend to suppress them or, at best, admit only a compromise solution which is no solution at all. This, however, is not correct—although, perhaps, there are not a few Catholic theologians whose manner of speaking and behaving would tend to confirm this opinion. They, I think, are incurring no slight responsibility; they are indeed guilty for their part in the fact that a great and ever-increasing number of people are being estranged from the Church....

Otto Karrer is no disciple of Thomas Aquinas [neither is Romano Guardini]. Werner Schöllgen, Professor of Theology in Munich, the Dominican Yves Congar, and the Jesuit Karl Rahner, are among those who today have finally broken that significant silence which so long has surrounded the topic, *Von der Freiheit des Christenmenschen.*

Saint Thomas has spoken about it; he even made it the high point of his ethical thought. In his Questions about the Old and the New Laws he has strewn about, liberally and profusely, the jewels of genuine, Catholic ethical thinking. Take them. Meditate on them. They are good bread and good wine for your intellect! I hope that every one of you, with the help of my few indications, will be able profitably to read and spiritually to enjoy these texts.

*h. Christian Legislation*

In a philosophy and theology which puts such an unmistakably strong emphasis, as does Saint Thomas, on inner experience, on the truth of our moral personality, the problem of *why* there is legislation, "legisposition," a "positing of law" (mainly concerning outer acts) naturally is very urgent. The New, Evangelical, or Christian, Era in which humanity has lived ever since the advent of Christ is dominated by a law principally consisting in inner, invisible, truth and rectitude. What about the "legisposition" in this era? What about the outer works of virtue, what about the social and ecclesiastical institutions?

Saint Thomas has a definite answer. I shall read a few texts, without comment, since I am anxious here to let Aquinas speak and Aquinas alone. I would not dare to interfere and the reason why will soon be apparent. In Part I-II, Question 108, Article 2, Aquinas states the question, "Whether the precepts of the new Law concern external acts," outer, visible works? In other words, what about the precise duties imposed on the Christian by the Evangelical Law? Are there any? If so, what are they?

> I answer that, as was stated above, the New Law had regarding these works, to establish only such precepts or prohibitions, either by which we are prepared for receiving grace, or which are necessary for our making good use of grace. Since we cannot of ourselves obtain grace, but through Christ alone, hence Christ Himself instituted the sacraments whereby we obtain grace. [There follow here short indications as to the institution of the seven sacraments.]—The right use of grace is made by the works of charity. One part of these works is strictly required lest there be no virtue, another part is not of such strict necessity.
>
> As for the first, there are here the moral precepts of the Old Law,

> thus especially the Decalogue. The New Law did not abolish these. But neither did it add new works to be done of this kind. The other part has not received legislative attention in the New Law itself where there are no determinations as to certain works to be done which are not necessarily presupposed for the possession of inner grace. The lawgiver left this to the judgment of the people. He left it to our own individual judgment when the matter concerns us and us alone. And He left it to the authorities, temporal as well as spiritual, when the matter concerns the common good.
>
> Accordingly there are in the Evangelical Law no precepts or prohibitions, except the sacraments and the Decalogue.[63]

In short, very few determinations. Viewed as a code, the New Law is a very small and inconspicuous book indeed. But do we not have in Christendom quite some legislation? The following text is found in Part I-II, Question 107, Article 4:

> The Old Law was a much heavier burden than the New one is; in numerous and minute ceremonial precepts, it prescribed quite a deal of works to be done, institutions to be established, and so on. The New Law, on the other hand, in the teaching of Christ and the Apostles, added very few precepts to those of Natural Law [which are codified in the Decalogue]. After the Apostolic times the Fathers established some ["some," ⟨that is⟩ a few more] laws. In regard to these new institutions, however, the warning of Augustine should be heeded; moderation should be observed lest the life of the Chri-

[63] "Dicendum quod sicut dictum est, lex nova in exterioribus illa solum praecipere debuit vel prohibere, per quae in gratiam introducimur, vel quae pertinent ad rectum gratiae usum ex necessitate. Et quia gratiam ex nobis consequi non possumus, sed per Christum solum, ideo sacramenta, per quae gratiam consequimur, ipse Dominus instituit per seipsum.... Rectus autem gratiae usus est per opera caritatis. Quae quidem secundum quod sunt de necessitate virtutis, pertinent ad praecepta moralia, quae etiam in veteri lege tradebantur. Unde addere non debuit circa exteriora agenda.... Et ideo quia istae determinationes non sunt secundum se de necessitate interioris gratiae, in qua lex consistit; idcirco non cadunt sub praecepto novae legis, sed relinquuntur humano arbitrio; quaedam quidem quantum ad subditos quae scilicet pertinent singillatim ad unumquemque; quaedam vero ad praelatos temporales vel spirituales, quae scilicet pertinent ad utilitatem communem.—Sic igitur lex nova nulla alia exteriora opera determinare debuit praecipiendo vel prohibendo, nisi sacramenta, et moralia praecepta...." ST 1-2, 108, 2, in corpore; t. 2, p. 1346a, ll. 9-17, 27-33; 38-51. Once more we have the advantage of Eschmann's paraphrase, rather than a strict translation of this text.

> stian become a burden again ⟨"again," that is, as it had been under the Old Law⟩. Augustine says, in reply to certain questions put to him by Januarius, "Whereas God in His mercy wished our religion to be a free religion, consisting of a very small number of sacramental celebrations, there are now certain people who make it a slave's burden, so much so that the condition of the Jews was more tolerable. And *they* were subject to divine ordinations, not to the presumptuous devices of men...."[64]

It is often said of Saint Thomas that he was a very abstract writer, not at all caring about what was going on in his time. This is not true, of course, and those who so judge either are unable to read Aquinas intelligently or are ignorant of the history of the thirteenth century. Still, I wonder what this text with the somehow pointed quotation of Saint Augustine really means.

I am tempted here to go into a discussion about the legal and juristic developments in the thirteenth century, called by some a century of "legal inflation." A few years after Saint Thomas's death, we have the *Liber sextus*[65] of Boniface VIII and the famous Constitution *Sacrosanctae.*[66] I resist this temptation. I have a notion that Aquinas here wrote a few lines of burning actuality in his own time. Exactly how far he might be involved in a criti-

[64] "Et quantum ad hoc lex vetus est multo gravior quam nova; quia ad plures actus exteriores obligabat lex vetus in multiplicibus caeremoniis quam lex nova, quae praeter praecepta legis naturae paucissima superaddidit in doctrina Christi et Apostolorum; licet aliqua sint postmodum superaddita ex institutione sanctorum Patrum. In quibus etiam Augustinus dicit esse moderationem attendendam; ne conversatio fidelium onerosa reddatur. Dicit enim, *Ad Inquis. Ianuarii*, de quibusdam, quod 'ipsam religionem nostram, quam in manifestissimis et paucissimis celebrationum sacramentis Dei voluit misericordia esse liberam, servilibus premunt oneribus, adeo ut tolerabilior sit conditio Iudaeorum, qui legalibus sacramentis, non humanis praesumptionibus subiiciuntur'." ST 1-2, 107, 4; t. 2, p. 1343a ll. 25-44. Here Eschmann has translated rather than paraphrased the text.

[65] The *Liber sextus* was issued by Pope Boniface VIII in 1298 (Pope from 1294 to 1303); it includes the so-called *Liber extra* (which had been promulgated in 1234 by Pope Gregory IX) and constitutes the third part of the *Corpus iuris canonici*, ed. E.L. Richter and E. Friedberg, 2 vols. (Leipzig: B. Tauchnitz, 1879, 1881). This collection with its additions was in force until the promulgation in 1917 of the new *Codex iuris canonici*. Historians and students of Church law give the *Liber sextus* higher marks than did Eschmann.

[66] "Sacrosancta Romana ecclesia" are the opening words of legislation on elections, promulgated under Pope Gregory IX (1227-1241); see *Corpus iuris canonici* (cited above), t. 1, Titulus 6, Caput 51.

cism that broke out some thirty to fifty years after his death, I am not prepared to say. A few years later again, Dante Alighieri wrote his *De monarchia* and those frightfully accusatory verses in the *Divina Commedia* about "lo principe d'i novi Farisei"![67]

[67] See Dante's *The Divine Comedy*, Inferno, Canto 27, ll. 85-93, in which the poet excoriates Pope Boniface VIII as "Prince of the new Pharisees"; the Pope was pilloried by the poet because he had waged war, not on Saracens and Jews, but on Christians:

Lo principe d'i novi Farisei, 85
avendo querro presso a Laterano,
e non con Saracin né con Guidei,
ché ciascun suo nimico era Cristiano,
e nessun era stato a vincer Acri
né mercatante in terra di Soldano,
né sommo officio né ordini sacri
guardò in sé, in me qui capestro
che solea fare i suoi cinti più macri. 93

# Bibliography

## A. Saint Thomas Aquinas

St. Thomas Aquinas, O.P. "De caritate." Ed. P.A. Odetto, O.P. In *Quaestiones disputatae*, 9th rev. ed., pp. 701-828. Turin/Rome: Marietti, 1953.

——. "De veritate." Ed. A. Dondaine, O.P. In *Quaestiones disputatae*. Rome: Sanctae Sabinae, 1970. [Opera omnia sancti Thomae Aquinatis, Commissio Leonina, t. 22.]

——. *The Division and Methods of the Science*. Transl. with introd. and notes, of Questions 5 and 6 of *Expositio super librum Boethii De trinitate* by A.A. Maurer, C.S.B. Mediaeval Sources in Translation 3. Toronto: Pontifical Institute of Mediaeval Studies, 1953; 4th rev. ed., 1986.

——. *Expositio super Iob ad litteram*. Ed. A. Dondaine, 1965. [Opera omnia sancti Thomae Aquinatis, Commissio Leonina, t. 26].

——. *Expositio super librum Boethii De trinitate*. Ed. B. Dekker. Leiden: Brill, 1955.

——. *In librum beati Dionysii De divinis nominibus expositio*. Ed. C. Pera, O.P., Turin: Marietti, 1950.

——. *In octo libros Physicorum Aristotelis expositio*. Ed. P.M. Maggoliolo, O.P. Turin/Rome: Marietti, 1954.

——. *Index Thomisticus. Sancti Thomae Aquinatis Operum omnium indices et concordantiae*. Ed. R. Busa, S.J. 50 vols. Stuttgart-Bad Cannstatt: Frommann-Holzboog, 1974-1980.

——. *On Kingship To the King of Cyprus*. Transl. by G.B. Phelan as *On the Governance of Rulers*; revised with introduction and notes by I.Th. Eschmann, O.P. Mediaeval Sources in Translation 2. Toronto: Pontifical Institute of Mediaeval Studies, 1949.

——. *Scriptum super libros Sententiarum Magistri Petri Lombardi Episcopi Parisiensis*. 4 vols.: vols. 1 and 2 ed. R.P. Mandonnet, O.P.; vols. 3 and 4 ed. R.P.M.F. Moos, O.P. Paris: Lethielleux, 1929-1947. Vol. 4 ends at Liber 4, Dist. 22, Quaestio 2.

——. *Sententia libri Ethicorum*. Ed. R.A. Gauthier O.P. Rome: Sanctae Sabinae, 1969. [Opera omnia sancti Thomae Aquinatis, Commissio Leonina, t. 47.]

——. *Sententia libri Politicorum*. Edd. H.-F. Dondaine, O.P. and L.-J. Bataillon, O.P. Rome: Sanctae Sabinae, 1971. [Opera omnia sancti Thomas Aquinatis, Commissio Leonina, t. 48].

——. *Summa contra gentiles.* "Editio manualis." Rome: Commissio Leonina, 1934.

——. *Summa theologiae.* Edd. Instituti Studiorum Medievalium Ottaviensis. 4 vols. Ottawa: Commissio Piana, 1941.

——. *Super librum De causis expositio.* Ed. H.-D. Saffrey, O.P. Fribourg: Societé philosophique, Louvain: Nauwelaerts, 1954.

## B. Other Sources

Alan of Lille. [*De virtutibus et vitiis*] "Le traité d'Alain de Lille sur les Vertus, les Vices et les Dons du Saint-Esprit". Ed. O. Lottin, O.S.B. *Mediaeval Studies* 12 (1959) 20-56.

Albert the Great, O.P. *Beati Alberti Magni Ratisbonensis episcopi, ordinis praedicatorum Opera omnia.* Ed. A. Borgnet. 38 vols. Paris: Vivès, 1890-1899.

Alexander of Hales, O.F.M. *Glossa in quatuor libros Sententiarum Petri Lombardi.* Quaracchi: Ex typogr. Collegii Sancti Bonaventurae, 1951 ff.

——. *Summa theologica. Dicta "Summa fratris Alexandri."* Quaracchi: Ex typogr. Collegii Sancti Bonaventurae, 1924-1948.

St. Anselm, O.S.B. "De veritate." ed. F.S. Schmitt, in: *Sancti Anselmi Cantuariensis Archiepiscopi opera omnia,* vol. 1, 176-199. Seckau: Abbey Press, 1938.

St. Augustine, Aurelius, Bishop of Hippo. *De ciuitate dei.* Edd. B. Dombart and A. Kalb. CCSL 47, 48. Turnhout: Brepols, 1955. Also PL 41: 13-804.

——. *Confessionum tredecim libri.* Edd. M. Skutella and L. Verheijen. CCSL 27. Turnhout: Brepols, 1981. Also PL 32: 659-868.

——. *Contra Faustum Manichaeum.* Ed. J. Zycka. CSEL 25.1. Prague: F. Tempsky, Leipzig: G. Freytag, 1890. Also PL 42: 207-518.

——. *De moribus ecclesiae.* Ed. J.B. Bauer. CSEL 90. Vienna: Hoelder-Pichler-Tempsky, 1992. Also PL 32: 1309-1378.

Averröes (Ibn Rushd). *Commentaria et introductiones in omnes libros Aristotelis cum eorum versione latina.* Venice: Ivntas, 1562-1574.

Bañez, Domingo, S.J. *Commentarios ineditos a la Prima secundae de Santo Tomas.* Ed. Vicente Beltrán de Heredia. Madrid: CSIC/Ministerio de Educació National, 1942, 1948.

St. Bernard, O.S.B. "Sermones super Cantica Canticorum." Edd. J. Leclercq, C.H. Talbot and H.M. Rochais. In *Sancti Bernardi opera.* Rome: Editiones Cistercienses, 1958. Also PL 183: 1018.

Boethius, A.M.S. *In Eisagogen Porphyrii commenta.* Edd. G. Schepss, S. Brandt. CSEL 48. Vienna: F. Tempsky, Leipzig: G. Freytag, 1906. Also PL 64: 9-48 (editio prima), 47-158 (editio secunda).

St. Bonaventure (John Fidenza), O.F.M. *Breviloquium*. Ed. R.P. A. Sépinski, O.F.M. In *Opera theologica selecta*, pp. 1-175. Quaracchi: Ex typogr. Collegii Sancti Bonaventurae, 1964.

——. *Commentaria in IV libros Sententiarum Magistri Petris Lombardi*, ed. minor. In *Opera theologica selecta*, vols. 1-4. Quaracchi: Ex typogr. Collegii Sancti Bonaventurae, 1934-1949.

Boyle, L.E., O.P. "The Setting of the *Summa theologiae* of Saint Thomas." The Etienne Gilson Series 5. Toronto: Pontifical Institute of Mediaeval Studies, 1982.

Chenu, M.-D., O.P. "Le plan de la *Somme théologique*." *Revue thomiste* 45 (1939) 93-107.

——. *Introduction à l'étude de saint Thomas d'Aquin*. Montréal: Institut des études médiévales, Paris: J. Vrin, 1950. English translation by A.-M. Landry, O.P. and D. Hughes, O.P. Chicago: Regnery, 1964.

Cicero, M.T. *De finibus bonorum et malorum*. The Loeb Classical Library. Cambridge, Mass.: Harvard University Press, London: Heinemann, 1951.

Dante Alighieri. *De monarchia*. Ed. B. Nardi. Milan/Naples: Riccardo Ricciardi, 1979.

——. *La divina commedia*. Ed. N. Sapegno. Milan/Naples: Riccardo Ricciardi, 1957.

De Burgh, W. G. *From morality to Religion*. Gifford Lectures, University of Aberdeen, 1938. London: MacDonald & Evans, 1938.

Eliot, T.S. "Little Gidding." In *The Complete Poems and Plays. 1909-1950*, pp. 138-145. New York: Harcourt, Brace & World, 1930; rprt 1952.

Freud, S. *The Psychopathology of Everyday Life*. Transl. A. Tyson, ed. J. Strachey, New York: Norton & Co., 1965.

Gilson, E.H. *L'esprit de la philosophie médiévale*. Gifford Lectures, University of Aberdeen, 1931-1932. Paris: J. Vrin, 1932.

——. *Dante et la philosophie*. Paris: Vrin, 1939.

——. *Dante the Philosopher*. Transl. D. Moore. London: Sheed & Ward, 1948.

——. *The Christian Philosophy of St. Thomas Aquinas*. With a Catalogue of St. Thomas's works by I. The. Eschmann, O.P.; transl. L.K. Shook, C.S.B. (from 5th edition of *Inroduction à la philosophie de saint Thomas d'Aquin*). New York: Random House, 1956.

Hubertus, Magister: Grabmann, M. "Notes sur la *Somme théologique* de Magister Hubertus." *Recherches de théologie ancienne et médiévale* 1 (1929) 229-239.

John of Rochelle, O.F.M. (*De Rupella*). *Summa de anima*. Ed. J.G. Bougerol, O.F.M. Paris: J. Vrin, 1995.

John of Saint Thomas, O.P. *Cursus theologicus*. Paris: Desclée De Brouwer, 1931.

Merkelbach, B.H., O.P. *Summa theologiae moralis ad mentem Thomae*. 3rd rev. ed. Paris: Desclée de Brouwer, ca 1939.

Peter the Chanter. *Verbum abbreviatum*. PL 205: 23-370.

Peter Lombard. *Libri IV Sententiarum*. 2nd ed. 2 vols. Quaracchi: typogr. Collegii Sancti Bonaventurae, 1919.

Peter of Poitiers. *Glossa super Sententias*. PL 211: 789-1279.

——: O. Lottin, O.S.B. "Le Prologue des glosses sur les Sentences attribuées à Pierre de Poitiers." *Recherches de théologie ancienne et médiévale* 7 (1935) 70.

——: P.S. Moore. *The Works of Peter of Poitiers, Master in Theology and Chancellor of Paris (1193-1205)*. Washington D.C.: The Catholic University of America, 1936.

Prevostin of Cremona: M. Grabmann. *Geschichte der scholastischen Methode*. 2 vols. Freiburg i B.: Herder, 1909-1911.

Ramirez, J. *De hominis beatitudine. Tractatus theologicus ad 1-2 Summa theologiae (Qq. 1-5)*. Madrid: Consejo Superior de invertigaciones Cientifices, 1942-1947.

Robert Courson: V.L. Kennedy, C.S.B. "Robert Courson on Penance." *Mediaeval Studies* 7 (1945) 291-336.

Stevens, G., O.S.B. "The Relations of Law and Obligation." *Proceeding of the American Catholic Philosophical Association* 24 (1955) 195-205.

Suárez, F., S.J. "De Incarnatione." In *Opera omnia*, vols. 25 and 26. Paris: Vivès, 1877.

——. "Tractatus de ultimo fine." In *Opera omnia*, vol. 4, pp. 25-39. Paris: Vivès, 1856.

Tertullian, Q.S.F. *Apologia*, 17. In *Florilegium patristicum*, ed. J. Martin, Fasc. 6, p. 73, ll. 10-11. Bonn: P. Hanstein, 1933.

William of Auxerre. *Summa aurea in quattuor libros Sententiarum....* Paris: P. Pigouchet, N. Vaultier, D. Gerlier, 1500.

Wittman, M. *Die Ethik des hl. Thomas von Aquin*. Munich: Max Herder, 1933.

# Index

## A. Index of Names

## B. Index of Subjects